Bargello Borders

Nancy Hall – Jean Riley

Copyright © 1974, Nancy Hall and Jean Riley

All rights reserved. No part of this book
may be reproduced or utilized in any
form or by any means without
permission of the publisher,
Needlemania, Inc.
P.O. Box 123
Franklin
Michigan 48025

Library of Congress Catalog Card Number 74-82108

2500 SOUTH STATE STREET / ANN ARBOR, MICHIGAN 48104
TELEPHONE 313 769-1000
BOOK MANUFACTURING SINCE 1893

To

Bill and Loren

. . . who dared us to do it . . .

SPECIAL THANKS TO:

JOYCE KLEIN for introducing us to needlepoint many years ago.

HI AND DAVE SMUCKER for allowing us to photograph in their home.

BARBARA HEMRICK for helping us set "type".
                and especially to
KITT HEIDEL for her encouragement and helpful advice.

Contents

DESIGN AND BORDERS   1
    COLOR   3–4

BEFORE YOU BEGIN   6
    SUPPLIES   6–13
    PREPARING CANVAS   14–16

CORNERS   17
    STEP-BY-STEP   17–25

BORDERS   40
    STEP-BY-STEP   40–48
    BIAS TENT CONVERSION   49
    LATTICE   70–74

OCTAGONS, ETC.   75
    STEP-BY-STEP   75–87
    PATCHWORKS   98–100

KALEIDOSCOPICS   102
    STEP-BY-STEP   102–112
    POMEGRANATE   114
    RECTANGULAR   143
    DESIGN YOUR OWN   145

FINISHING   146
    KNITTED CORDING   150
    BINDING STITCH   151–155

INDEX OF PHOTOGRAPHS   157

. . . a ridiculous word? No, not really! By definition, a mania is an excessive excitement or enthusiasm. For those of us addicted to needlepoint, it is a very descriptive word.

BARGELLO BORDERS is a collection of design elements for those who want to create their own canvasses. Our borders provide the perfect supplement for your designs. The Intertwining Borders are like mitered ribbons - very effective around a simple motif. The Ornamental Corners can be used as another type of border, dramatizing an often neglected part of the canvas.

Classic Geometrics and Modern Patchworks will appeal to those who enjoy working with textured stitches. The planned symmetry of lines and angles divide the canvas into interesting design areas. Our new, easy Kaleidoscopics offer a fast, fun way to make Bargello more exciting.

The color photographs beginning on page 88 show examples of our work. You can easily duplicate our patterns and before you know it, you will be creating "Originals".

Please read "Before You Begin". It lays the ground rules for our type of canvas work, contains information on supplies, planning, and techniques which we feel are important.

Each chapter includes step-by-step directions for basic procedures, clearly diagrammed stitch charts, and suggestions for easy variations.

Design and Borders

DESIGN is really nothing more than the careful planning and co-ordinating of colors, shapes, and textures into a pleasing, well proportioned composition.

Borders have simplified the problem of designing your own needlepoint. They are like picture frames - they outline and define the composition, set it apart from its surroundings, and make it a complete unit. An attractive border can act as a secondary pattern to a simple design; a plain border can just frame a more complicated central motif.

Every piece of needlepoint should have a border of some kind. If your design incorporates much detail, color, and texture, use a plain border - maybe nothing more than just cording. With a simple design, a border allows you to carry color and texture to the perimeter of your canvas - adding interest to the background area.

Our Chapter headings illustrate the interaction between the border and a simple motif. Lettering alone looks insignificant. The borders add the necessary supplemental pattern.

In planning a project, first select your central motif, then choose a border to complement it. Your design determines what type of border you should use, and how it should be treated. We will give you the borders; you must supply the rest.

If you are not artistic - don't worry! It is very easy to copy, trace, or adapt. Design ideas are everywhere.

Look around your home. Perhaps your drapery fabric or upholstery will inspire you. One of our friends used her bedroom wallpaper as the design source for a pillow. Using the same colors, she combined one small bouquet and a border. The result is the simple, unified design shown in color picture (B-1).

Your china pattern, a porcelain figurine, or an antique vase could provide you with a perfect motif. Royal Dolton's "Bedtime" was used as the subject for a small picture, (A-1). The muted border acts as a subtle frame, enlarging and completing the design.

Color picture G-1 shows an Alaskan bird used as the subject for a pillow. The carefully limited color scheme and the simple shapes have been sparked by the bright green eyes, and set off by the ribbon-like border. The source for this design was a calendar print.

Some Decoupage prints or magazine illustrations are design sources for wild flowers, herbs, fruits, or vegetables.

"Favorite things" or hobbies can be good subject material. A stamp collector might like a careful rendition of a rare stamp; a bridge player might like "the perfect hand".

Sports suggest a variety of ideas; decoys for the hunter, something nautical for the sailor, a personalized racquet cover for the tennis player.

Children's books, greeting cards, and coloring books offer simple shapes. Tweety Bird (F) was traced from a giant size greeting card. Much needlepoint design is frankly whimsical. Find some silly design that makes you smile and adapt it.

Zodiac signs, favorite sayings, or monograms lend a personal touch to your needlepoint project. Monogrammed items are especially appreciated when given as gifts. Until now, the biggest problem of designing monograms has been that the letters had to be very large or fancy to be effective; and still something was lacking. Our borders provide the perfect solution.

GOOD DESIGN results when all elements work together for a total effect; and SIMPLICITY is the keynote to good design.

You should eliminate all unnecessary detail and work with:

1. a central motif - a single focal point
2. a border
3. a carefully planned color scheme. A limited and well-chosen color scheme can help you achieve unity between the central design and the border.

Because COLOR is such a personal decision, we hesitate to set rules for its use. What might be appealing to one, would appear very unattractive to another. In general, you should use colors that make you happy, colors that go well in your room, or the natural color for the item you are depicting.

We make color selections every day when we dress. Fashion experts tell us to pick a basic color scheme and build our wardrobe around it - accent colors are chosen for accessories. This idea doesn't bother us, but when faced with the decision of choosing yarns, many of us feel overwhelmed. Either we play it safe and end up with a "blob" or we get carried away and use too many colors. Remember, we are stressing simplicity in design and color.

The first question you must answer is "What am I going to make and where will it go?" A pillow for the living room couch? Fine! Once you determine this, let the fabric on the couch help you in your color selection.

In planning pillows for a gold couch piped in navy, the blue was chosen as the background color for the pillows. The gold was used for the border and as a secondary color of the design. A bit of white was added to lighten the scheme. By using the accent color of the couch (navy) as the primary color of the pillow, and the dominate color of the couch (gold) as the secondary color, the pillows and the couch have been successfully co-ordinated. If gold had been used as the background for the pillows, there would have been no contrast, no interest, and no oomph.

Take a sample of your upholstery material with you when you select your yarns. "Carrying" colors in your head sounds easy until you try it. If you are working with unusual colors, buy your backing fabric first. It is easier to match or blend yarns to the fabric than to search for a fabric to back a finished piece. Consider using the color of the backing fabric as one of your secondary colors. This provides a nice contrast.

What a world of color awaits you! Manufacturers have created more than 300 shades of Persian yarn to amuse, delight, and sometimes confuse you. How can you possibly choose just three or four? Which three or four?

Color combinations can be bright, bold and cheerful; or pale, subdued and restful. It depends on how they are used. What kind of effect do you want to create?

Because your background color will predominate, it should be selected first. Spread out the background yarn, and lay your secondary choices around it. Do they react well with each other and the background? If not, experiment until you are satisfied with the combination. Remember, this is your pillow, it will reflect your taste and be in your home. It should make you happy!

WHICH CAPTION WOULD YOU CHOOSE? CHECK ONE:

1. Knee deep in needlepoint.

2. What the world really needs - another needlepoint pillow.

3. All it takes is time.

4. No place left to sit.

Observer & Eccentric Photo by Art Emanuel

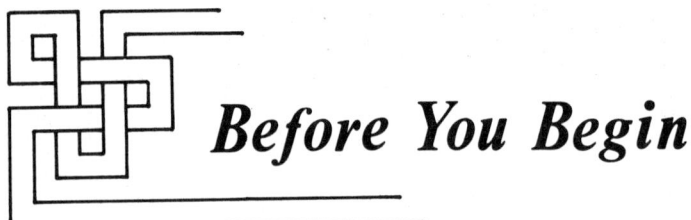

Before You Begin

The supplies that you will need for your needlepoint project are easily assembled and relatively inexpensive. The canvas, yarn, needles, etc. can be obtained from needlepoint shops. Tracing paper, masking tape, graph paper, marking pens and #4-very hard pencils can be purchased at an Artist or Office supply store.

Always buy the best materials. There is very little difference in price between good and poor quality. Your time is your biggest investment; don't waste it on inferior materials.

YARNS   The ideal wool to use for needlepoint is PERSIAN. Most shops recommend it because of its hard wearing and serviceable qualities. Each strand is composed of 3 smaller strands or ply which can be easily separated or combined for different stitch requirements. It is a versatile wool which works equally well for small, tight stitches (Bias Tent) or for larger, softer stitches (Bargello). It comes in an outstanding range of colors - from the palest, softest pastels to the brightest, most vivid hues.

CREWEL WOOL is single ply and is also suitable for canvas work. You must experiment to see how many strands are needed to cover the canvas adequately.

TAPESTRY WOOL is not suitable for our projects because it is tightly twisted and can not be divided into smaller ply. When doubled, it is too thick to be used for most stitches.

D.M.C. PERLE is a shiny cotton yarn. It is especially good to use for lettering as it does not fluff or fuzz over your background stitches. It does not work well for Bargello because it is tightly twisted and does not spread to cover the canvas. Size 5 can be used for Tent on #18 canvas, and can be doubled for Tent on #14 canvas. #5 comes in a larger selection of colors than #3 which can be used only on a #14 canvas.

CANVAS CANVAS is the foundation material for needlepoint. It is a heavy cotton open-weave fabric. Mono canvas is constructed of single vertical threads and single horizontal threads woven over and under each other. It is the only type to use for our projects. Penelope (double threaded) canvas is not suitable for Bargello.

Look for smooth, polished canvas threads that have been squarely woven. The holes should be clear and open, and the canvas should feel firm - not limp or rough. Beware of crooked, uneven threads, knots, or any other obvious flaws. Hold it up to the light - are the holes fuzzy? This indicates an inferior sizing has been used for body. These fuzzies will shred your yarn as you work and will cause you nothing but aggravation.

Mono canvas is available in a variety of sizes, determined by the number of holes to a running inch. The fewer the holes; the larger the canvas.

We prefer working on a #14 mono canvas because we combine Bargello stitches (border) and Bias Tent (design area). On this size we are able to use Persian yarn to its best advantage. Used 3-ply (full strand) for Bargello, the yarn covers perfectly and the stitches lie smooth and flat. The Bias Tent area requires 2-ply. Unless otherwise noted, all our designs have been planned and worked on #14 canvas.

You may be tempted to select a #10 canvas. The larger holes look very appealing. True, your Bias Tent (3-ply) will work up more quickly, but you will soon discover that your border will look bulky and out of proportion. Because you are working on a larger gauge canvas, you have to increase your yarn requirements. On #10, your Bargello uses 4-6 ply, and it is more difficult to keep your stitches flat and the yarn untwisted.

For some strange reason, #12 was introduced as a compromise between a #14 and a #10. It sounds logical; but in reality, it doesn't work. When treated as a #14, the yarn does not cover adequately; and when treated as a #10, the yarn is crowded in the holes.

If you want more detail in your design, or are working in a limited space (checkbook cover, eye glass case, or a narrow belt), you might try a #18. 2-ply is suitable for Bargello, and 1-ply is used for the Bias Tent.

Get your glasses checked before you start on a #24. Fun for a small project such as a name tag or a book mark. Use full strand (6-ply) cotton embroidery floss for the Bargello, and 3 or 4 ply for the Bias Tent.

NEEDLES	Use a blunt tapestry needle. They come in assorted sizes from 13-24. The larger the number, the smaller the "eye". Choose your needle according to your yarn requirements; use the smallest one that you can easily thread. If your needle is too large, you will have difficulty pulling it through the canvas, and it will keep coming unthreaded.

Canvas Size	Yarn Bias Tent	Yarn Bargello	Needle Size
5	1 strand (rug wool)	No	13
10	3 ply (Persian)	4-6 ply (Persian)	18 or 20
12	2-3 ply (Persian)	3-4 ply (Persian)	18 or 20
14	2 ply (Persian)	3 ply (Persian)	20
18	1 ply (Persian)	2 ply (Persian)	22

THIMBLES   Some needlepointers can't thread up until their thimble is in place; to others it feels very awkward. If you do a lot of needlework you will find your "pushing" finger will get sore. If a metal or plastic thimble is uncomfortable, try a rubber finger guard. They come in different sizes and can be purchased at an Office Supply Store.

MARKERS   BEWARE OF THE MARKER THAT CLAIMS TO BE WATERPROOF. IT MIGHT NOT BE! Waterproof markers have ruined many projects. If the marker has not been specifically designed for canvas, the marks sit on top of the sizing instead of penetrating the fibers. When dampened for blocking, the sizing releases the ink into the wool. Once it permeates the wool, it <u>is</u> permanent and nothing will get it out.

"Nepo" markers by Sanford are guaranteed not to bleed. You must follow their directions, however, or the guarantee is void. They are available in sets of six colors (red, yellow, orange, black, blue, and green), or individually, plus gray. You may choose either broad points (for coloring large areas) or sharp points (for fine marking). For our method of marking, we recommend the sharp point because you can dot the mesh precisely.

A #4-very hard pencil (not a regular #2) works well as an alternative to the marker. For outlining, the faint line it makes will not show through even the palest stitches. In laying on our Borders, only a few dots at each corner are needed. The pencil marks will not smudge your wool, and they will stay on long enough to complete your Border. You can make the pencil marks permanent (for Geometrics and Kaleidoscopics) with a light spray of Acrylic sealer. For Patchworks, use the pencil for the grid lines, and a marker for the pattern lines.

The marks on your canvas are there to guide you; they should be just <u>barely</u> dark enough to see. Never make any unnecessary marks; but if you goof, several coats of white acrylic paint should cover your mistake. Dampen your brush, and use the white full strength.

If you want to paint your central motif, the acrylics are ideal. However, they cannot be used for preparing the canvas for any of our techniques. Even the finest brush cannot make the precise dots and lines needed.

MASKING TAPE Binding the edges with masking tape will keep the canvas threads from unraveling. The tape also provides a smooth edge so the threads will not snag your yarn. 1" or 1½" tape is preferable for large projects and will stay intact through the blocking process. For small items such as pin cushions or belts, the 3/4" width is sufficient.

GRAPH PAPER A supply of graph paper is invaluable for some of the patterns we offer. It is not necessary that it be the same size as your canvas, or the same gauge (# of holes per inch). The inexpensive green Science Filler available at any drug store is fine.

It is easy to convert the stitch pattern on your graph paper to an inch size for your canvas. Merely count the number of squares the design uses on the graph, and divide the figure by the size canvas you are using. If your charted design uses 119 squares, and the canvas size is 14, your design will be 8½". Once you try our method of charting, you will realize how very simple it is.

TRACING PAPER All designs should be planned and drawn to size on tracing paper; no "free-hand" work should be done directly on the canvas. Marks on the paper can be changed or ignored; wrong marks on the canvas can show through your stitches - no matter how carefully you paint them out. A pad of 11" x 14" tracing paper is much less expensive than a piece of 'ruined' canvas.

STITCH TIPS It is imperative that you ANCHOR YOUR YARN securely. Because Bargello stitches are loose, it is wise to weave through the back of completed work and then reverse weave. This double weaving prevents the yarn from pulling out. It is just as important at the beginning as at the end of a strand.

Keep the back of your work NEAT with all ends well secured and closely clipped; this prevents knots, tangles, and fuzzies. Always bring any unused yarn to the front of your canvas when changing colors, eliminating the risk of splitting or stitching it to the back. To continue with a color, merely pull it to the back and rethread.

Develop an EVEN TENSION. Pull your yarn until it lies smooth and taut on the canvas. Do not give it an extra tug.

Keep your yarn SMOOTH and UNTWISTED. When it begins to curl, drop the needle and gently shake until the yarn unwinds.

Never 'scrunch' your canvas. If you are comfortable using a frame, great; if not, roll the canvas scroll fashion for stitching ease.

Always bring your needle UP (back of canvas to front) at the bottom of a stitch and DOWN (front to back) at the top. This will allow your yarn to pad the back of the canvas for durability and will prevent your stitches from slipping. If you must come up in a "filled" hole, stitch carefully so you do not split the yarn.

MISTAKES . . . are inevitable. No matter how carefully you work, you are bound to make one sooner or later. If you catch it right away, simply unthread your needle and pick out the mistake. Rethread and continue. Never "unstitch" with your needle; you will only make matters worse.

If you do not see the mistake immediately, you must cut <u>all</u> the stitches back to your "boo-boo". Our patterns are based <u>on</u> precise stitch count and a mistake way back will keep the pattern from fitting properly.

Bargello stitches are easy to remove. Using sharp pointed embroidery scissors, slip the tip under the <u>right</u> side of the stitches and cut. Keep the tip <u>up</u> so that you <u>do</u> not cut the canvas threads. Turn your canvas to the wrong side, scratch the back of the stitches you have cut to loosen them and pull out the fluff. Undo enough stitches at the ends of the cut so that you can thread your needle and secure the yarn.

Wrap a piece of masking tape over your fingers, sticky side out. Rub this over the area you have corrected, both front and back. This will remove all the "fuzzies" you cannot see but which would show through your new stitches.

If you must remove Bias Tent, a pointed seam ripper is invaluable. Cut and remove the tent stitches along the diagonal line in the opposite direction from which they were stitched.

KNOW YOUR YARN

Persian yarn is manufactured and packaged for retail sale in different quantities by different companies. You can buy an 8½ yard skein, a 40 yard skein, a 4 ounce skein (approximately 180 yards), or by the ounce. Most needlepoint specialty shops carry the 4 ounce skeins, and will gladly cut them and sell you as little as 1 ounce or a single strand. An ounce is approximately 22-25 strands and is more economical. Ten "strands" cost about as much as a full ounce. If you are going to use the same color yarn for several projects, or if you need a long continuous strand (for the self cording described in the Finishing chapter), buy an <u>uncut</u> 4 ounce skein.

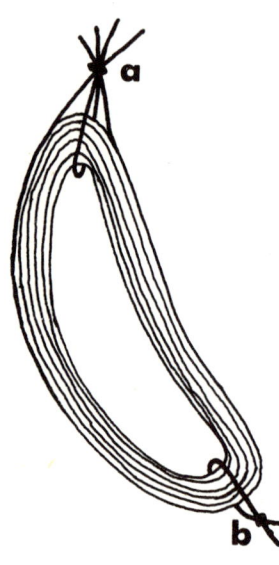

When you untwist the skein into a ring, you will see two knots. Look for knot A - the one composed of 4 ends of yarn; the beginning of the skein, the end of the skein, and the two ends of a small loop. Knot B is just a small loop. Cut off the knots, discard the loops, and:
1. Measure off the amount you will need if you want to make the knitted cording. Wind it into a ball and set it aside.
2. Cut through the "remaining" skein. This will give you strands of yarn that are approximately 60" long. A 4 ounce skein cut <u>once</u> is about 100 strands.

Never buy yarn that is less than 60" long - cut <u>once</u> from the skein. Because Bargello works up quickly, we pre<u>fer</u> the 60" length. Thread your needle, start with a long fold-over and keep moving the needle toward the end as the yarn gets shorter. Your yarn will not fray or wear thin because it is being used up so quickly.

For anything other than Bargello, work with a strand about half this length. On a #14 canvas, 30" is suitable; but, a #18 canvas works better with a 20" strand. Purchasing long strands gives you the option to cut them as <u>you</u> need them.

12

Because many of the new kits have been prepared on the odd size canvas - #12, there is a simple trick to make the stitches look fuller. Separate the ply and lay them back together - do not twist them. Keep the strands flat and loosen your tension just a bit. This method allows the yarn to spread and you get better coverage.

How much yarn should you buy? Don't buy "just enough" yarn; it is better to end up with a little extra than to run short. Dye lots do change and the difference is very obvious on the canvas. You can always use leftover yarn on a patchwork or small project. The 3½" pin cushions in color picture B use 3 strands - 60" long for the pattern row, and 4-5 strands - 60" long for the background. The butterfly shown in color picture C is 14" square. One ounce of white, 1 ounce of yellow, and 2½ ounces of green were enough to complete the border and the design area. The bench pad in the same picture is 14" x 27" and used 2 ounces of yellow, 2 ounces of green and 6 ounces of white.

Not only is Bargello faster than Bias Tent, it requires much less yarn. In planning a Kaleidoscopic, you would need about 4-5 ounces of yarn for a 14" pillow. The background takes 2-3 ounces and the medallion will use about ½ ounce of 3 other colors. If you are buying by the ounce, you will have enough yarn to do a companion pillow. A chair seat requires more background around the medallion so allow for this in your purchase plan.

An estimate for a set of 6 dining room chairs would include 1 skein of background for each chair plus 1 extra for good measure. A total of 4 ounces each of 3 or 4 colors (1/2 - 3/4 for each chair) should be enough for the medallions. The yarn and canvas will be your only expense - a substantial saving if you consider the cost of 6 painted canvasses.

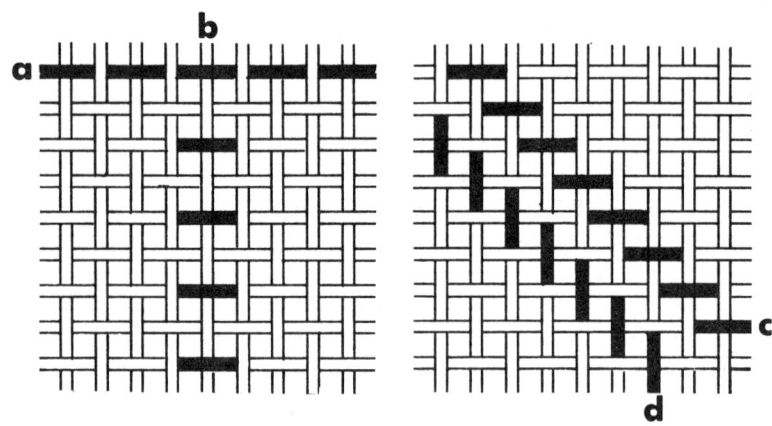 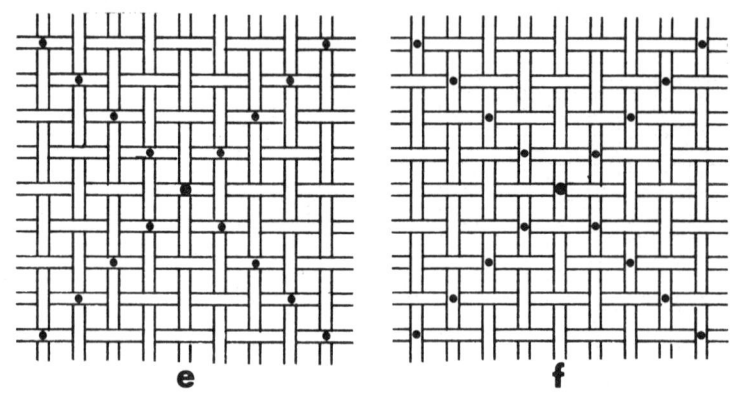

KNOW YOUR CANVAS

Look at your canvas. It contains holes which you can easily see. It is constructed of single threads running horizontally (side to side) and vertically (up and down). The intersection of a horizontal thread and a vertical thread is called a MESH - not the threads or the holes between the threads, but the intersection itself.

Follow line A. Notice the over and under of the weave. Because it is an even weave canvas, the mesh alternate. The horizontal thread is on top of every other mesh. These are called horizontal mesh, and alternate with vertical mesh (the vertical thread is on top).

Follow line B. The principle of alternating mesh applies across the canvas from side to side and down a row from top to bottom

In diagonal rows, the mesh do not alternate. Follow line C, the mesh are all horizontal. Follow line D, the mesh are all vertical.

A corner is a right angle, and a miter is a diagonal cut of a corner. In order to mark your canvas properly for a miter, you must SEE diagonal rows.

You can draw a diagonal in four directions from one central mesh. The threads that are on top of each mesh in any diagonal direction will all be the same: Horizontal mesh (E), vertical mesh (F).

PREPARING YOUR CANVAS

1. Determine the dimension of your finished piece and add 2" on each side for a blank margin. You will need this for blocking and finishing.
2. Cut your canvas straight - in the row of holes between two threads.
3. Bind the edges with masking tape.

Each of our techniques requires a different marking procedure and will be treated individually.

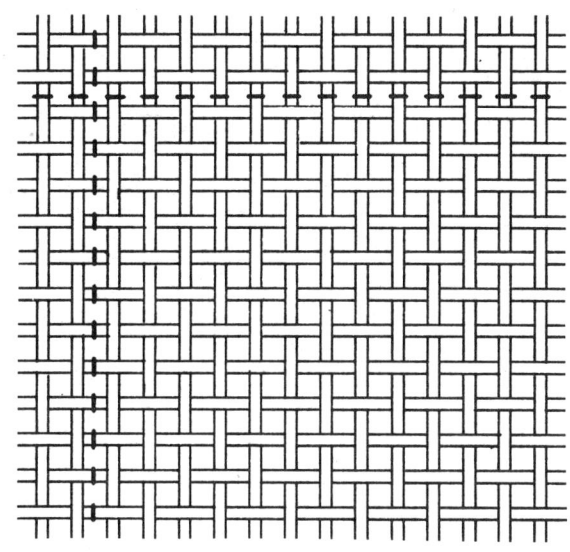

MARKING FOR CORNERS

All you need is a simple outline on your canvas. Measure down 2" from the top edge and run a #4 hard pencil in the row of holes between two threads all the way across your canvas. We mark in the channel between two threads because the mark is then recessed and will not show through your stitches. Don't mark on a thread; the marks show. Measure 2" from the side and mark another line in a channel of holes. Draw the outline for the other two sides in the same way. The Corner patterns fit into the outline you have marked. The chapter on CORNERS thoroughly explains our techniques.

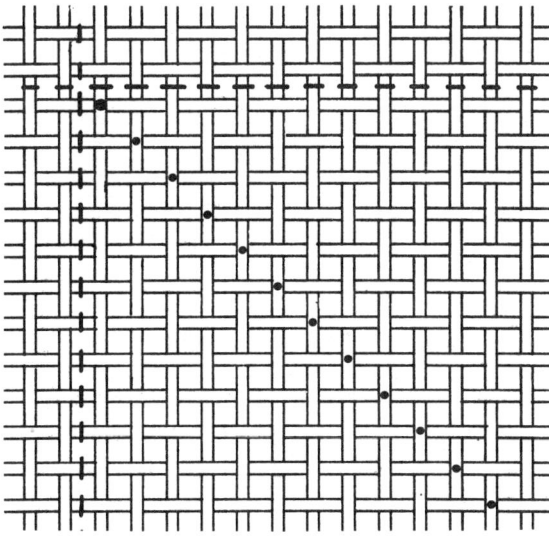

MARKING FOR BORDERS

Read the chapter on BORDERS. It tells you how to measure and plan for a Border. Cut your canvas to the proper size and bind.

In the upper left corner, mark two straight lines; one 2" down from the top, and the other 2" in from the side. With this right angle on your canvas, you are able to find a Miter line. Look at the first mesh <u>inside</u> that corner (it doesn't matter if it is a horizontal or a vertical mesh). Dot it! Continue dotting in a diagonal line for about 2". <u>Do</u> <u>not</u> try and mark the other three corners now. As your border pattern progresses around the canvas, you will be able to determine where your remaining Miter lines will be needed.

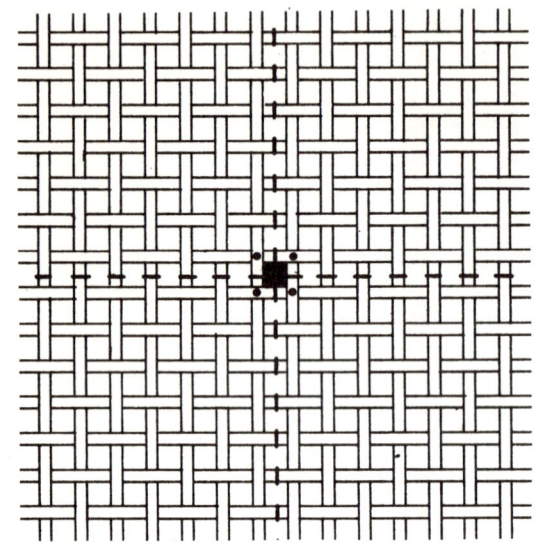

MARKING FOR KALEIDOSCOPICS AND GEOMETRICS

The chapters on OCTAGONS, ETC., and KALEIDOSCOPICS tell you how to plan your project. Cut your canvas to the proper size and bind.

Find the center row of holes vertically by folding your canvas from side to side so that the taped edges meet. Make a small mark on the tape along the fold. Open the canvas and run your marker or #4 pencil down the row of holes between two threads. To find the horizontal center row of holes, fold your canvas in half the other way and repeat the procedure. Your canvas is now divided into four sections.

The CENTER HOLE is at the junction of the vertical row of holes and the horizontal row of holes. THIS CENTER HOLE IS YOUR MOST IMPORTANT REFERENCE POINT. Mark the four mesh surrounding it.

In a diagonal line, all mesh are the same. The mesh to the upper right and the lower left (of this diagram) are horizontal mesh. Mark the diagonal line from the Center Hole to the upper right and from the Center Hole to the lower left. You must "dot" mesh by mesh with your marker. Do not use a ruler and draw a line.

The upper left and lower right mesh are both the same - vertical. Dot the diagonal line from the Center Hole to the upper left and from the Center Hole to the lower right.

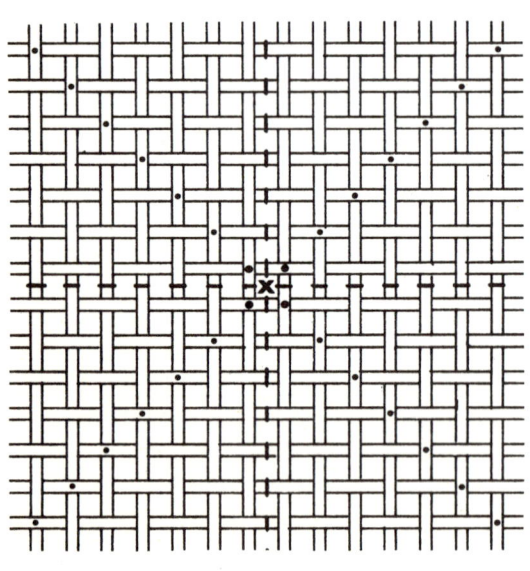

Your canvas is now divided into eight segments and you are ready to stitch an Octagon, an Eight-pointed Star, or a Kaleidoscopic. If you have marked with a #4 pencil, a quick spray with an acrylic sealer (Krylon or a Decoupage spray) will seal your marks and keep them visible throughout your project. Be sure and spray before you start stitching.

Ornamental knotwork patterns are intriguingly simple. They are created by a line or band flowing over and under itself in a continuous motion. More complicated patterns can be achieved by adding more interweaving lines. Fabrics, leather goods, jewelry, inlaid wood work, plaster relief, and ornamental grillwork offer examples of this type of design.

The patterns we have developed for Bargello use a type of squared open knotwork in the four corners of a design as part of the border. Follow the lines in the photograph above. You will see how they pass over and under one another; move into and out of each corner; and finally, reconnect with themselves. This type of border may be applied even after your central design is on the canvas - either marked or stitched.

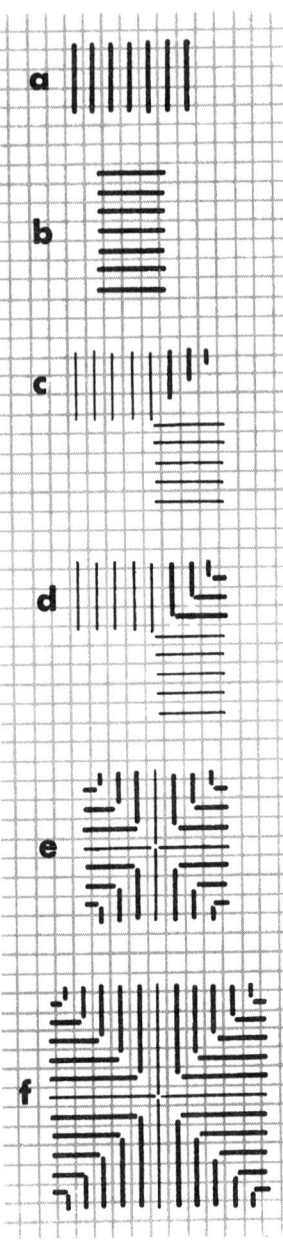

MITERED GOBELIN

One of the simplest and most effective stitches for canvas is the Satin stitch or Gobelin. It is nothing more than a series of straight stitches of the same length placed side by side. Each stitch is vertical and uses 5 holes (Covers 4 threads). The Gobelin is worked in horizontal rows across the canvas (a). Because of the nature of mono canvas, Gobelin can also be worked in vertical rows - the stitches themselves are horizontal (b).

Gobelin is especially useable for a border or simple frame. The problem of fitting the rows together neatly at the corners is solved by mitering. The pale lines (c) are Gobelin and the bold lines show how you gradually decrease the length of each stitch. The final stitch uses only 2 holes- covers 1 thread. Be very careful that you do not pull your yarn too tightly or this stitch will disappear between the canvas threads.

The bold lines (d) show a complete miter. ALONG THE MITER LINE, STITCHES OF THE SAME LENGTH ARE AT RIGHT ANGLES TO EACH OTHER AND SHARE A COMMON HOLE. You will know that your miter is complete when the longest stitches meet, and you may continue with your Gobelin.

The Triangle stitch (e and f) is nothing more than four complete miters. The center stitches are always the longest and can be any length from 5 holes on up.

It is important that you understand mitering as it is the basis for all of our diagrams.

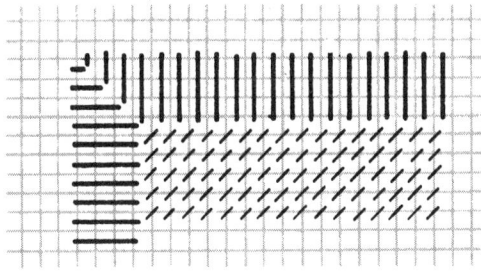

A single row of Mitered Gobelin is a perfect frame for almost any design. It gives a finished edge and eliminates the necessity of applying bias-covered cording when assembling your pillow. It can be done in your background color or in a contrasting color. A super frame - especially good because it can be applied <u>after</u> the background is finished. The Gobelin stitches <u>share</u> holes with the Tent stitches so that all canvas threads are covered.

Two or three rows of Mitered Gobelin can act as a heavier frame. They can be of the same, contrasting, or graduating colors. The Tweety Bird wall hanging used two rows of black Mitered Gobelin. This soft "frame" looks real. When one row of Mitered Gobelin is stitched <u>outside</u> of another, your last long stitch will fit into the empty hole at the corner of the previous row. Complete your miter and continue.

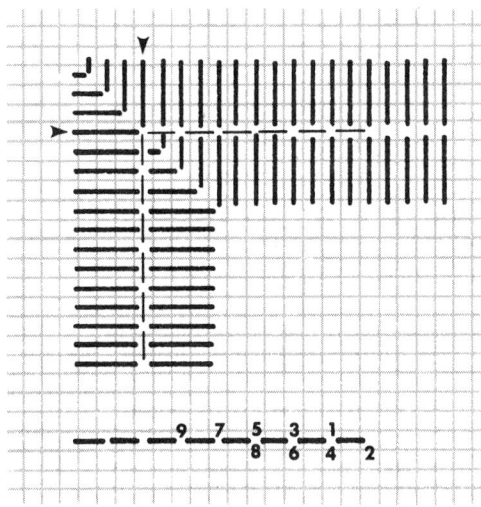

When doing several rows of Mitered Gobelin, especially in dark colors, you might notice the canvas threads showing between the rows. This can be covered by a back stitch using 2 ply on #14 canvas. The yarn is carried backward <u>over</u> 2 threads, and forward <u>under</u> 4 threads to come up <u>for</u> the next stitch. This makes a nice dimple or shadow on the border. For a daintier look, use 1 ply over 1 thread.

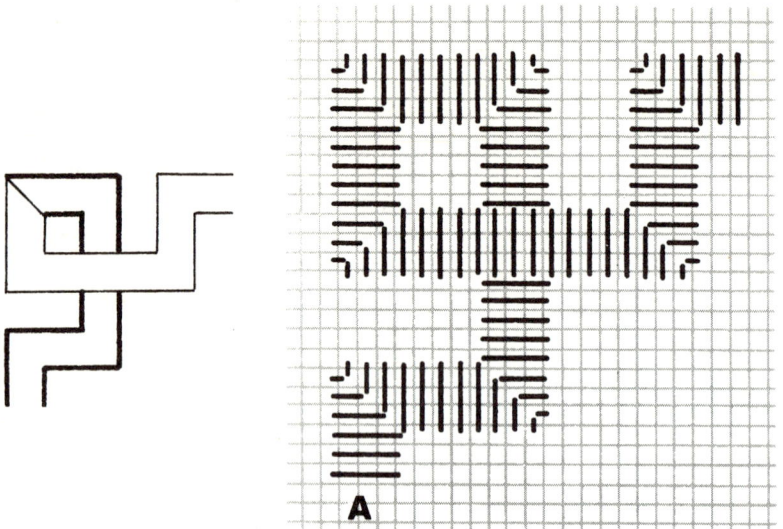
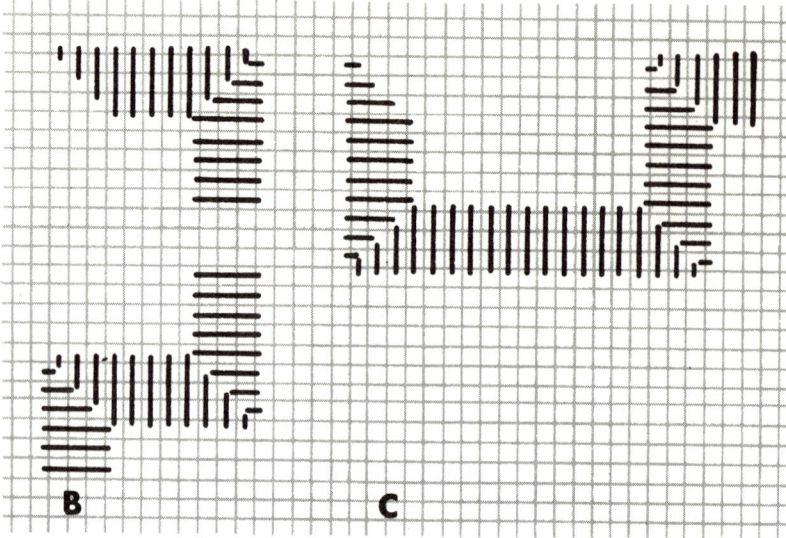

Carrying our Mitered Gobelin technique one step further, we are able to create interesting Corner designs. Diagram A shows a complete Corner. To make it easier for you to see how it is constructed, we have broken it at the upper left corner into two sections. You will have less trouble if you visually separate the two sections and stitch just one at a time. The bold lines of the small line drawing correspond to Diagram B; the pale lines correspond to Diagram C. The pattern looks incomplete until the second section fits into the first. You must count your stitches carefully. Your pattern will not fit properly if you use <u>even</u> one stitch too many or too few.

Look at B. Start counting at the upper left with half a miter. How many 5 hole Gobelins are there before the next miter? Yes, there are 5. The pattern continues with another complete miter - 5 Gobelins - skip 3 rows of holes - 5 Gobelins - a complete miter - 5 Gobelins - and a complete miter. At this point you may carry your straight Gobelin as far as you need.

C is the second section of your corner. Again count from the upper left. Half a miter - 5 Gobelins - a complete miter - 13 Gobelins - a complete miter - 5 Gobelins - and a complete miter finishes this section. Again, work as much straight Gobelin as you need. Notice that the 3 rows of holes that were skipped in B merely leave room for the stitches in C to pass over. You will have to sneak your stitches into holes that are partially covered by yarn, so be careful.

We have taken you through the basic mechanics of mitering and counting. Now, let's have fun stitching this pattern. It can be made into a coaster, pin cushion, or needle case. The finishing techniques are explained in the last chapter.

1. Cut a 6" square of #14 mono canvas and bind the edges with masking tape.

2. The dark line is your pattern row. Start at a corner - 1½" down from the top and 1½" in from the side. Break the pattern and stitch half a miter. Remember to count carefully and skip when necessary. Whenever a line passes under, you must leave 3 rows of holes so that the other line may pass over.

3. The background is completely diagrammed for you in pale lines, and will give you more practice in mitering.

4. The three small pin cushions in color picture B show the various ways your colors can be used.

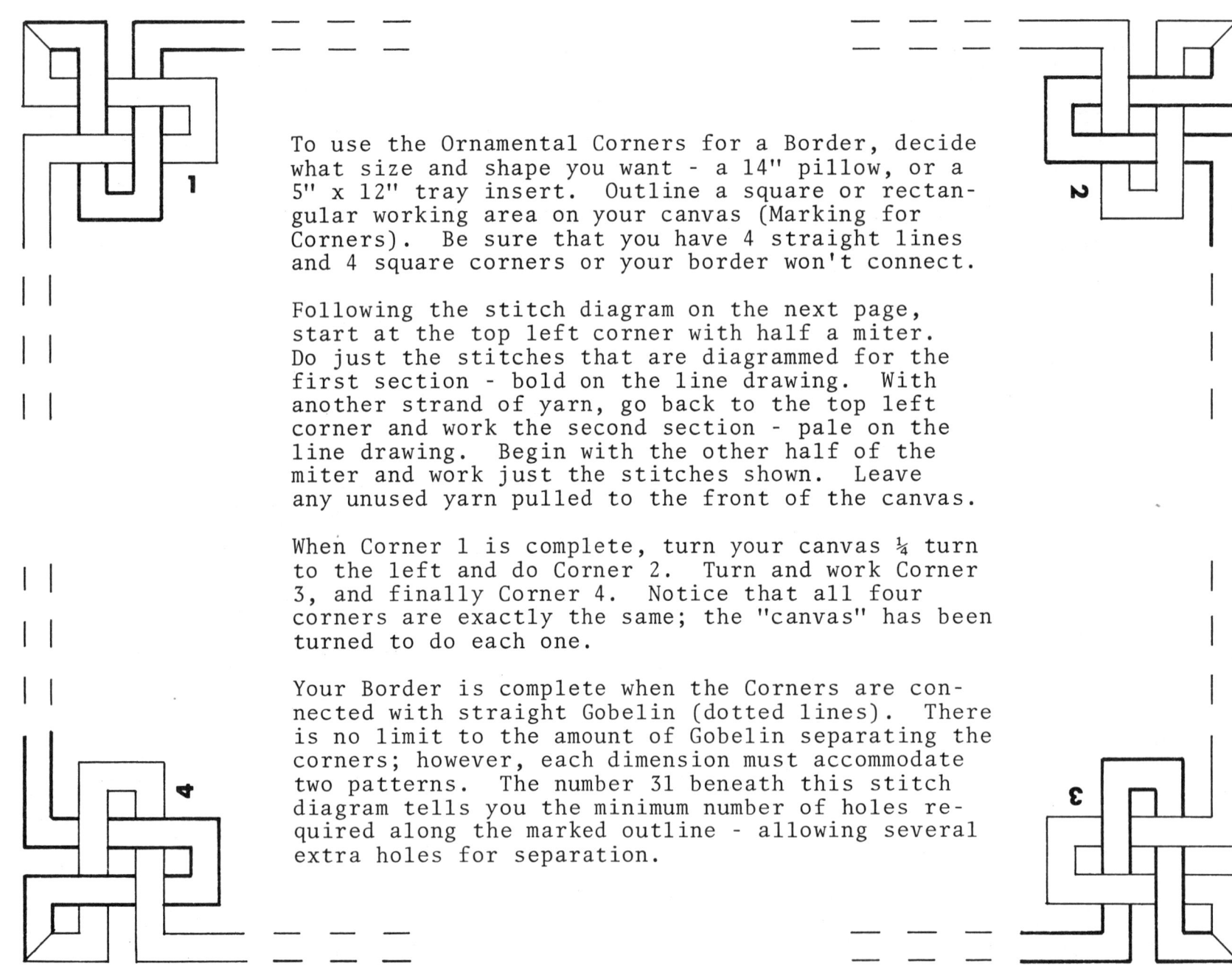

To use the Ornamental Corners for a Border, decide what size and shape you want - a 14" pillow, or a 5" x 12" tray insert. Outline a square or rectangular working area on your canvas (Marking for Corners). Be sure that you have 4 straight lines and 4 square corners or your border won't connect.

Following the stitch diagram on the next page, start at the top left corner with half a miter. Do just the stitches that are diagrammed for the first section - bold on the line drawing. With another strand of yarn, go back to the top left corner and work the second section - pale on the line drawing. Begin with the other half of the miter and work just the stitches shown. Leave any unused yarn pulled to the front of the canvas.

When Corner 1 is complete, turn your canvas ¼ turn to the left and do Corner 2. Turn and work Corner 3, and finally Corner 4. Notice that all four corners are exactly the same; the "canvas" has been turned to do each one.

Your Border is complete when the Corners are connected with straight Gobelin (dotted lines). There is no limit to the amount of Gobelin separating the corners; however, each dimension must accommodate two patterns. The number 31 beneath this stitch diagram tells you the minimum number of holes required along the marked outline - allowing several extra holes for separation.

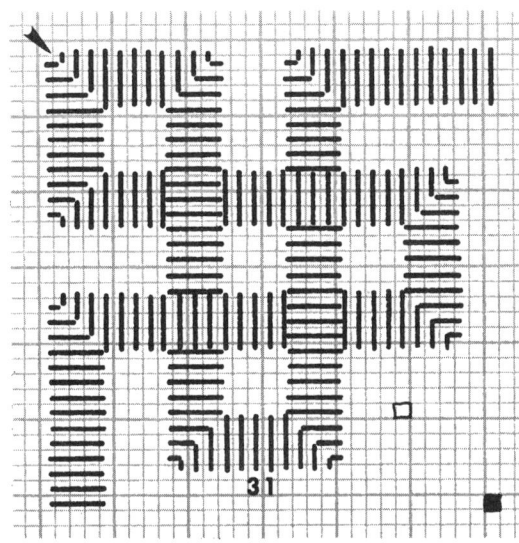

There are several different ways to work the background areas. The soft, raised effect of these patterns can be enhanced by using Bias Tent. These flat stitches provide a contrasting texture which highlights the pattern.

Some of the areas created by the intertwining lines can benefit by the use of textured stitches. The Triangle stitch (p. 18) fits perfectly into an opening of 9 x 9 holes or larger. The smaller openings (5 x 5) are perfect for the Double Leviathan.

To make sure that you have room for both patterns, merely double the hole count, and divide by the size canvas you are using. This will give you an approximate measurement to compare with your working area.

    62 ÷ #18 = 3½"   62 ÷ #14 = 4½"
    62 ÷ #12 = 5"   62 ÷ #10 = 6"

The starting point for any Corner is the upper left Miter, and has been indicated by a large arrow on the stitch diagram. When you begin stitching, leave the very corner hole empty. This will allow the outer edges of the pattern to fit into the outline you have marked. Count your stitches carefully! If you use <u>even</u> one extra stitch, your pattern will <u>not</u> fit.

DOUBLE LEVIATHAN

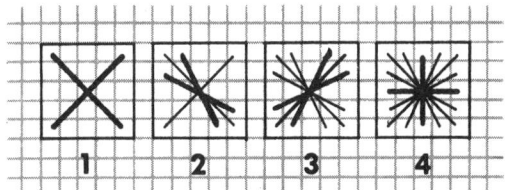

1. Make a basic X from corner to corner.
2. The basic X is pale and the overlay stitches of one "leg" of the X are bold. Notice that they cross at the very center.
3. The other "leg" of the X is overlaid.
4. The Leviathan is completed by a horizontal and a vertical stitch.

23

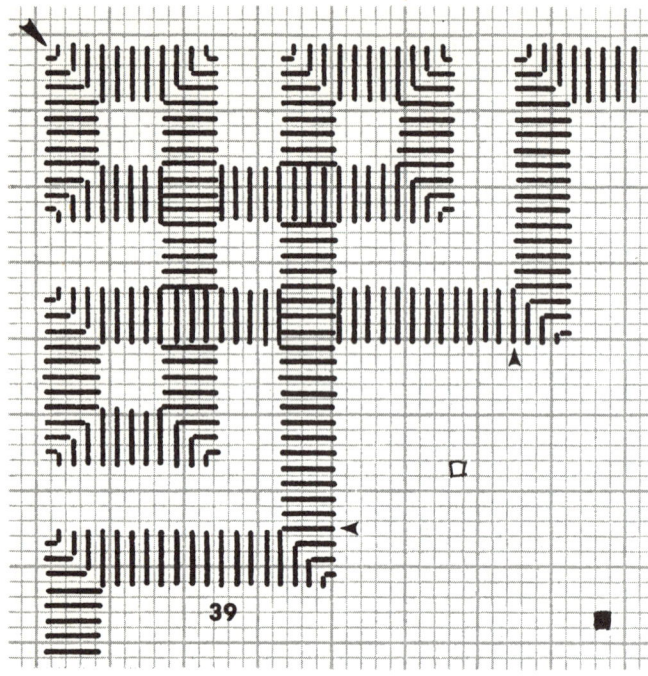

The Chapter heading on page 17 illustrates how a pattern can be used for a rectangular shape. At the top and bottom, the light line comes out of the corner and miters; but along the sides, it continues straight. Several of our Corner patterns offer this option.

On the stitch diagrams, a small arrow points to the last stitch before the miter. If you wish to use the option (dotted lines), ignore the miter and continue with straight Gobelin. If the diagrammed version is too large, try the option; it requires fewer holes.

The drawing below is the work plan for the tray F-4. The short sides follow the option and the full pattern was used along the top and bottom. The row of yellow Gobelin around the outside "frames the border".

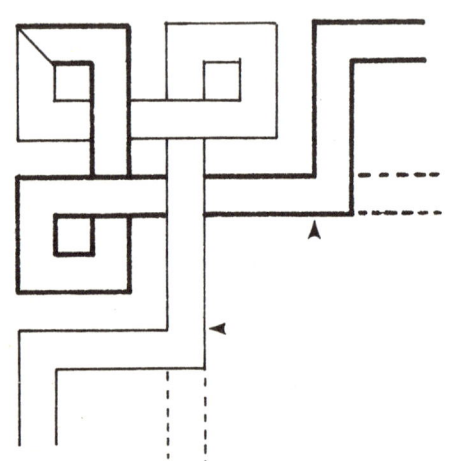
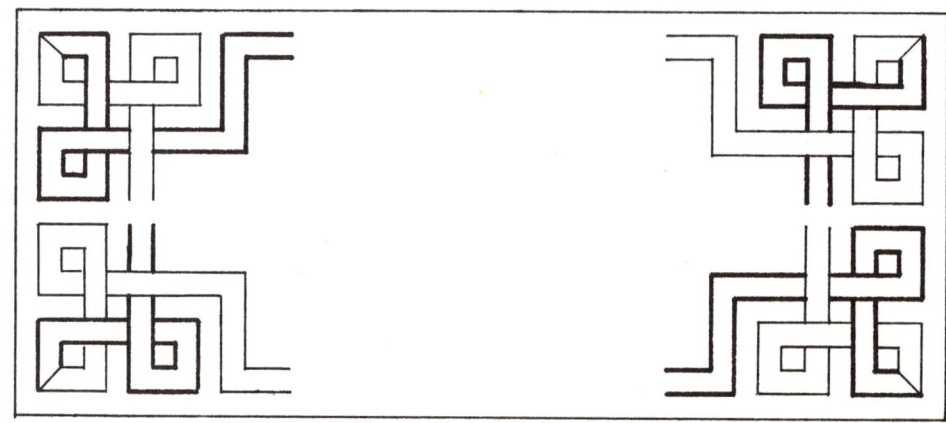

24

Many of our Corners do not "fill a square" and can be used successfully around an oval design. Some of our Kaleidoscopics (✱) can accommodate a Corner as a secondary pattern. Stitch the medallion first; then draw the outline (p. 109). Select your Corner and check the hole count.

On the stitch diagram, the figure 27 tells you the number of holes the Corner requires along the outline. The black dot finishes the imaginary square and the pattern does not fill the entire area (27 x 27).

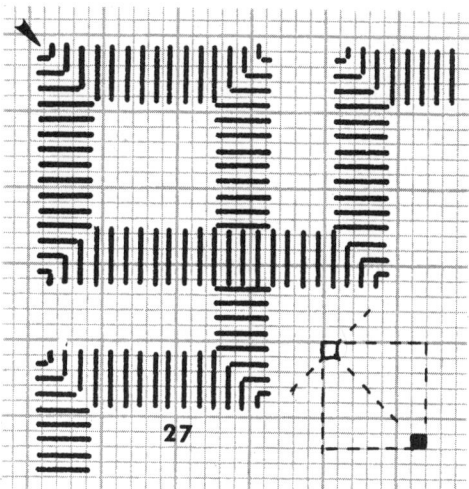

To determine how many holes the Corner uses along the diagonal (Miter line), subtract the number of unused holes. Count diagonally back from the black dot to one hole before the outlined hole. Subtract this figure (6) from 27 (the Corner count) to give you the number of holes needed along the diagonal. The larger Corner uses 47 holes along the outline, but only 33 along the miter. This procedure is only used when combining a Corner and a Kaleidoscopic.

The Miter line on your canvas will correspond to an imaginary Miter line on your diagram (from the arrow to the black dot). Ignore it when you are stitching the Corner. It may bother you, but don't paint it out; you will need it when you stitch the background for the Kaleidoscopic.

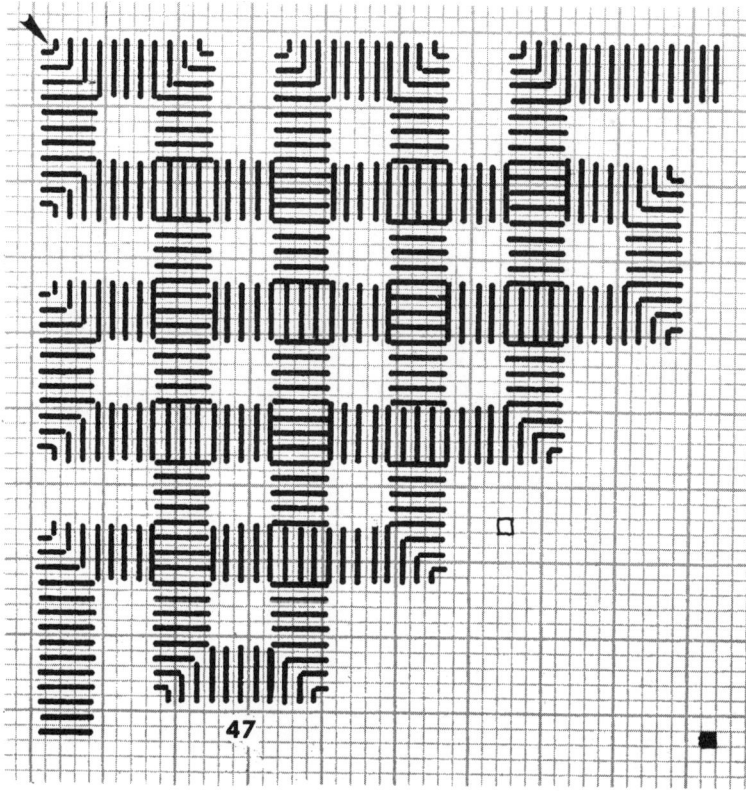

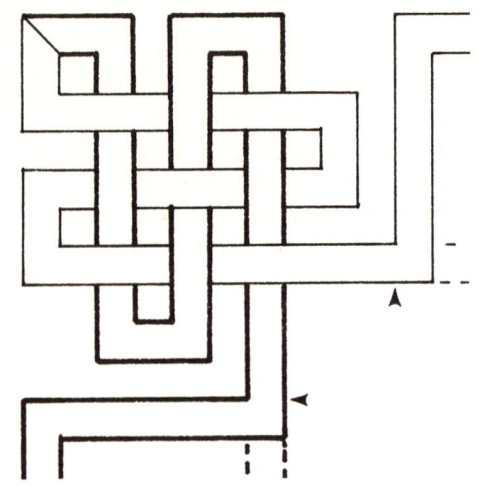

The purse flap (B-5) used the diagram on the left. It miters out to the edge along each side; but at the bottom of the flap, it continues straight by following the option. Yes, there were enough holes along the bottom to miter the pattern; but it looked heavy and unattractive. By following the option, there was room to add an initial. Bias Tent was used between the pattern lines and the Diamond stitch in the interior added texture.

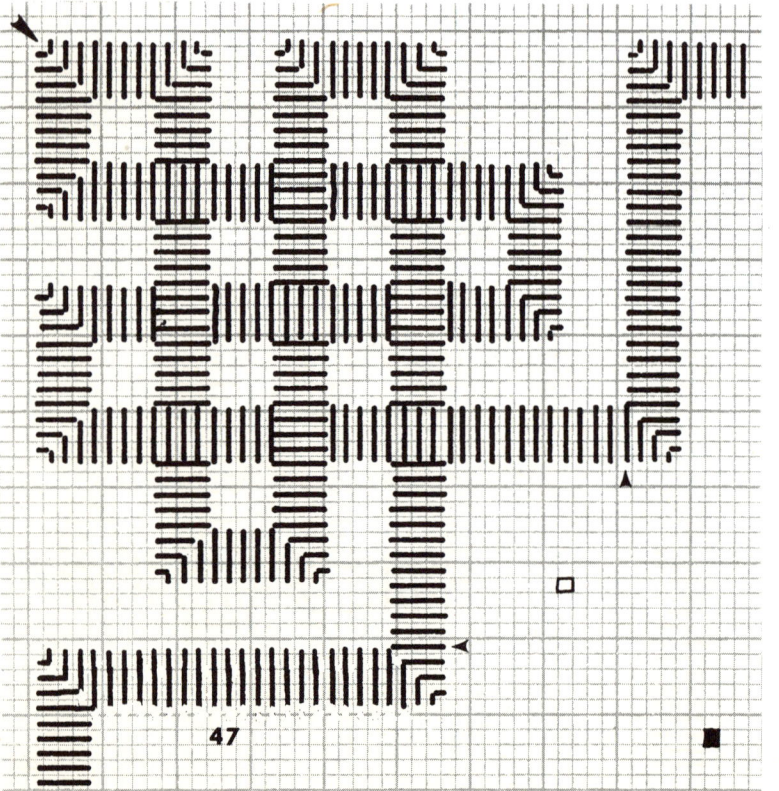

47

47

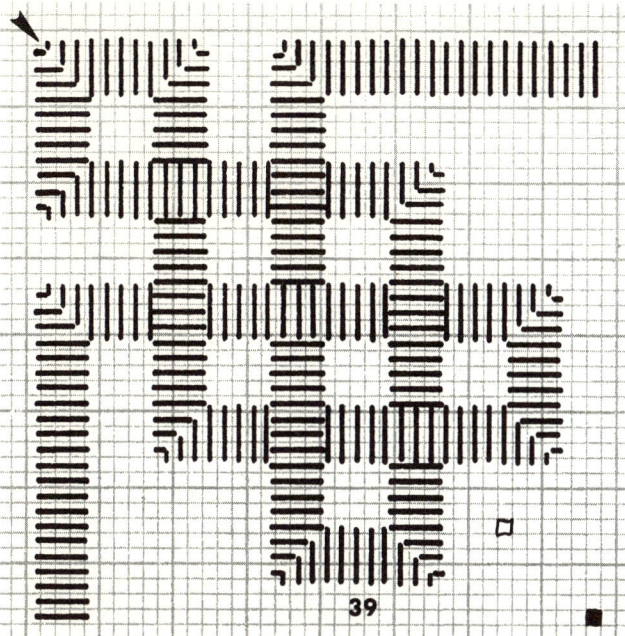

The pattern on the left was used in the corners of J-5. Because the background was dark, the gold Corner pattern looks like brass escutcheons on an antique wooden cabinet.

The expanded version of this pattern, on the right, could be used for a larger project.

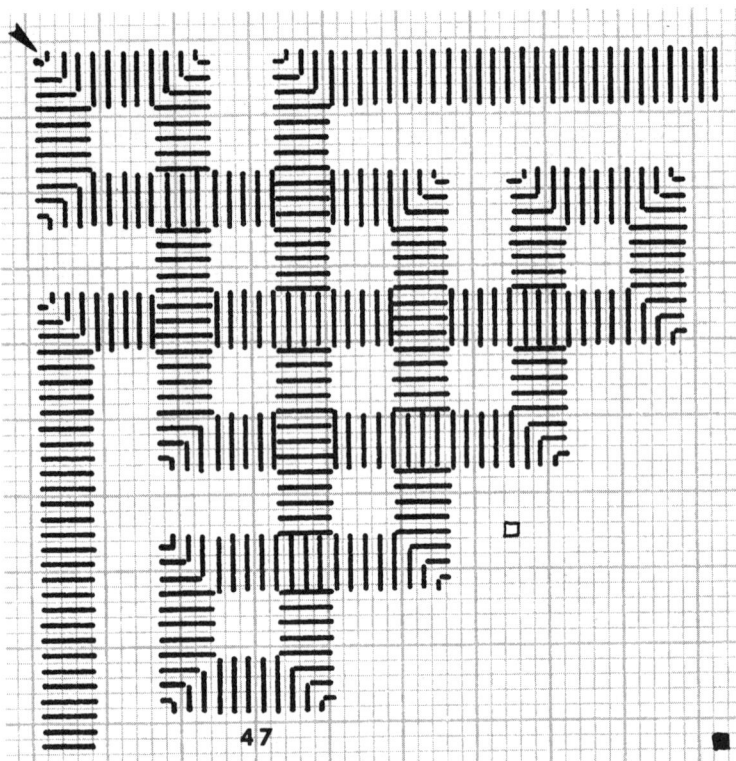

47

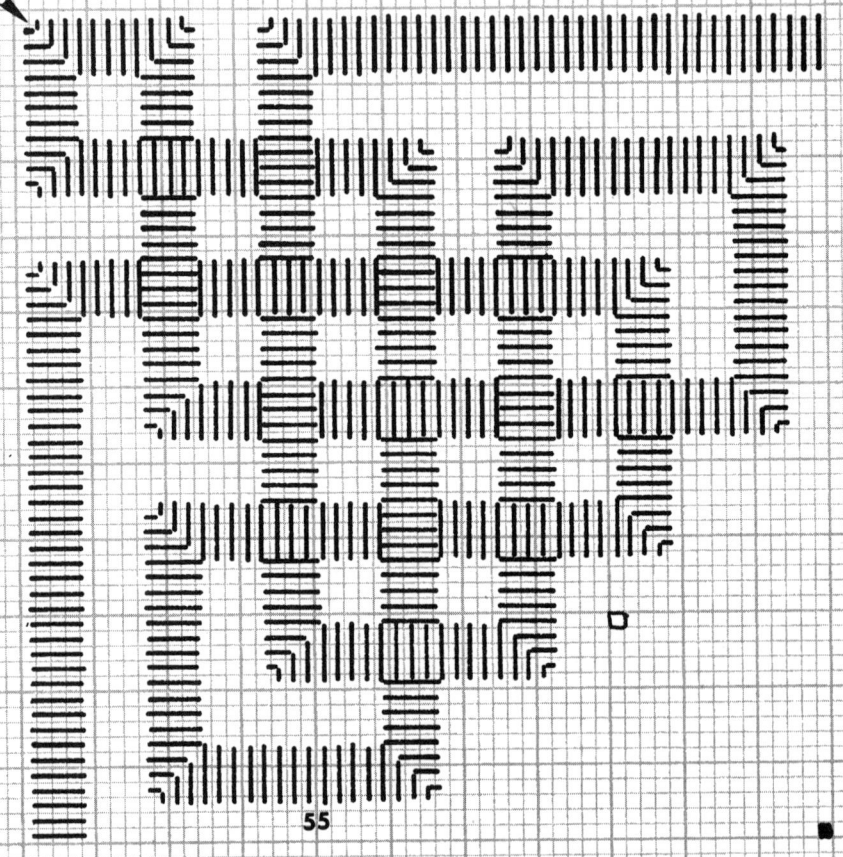

This pattern was used for the brown corners on N-13.

55

This pattern should not be combined with a Kaleidoscopic; it is too large and involved to be used as a secondary pattern. This would be perfect around a monogram or any small design.

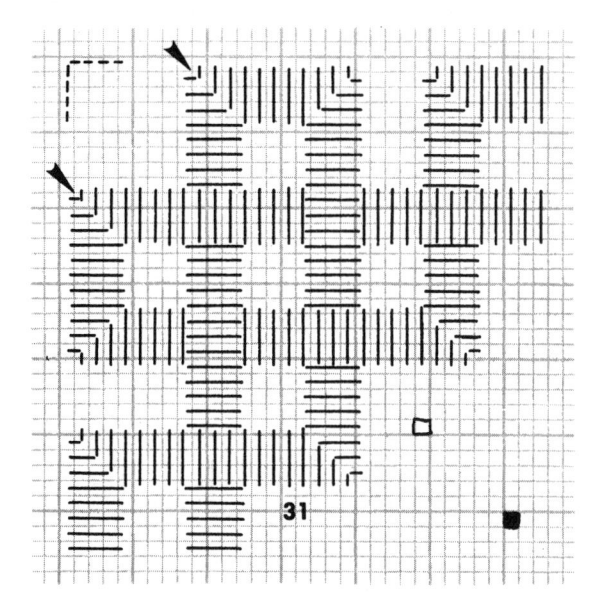

The upper left pattern was used on J-3, a Kaleidoscopic. The lower left Corner was used on the tray, N-25. These are both double line patterns; but, both lines should be stitched in a single color. The dotted lines in the corners correspond to the outline on your canvas. The arrows indicate the starting point for each line.

The pattern below is another double line Corner. Although diagrammed dark and pale, both lines should be stitched in the same color. Always stitch the dark line first, starting at the arrow, even when working a single color.

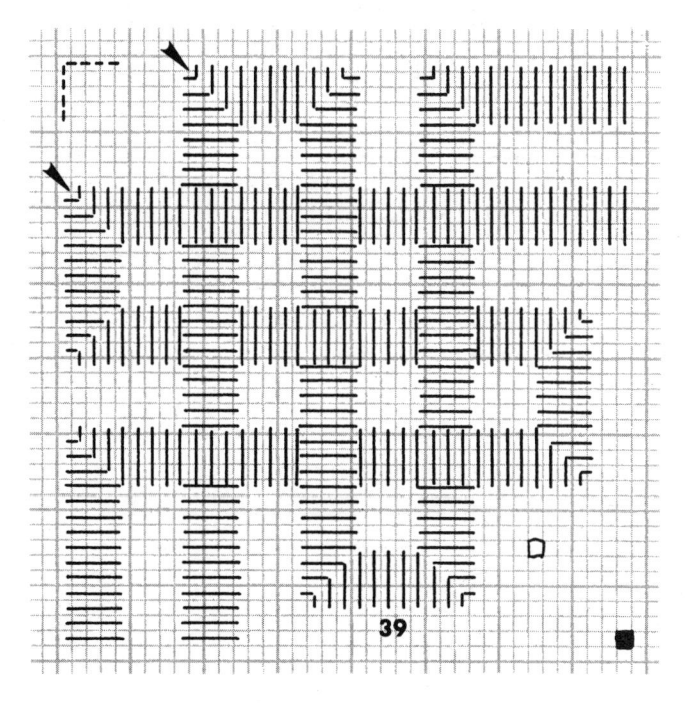

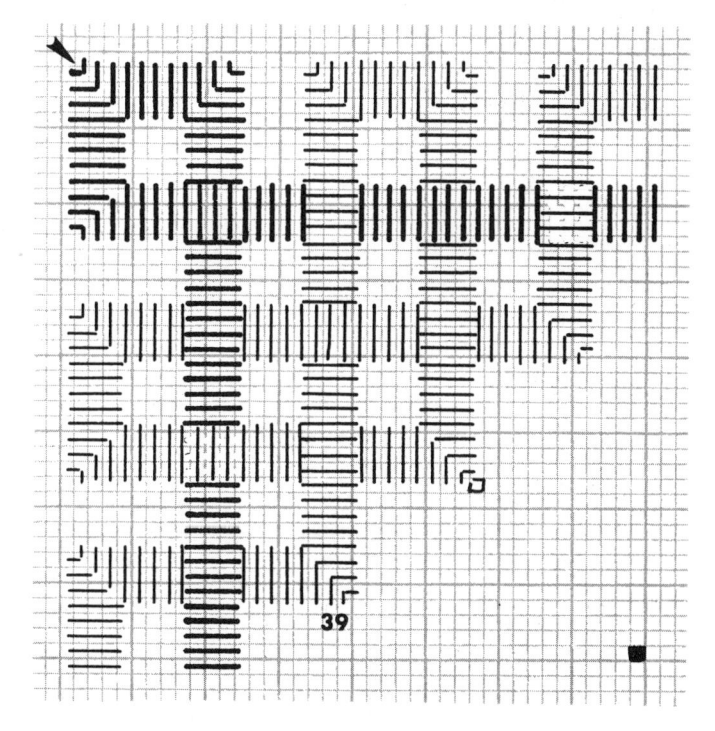

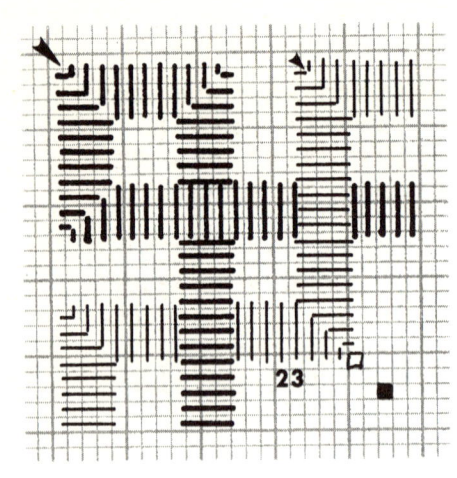

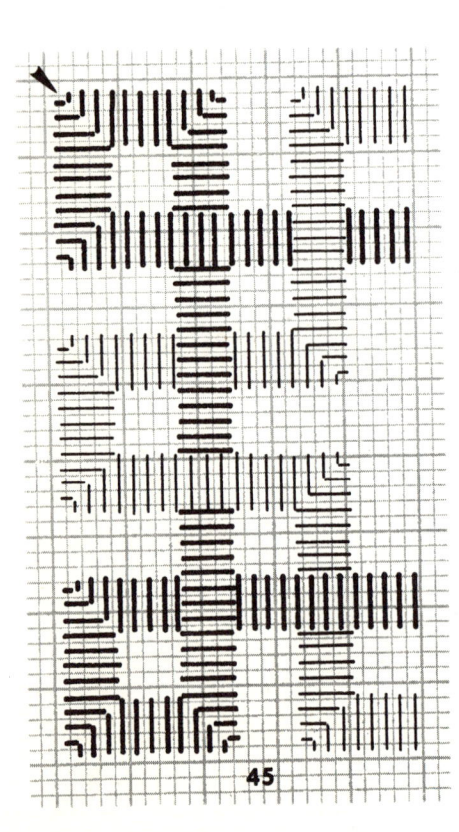

This double line Corner would be perfect for a small item. Once the dark line has been stitched, use it as a guide to find the starting point for the pale line (small arrow).

The straw purse (N-11) used the diagram on the bottom. It is nothing more than two Corners (corner 1 and corner 4) placed as close as possible. This forms an open pattern at each end which can be connected by any amount of straight Gobelin.

The arrows on the line drawing show how the pattern was placed at either end of the purse patch. This type of Corner placement is perfect for a long, narrow design area. The tray on page 24 was a single line rectangle. You must be a bit more careful when working a double line.

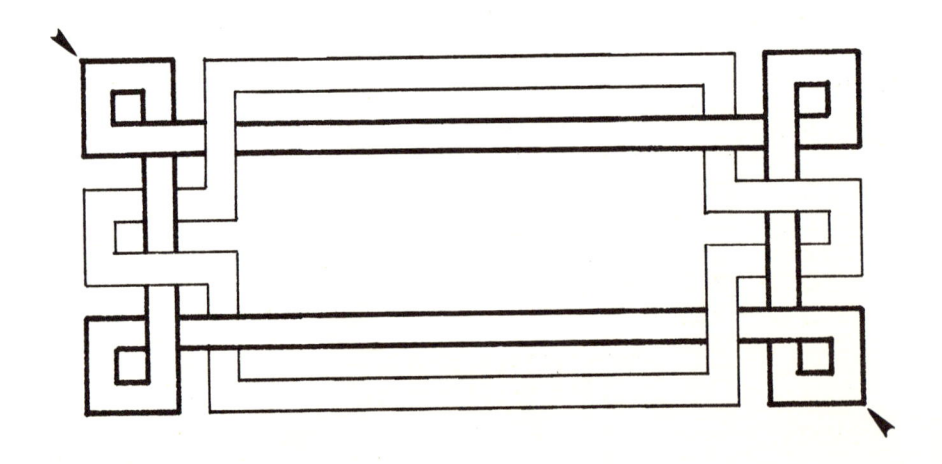

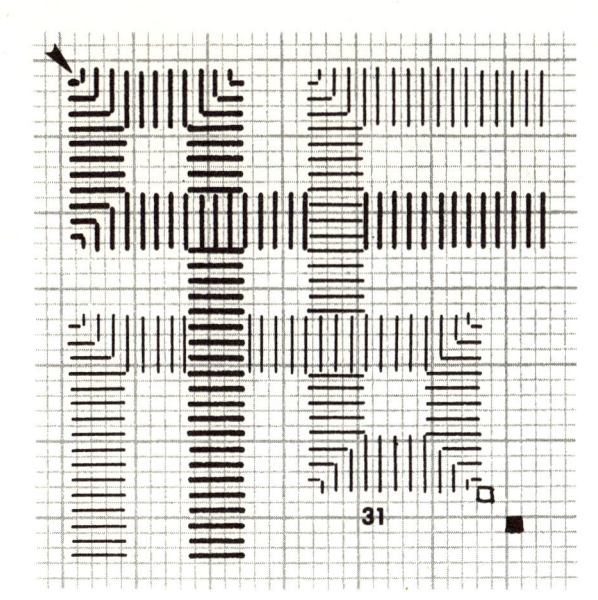

In N-22, this small double line pattern was worked in a single color. N-23 used the same corner in two colors as diagrammed. This illustrates how the use of color can change the appearance of a pattern.

The larger version below is seen in L-4 and I-5. The Triangle stitch was inserted in the 9 x 9 openings and the Brick stitch was used between the pattern lines. It is an attractive textured stitch; it works up quickly and does not detract from the primary pattern.

31

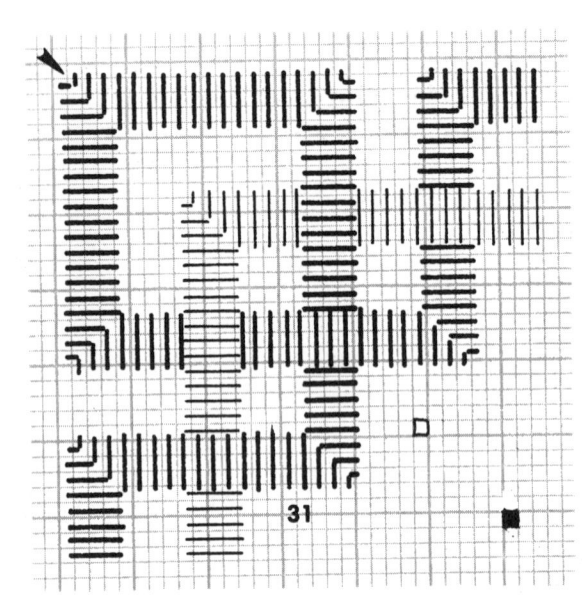

The upper left pattern can be seen on the canvas purse, P-3. Because the interlaced initial was rather large, this small corner was used.

The same size area could accommodate a smaller monogram and a larger Corner, such as the pattern on the lower right.

The lower left corner would "crowd" a monogram. Because it fills the square, it needs a larger area.

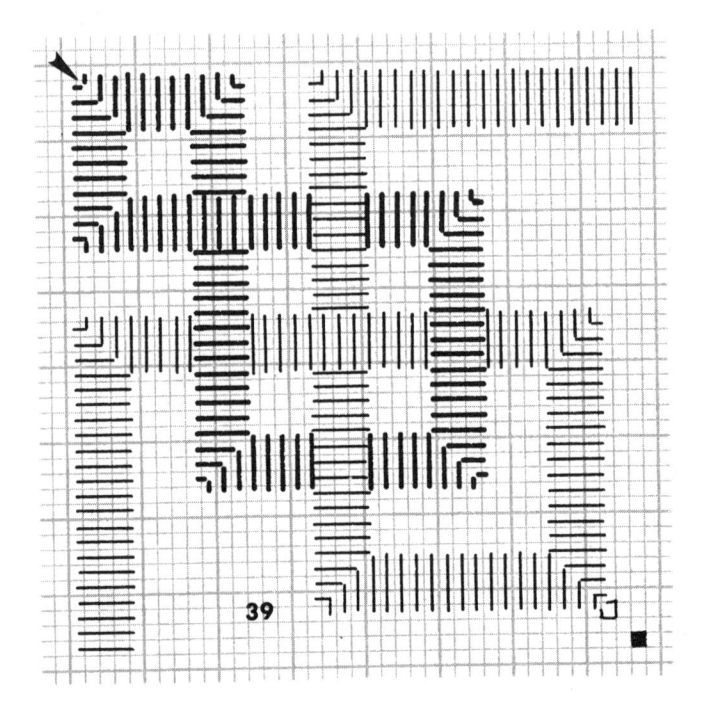

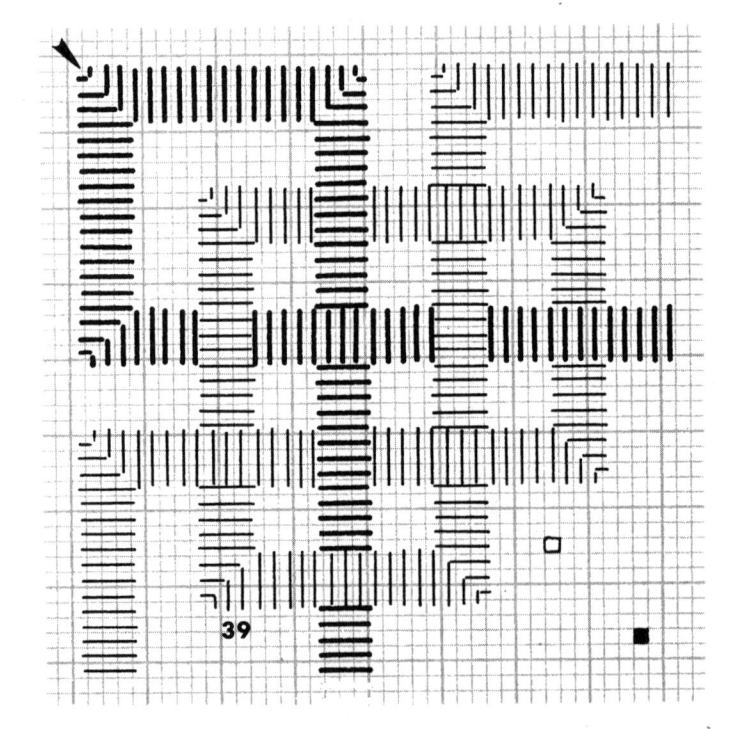

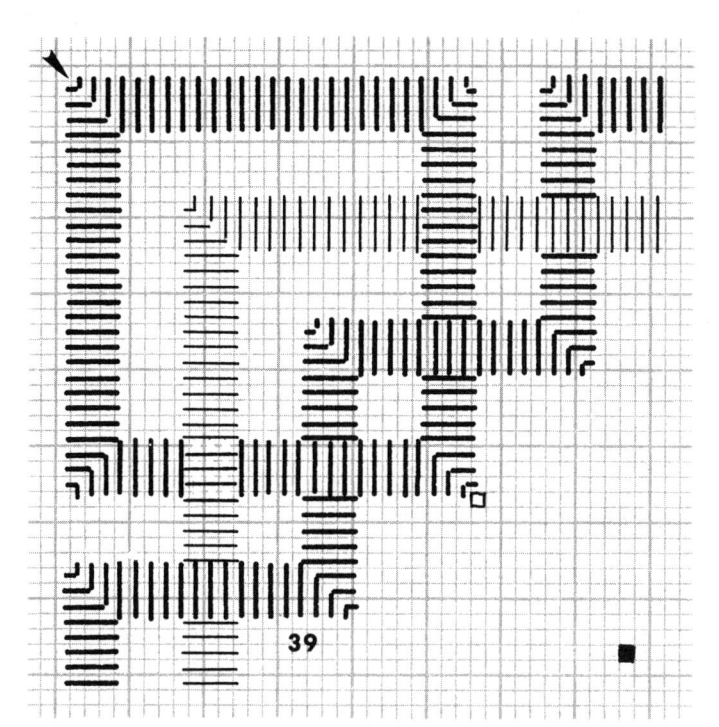

This is a triple line Corner. The bold lines should be done in the same color. This would be smashing around a monogram.

This double line Corner offers the option. Remember the option? This pattern would look entirely different if the pale line continued straight.

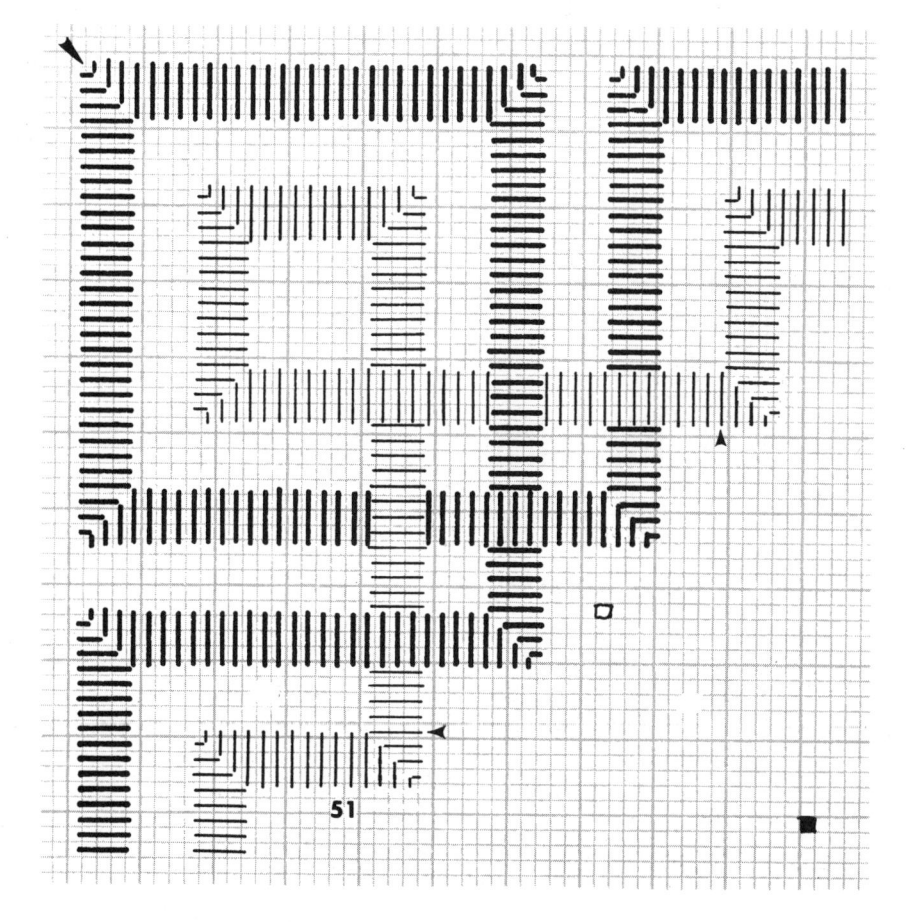

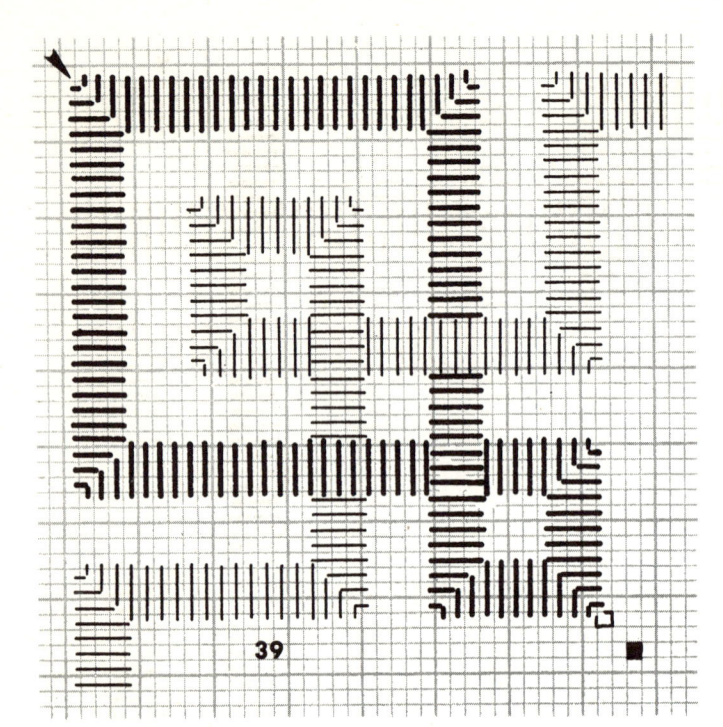

This Corner has not been photographed. Although it has been diagrammed dark and pale, it would be more effective stitched in a single color.

This is a larger double line version. Because the bold line is off-set, you should be careful in your choice of colors - they should be of equal value. Red and black, or light and dark blue would look off balance. Two closely related colors such as medium blue and medium green would work well together.

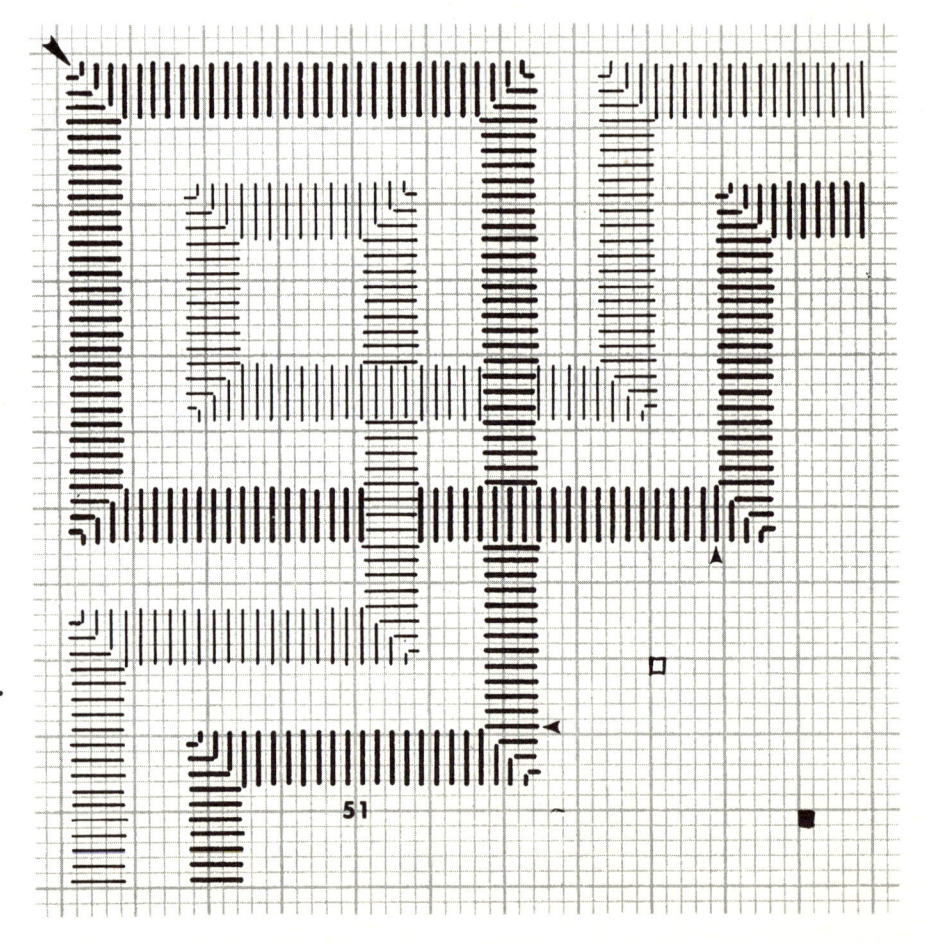

The large square opening can be filled with a Triangle stitch, 13 by 13. Although this pattern has been diagrammed dark and light, it would be more effective if both lines were stitched in the same color.

This is a 4-line Corner. Two pale links criss-cross and separate the two dark lines. Although the Corner pattern itself is rather large, it would fill out the "hollows" of a round or oval design on a square canvas.

The pin cushion, F-3 used this pattern. The small arrows indicate the last long stitch before the miter.

35

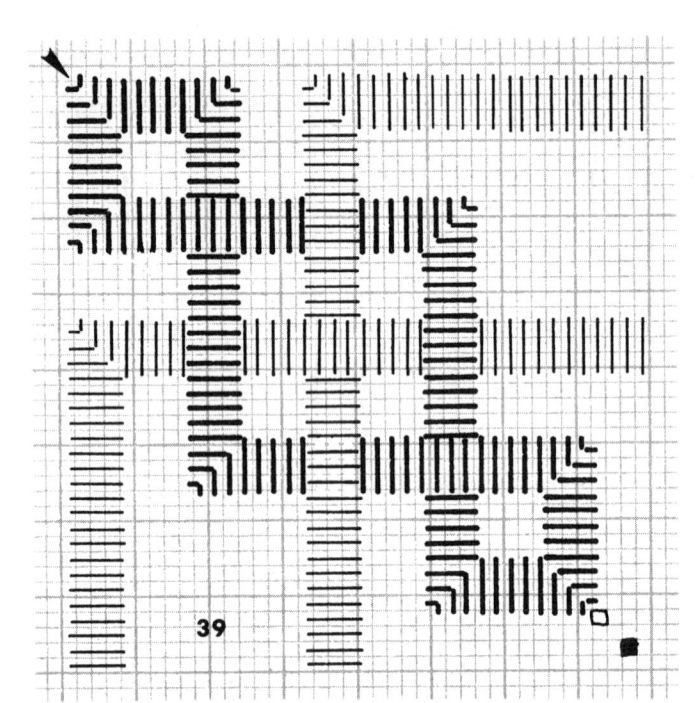

Two different colors could be used on this triple line Corner. Textured stitches would work especially well between the pale lines.

This is the pattern used at the beginning of the Chapter. It can also be seen on the check book cover, N-26. Here it follows the option along the bottom to allow room for a small monogram. Along the sides, the pattern miters out to the edge as diagrammed. The pattern lines were stitched in navy and red against an ecru background of Bias Tent. A row of ecru Mitered Gobelin was worked <u>inside</u> this Border to highlight it and separate it from the red Brick stitch interior.

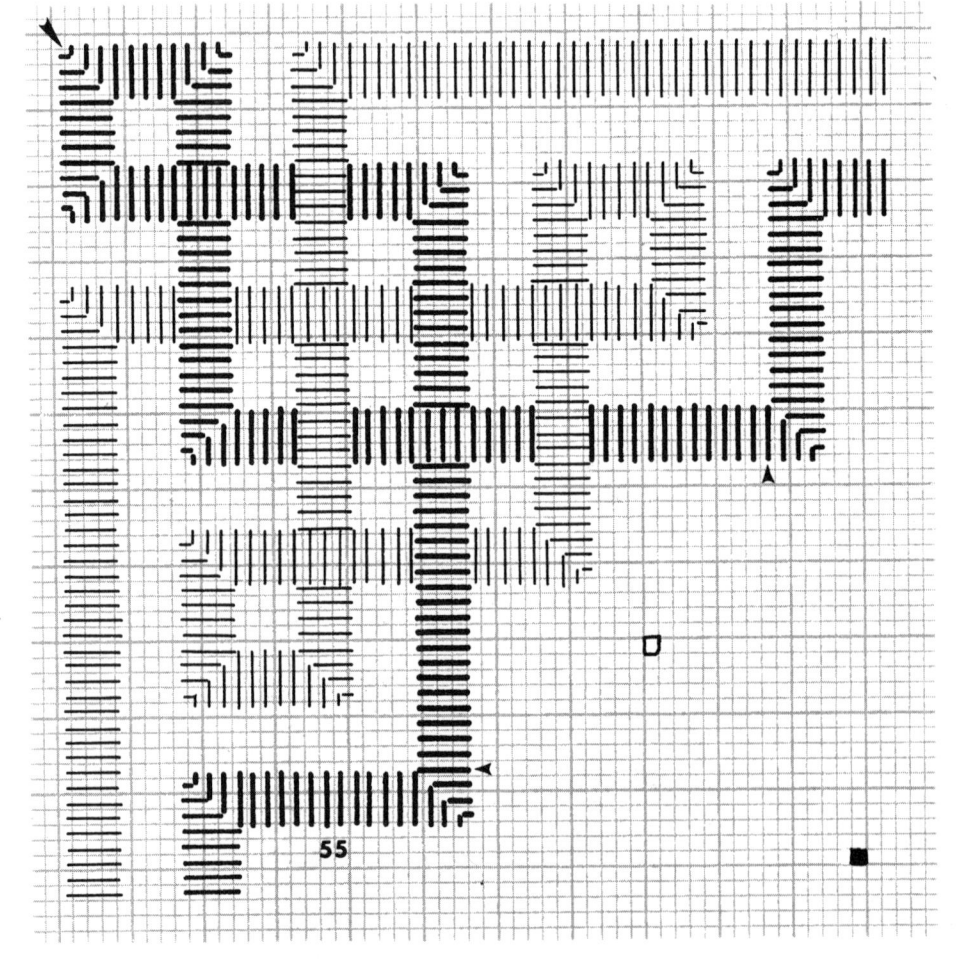

There is no stitch diagram for this surprise pattern. Start at the upper left corner with ½ a miter and do 17 Gobelins (5 holes high). The numbers in each section tell you how many 5 hole Gobelins to do <u>in addition to the miter</u>. A row of Mitered Gobelin around the outside is optional.

If you understand our mitering technique, you will have no trouble with this fun pattern. It is 65 holes square; 5" on a #14 canvas or 3½" on a #18 . When you cut your canvas, be sure to leave adequate margin.

In planning your colors, let your eye follow one line, and then another, around the pattern. Use no more than 3 colors plus the background; they may be shaded, or completely unrelated. Just be careful to keep them in their proper order. Although this pattern has not been photographed, it is intriguing and fun to do.

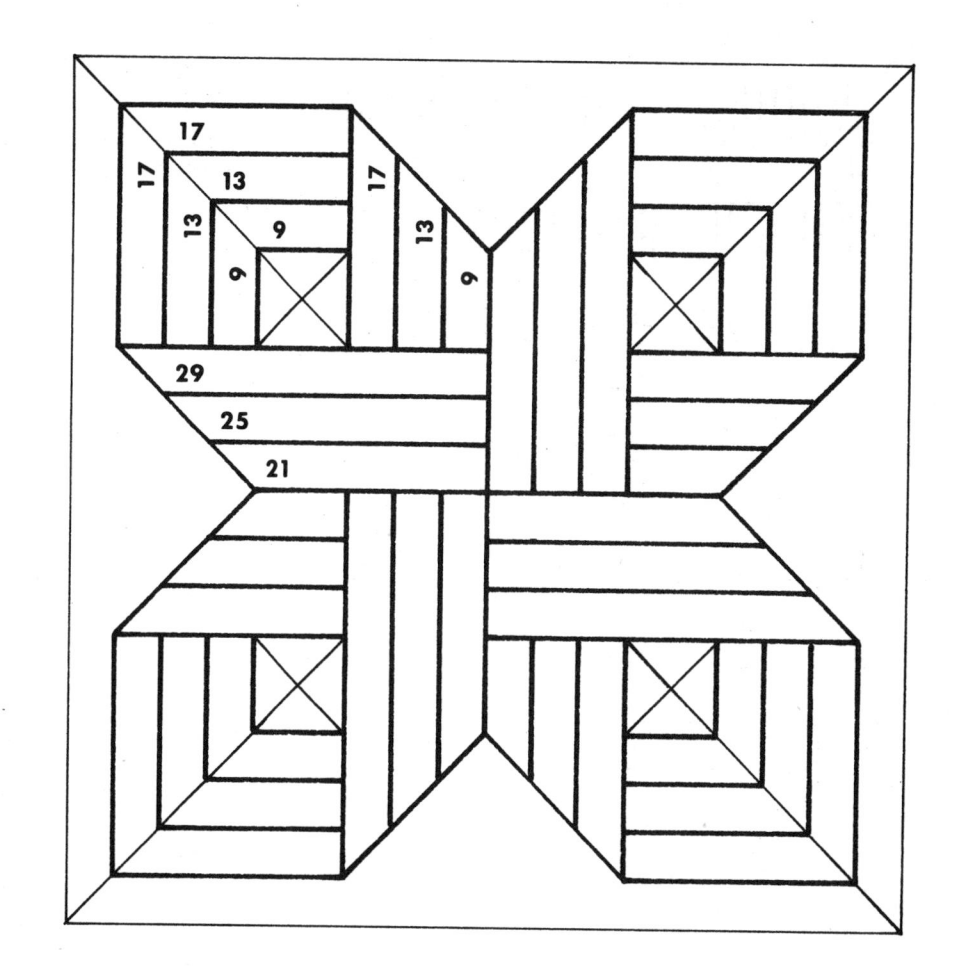

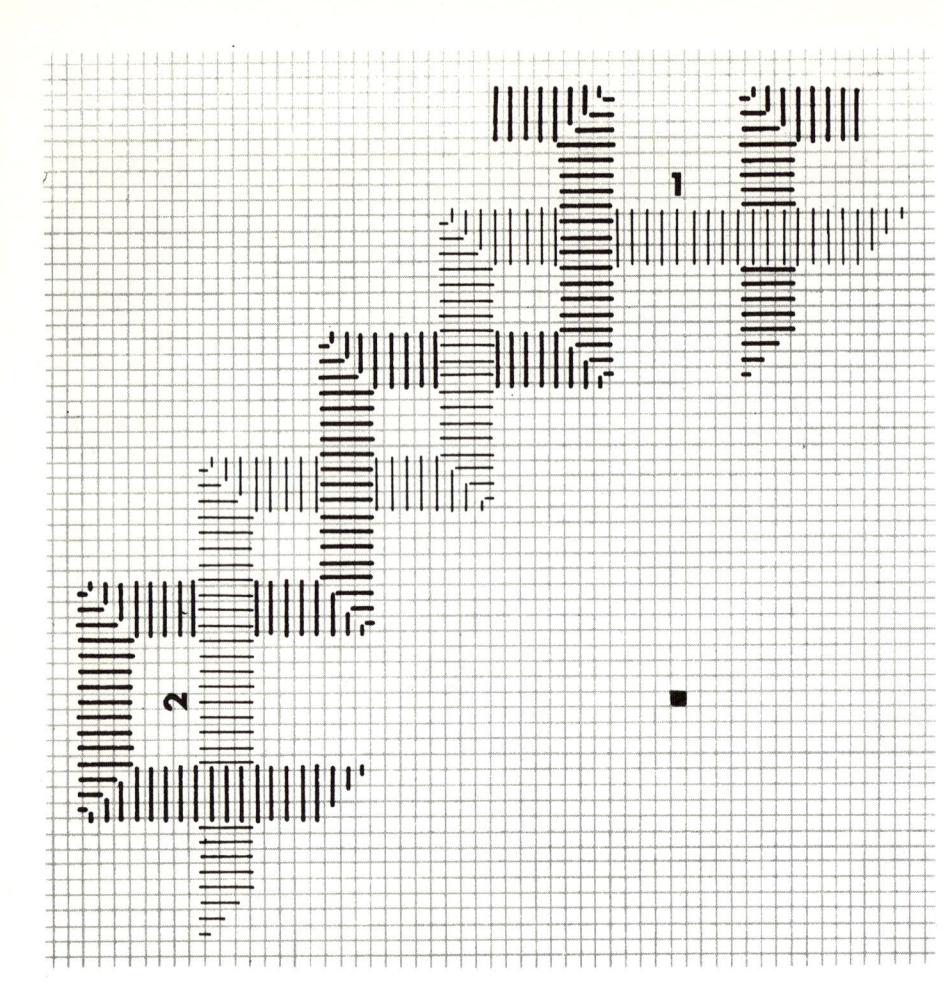

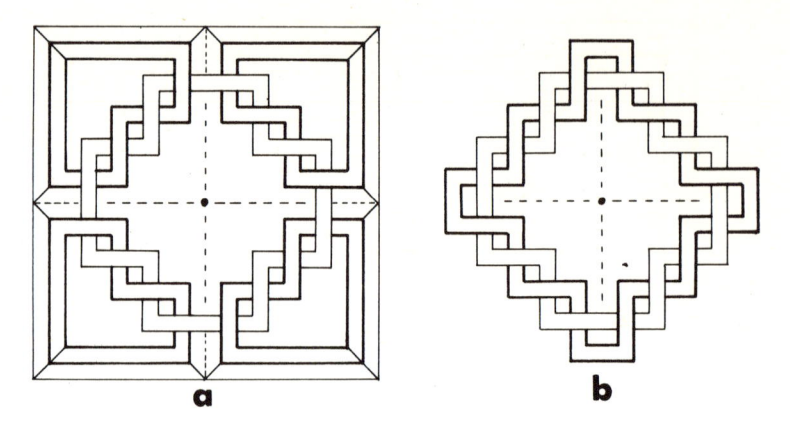

This is one of the most interesting and versatile patterns. The stitch diagram shows 2 options. Option 1 corresponds to Diagram A which has been used as a 6½" square patch for a straw purse (N-15). Option 2 corresponds to Diagram B which has been used on a pre-finished canvas purse (N-20).

Color picture N-19 (Diagram C) is simply an enlarged version of Diagram A. As you can see, more mitered lines have increased the size for a 12" pillow. The bold lines of the pattern (1) are red and intertwine with the pale lines (2) which are navy. All other areas are white. One row of plain Mitered Gobelin in navy was done around the white background to complete the color sequence.

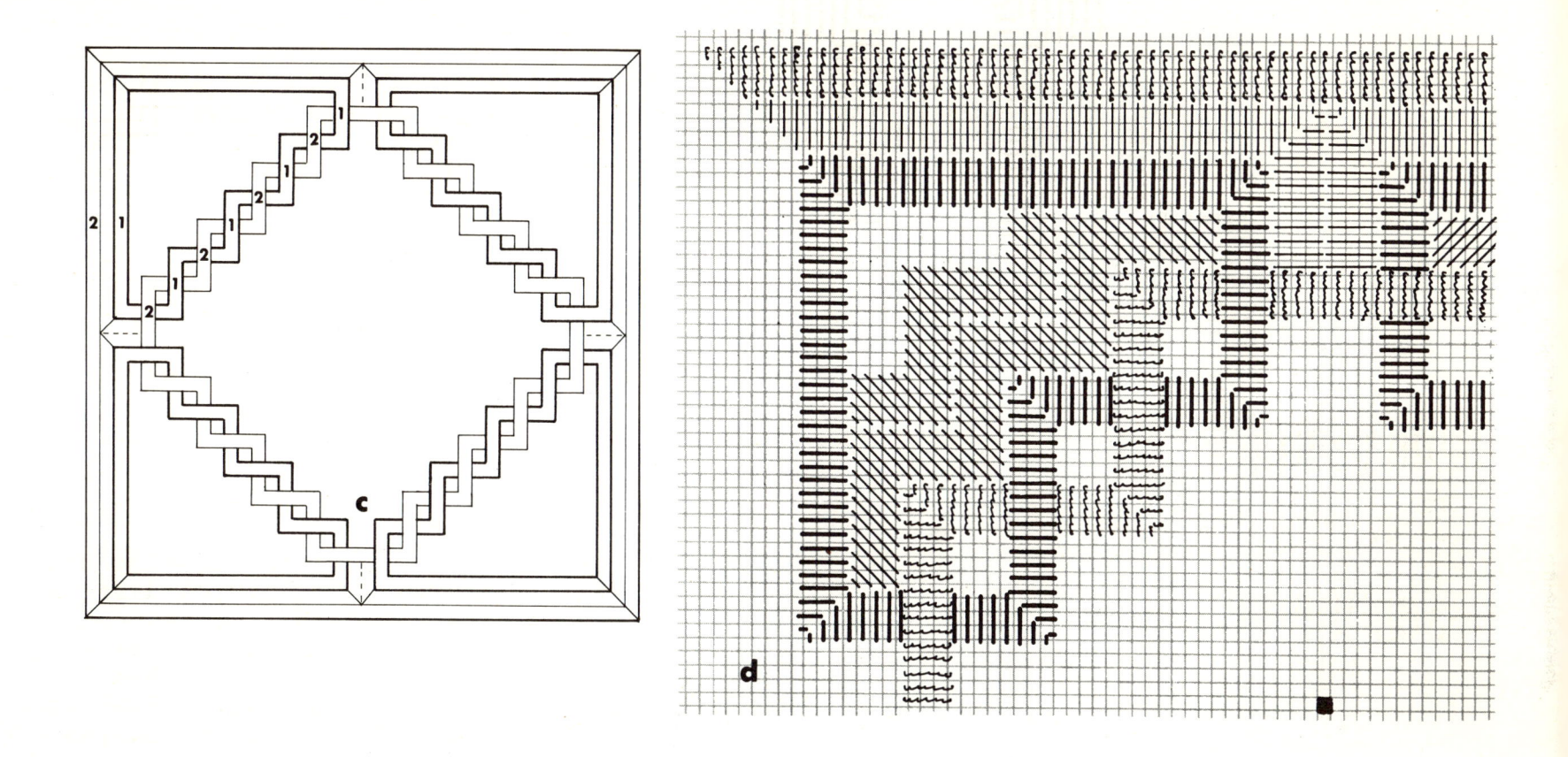

This is a good example of the proper use of textured stitches. The monogram and the background within the pattern line were done in Bias Tent. The Double Leviathan stitch creates a bumpy texture in the center of the pattern line. The Byzantine stitch was enlarged to follow the established pattern and used in the four corners. The detailed stitch diagram (D) shows the enlarged Byzantine following the pattern line. Yes, the Byzantine will slant the "wrong" way in the upper left and lower right sections. This opposite slant causes distortion of the canvas but it will block out.

39

Bargello borders are symmetrical, work up quickly, and cause little distortion of the canvas. Our braid type patterns work on the principle of 2,3, or 4 lines passing alternately over and under one another, as in weaving or plaiting. The wide variety of trims and braids available in fabric shops reflect the growing interest in this type of supplemental design. The spark they lend to clothing, curtains, etc. is a welcome decorative addition.

Because texture is visual as well as tactile, a Bargello border provides a bas-relief or raised effect around a Bias Tent design. By repeating some of the colors of the central motif, the border can be a reinforcement of the total color scheme. For a subtle effect, the intertwining lines and the background can all be done in a single color and the stitch pattern looks as if it had been carved.

Study the photograph carefully. You will see that this Scallop border consists of two intertwining lines. The movement of these lines throughout the border creates a rhythm for the eye to follow. The pattern continues without interruption because we have planned the mitered corners as an integral part of the border design.

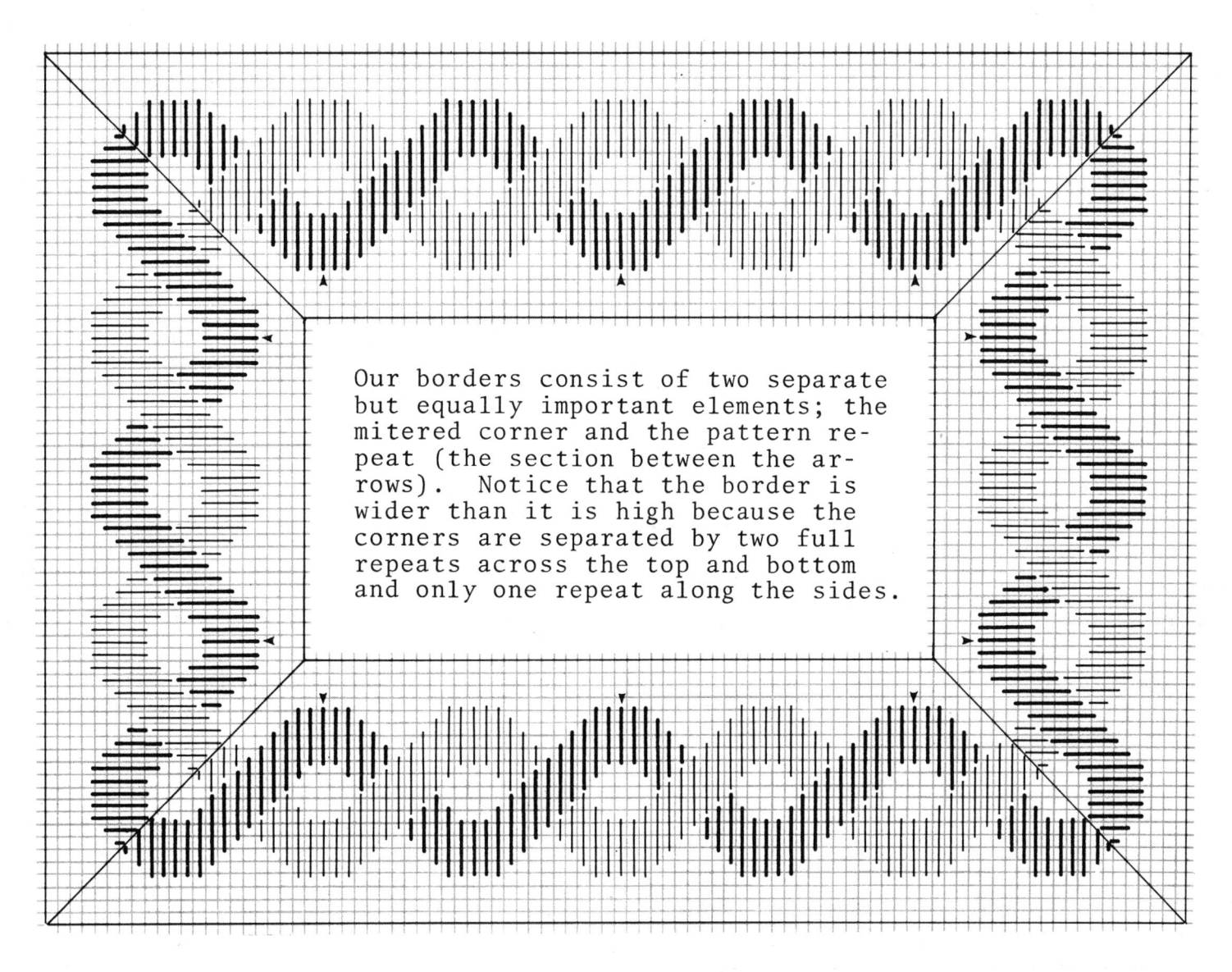

Our borders consist of two separate but equally important elements; the mitered corner and the pattern repeat (the section between the arrows). Notice that the border is wider than it is high because the corners are separated by two full repeats across the top and bottom and only one repeat along the sides.

Pattern depth = 21 holes
Repeat width = 24 holes
Corner width = 23 holes

Think of each side of your border as a corner - any number of repeats - and another corner. You may use as many repeats as you need, but you must use full repeats. This means that you may break your pattern only at the arrows. They indicate where you may either continue into another repeat, or miter into a corner. Notice that both lines are alike except at the corners, and that all four corners are identical.

Because of the limitations of working with full repeats, it is imperative that your border be stitched first. Allow enough room for the central motif which will be traced onto the canvas after the border is finished. Do not work backward and attempt a border of this kind after your central design is on the canvas. It does not work successfully. You may use one of our Corner patterns if you want a border around something you have already started.

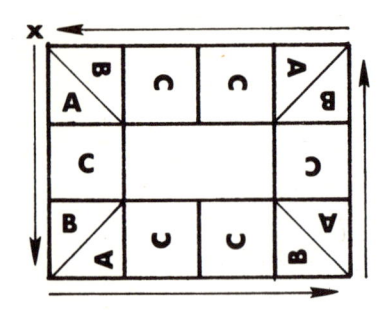

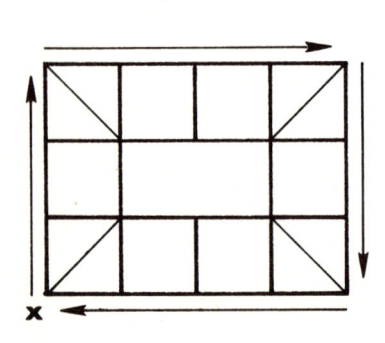

This diagram shows how the border segments fit together. Start at the top left corner. It has been broken diagonally (mitered) into two sections - A and B. Section A carries you out of the corner, through one repeat (C), and miters into the lower left corner at B. Turn your canvas and miter out of this corner at A, through two repeats, and into the next corner at B. Turn your canvas again and miter out at A. Continue working around your canvas until your border re-connects with itself in the upper left corner (B/A).

In laying on a border, you must start at a miter. It doesn't matter which miter, which corner, or in which direction you stitch. For consistancy, we always start in the upper left corner. The important thing is that you start at a miter, and work your way continuously around the canvas.

Our border patterns are not difficult, but they are very precise. Every hole on the chart is important and corresponds to a hole on your canvas. An incorrect count in either the number of stitches, their length, or their placement will throw your border off track. Once you get out of the corner, a stitching rhythm will develop and you will not have to refer to the chart for every stitch.

42

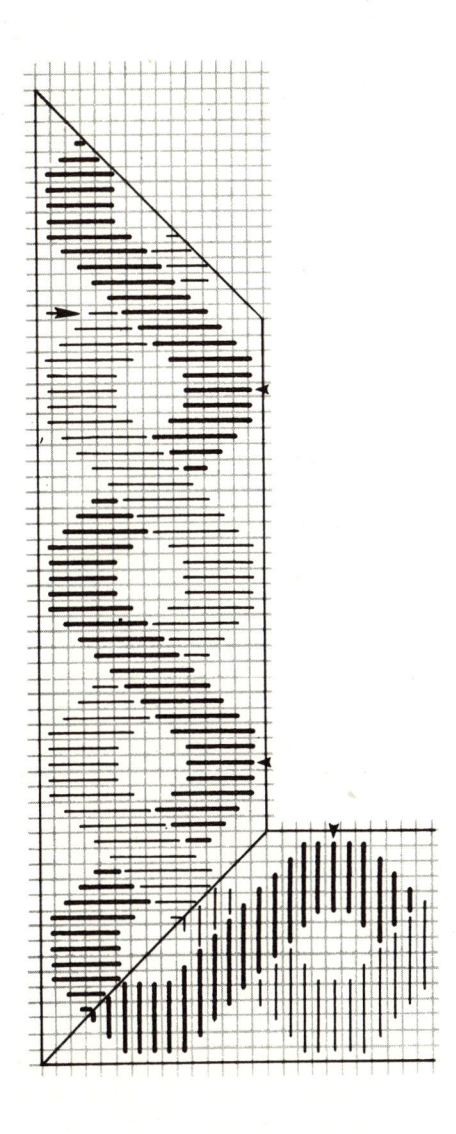

Let's look at this pattern. As you can see, it miters out of the corner (A), continues through one repeat, miters into (B), and out of (A), the next corner. You must learn how to visually separate the pattern because you will be working just one line at a time.

Start at the miter and stitch only the dark line. Count the length of each stitch and notice its placement. The first stitch uses only 2 holes (do not pull your yarn tightly or it will bury itself between the canvas threads). The second stitch expands to 4 holes. There are four stitches that are 6 holes high. The next stitch is the first of a group of nine that use 7 holes. Add the three stitches that are 6 holes high, the two 7's, a 5 and a 3. Skip a row of holes and place your next stitch as indicated on the diagram, leaving room for the other row of stitches to pass over. Continue counting and stitching. Remember - every hole and every stitch is vital.

The second line is counted and stitched in the same manner. The arrow shows the easiest starting point. You will have no trouble stitching your pale line "over" the dark line or ending it as you prepare to go "under". On the diagram it is easy to see where the pale line emerges - not as easy on the canvas. This is the point where most mistakes occur. Your border will fit together perfectly if you have counted and stitched accurately.

There are a few simple steps which must be followed in planning a border project.

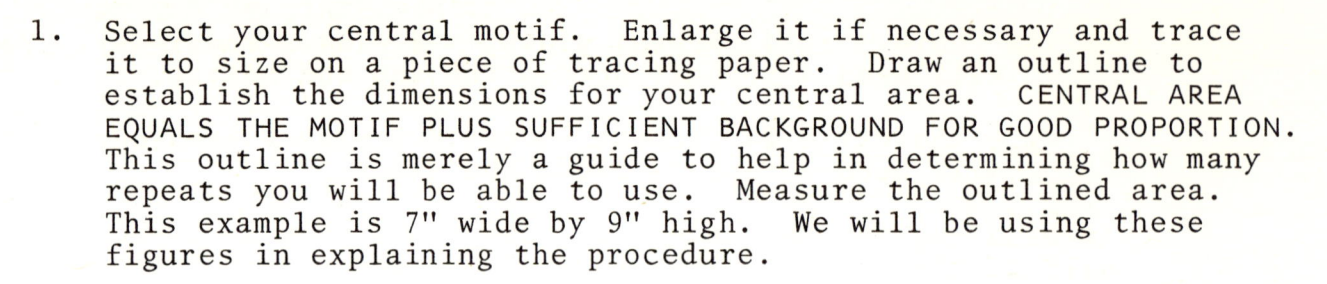

1. Select your central motif. Enlarge it if necessary and trace it to size on a piece of tracing paper. Draw an outline to establish the dimensions for your central area. CENTRAL AREA EQUALS THE MOTIF PLUS SUFFICIENT BACKGROUND FOR GOOD PROPORTION. This outline is merely a guide to help in determining how many repeats you will be able to use. Measure the outlined area. This example is 7" wide by 9" high. We will be using these figures in explaining the procedure.

2. Select your border. Refer to the legend that accompanies it.

    Pattern depth = 21 holes (The number of holes between the top and bottom of the pattern including the border background).
    Repeat width = 24 holes (The number of holes from one arrow to the hole <u>before</u> the next arrow inclusive).
    Corner width = 23 holes (The number of holes needed to complete a corner).

The inside dimensions of the border must be large enough to accommodate your central area. How many pattern repeats will you need? The repeats are figured by hole count, so you must convert your inch measurements to holes also. This is done mathematically - but don't panic!

3. Multiply your central area dimension (7" x 9") by the size canvas you are going to use.

    7" wide x 14 (canvas size) = 98 holes
    9" high x 14 (canvas size) = 126 holes

Your inside measurements should be approximately 98 holes wide by 126 holes high.

This silhouette will be a personal "portrait", because photographic realism in needlepoint is impossible.

44

4. To figure the number of repeats that will fit, divide these figures (98 holes and 126 holes) by the Repeat width (24).

   98 (holes) ÷ 24 (Repeat width) = 4 plus a remainder. You will need 4 repeats across the top and bottom.

   126 (holes) ÷ 24 (Repeat width) = 5 plus a remainder. You will need 5 repeats along the sides.

In handling the remainder, we have found that any fraction over half of the Repeat width requires another repeat. It all depends on how close to your motif you drew your outline. ¼ of this repeat is 6 holes or about ½" on #14 canvas. Can your border encroach on the central area ¼" on each side and still be in proportion? If so, forget the remainder and don't add another repeat.

   If you were using a #10 canvas which has fewer holes per inch, your total hole count would be <u>less</u> for the measurement. (70 x 90). Here you would have $\overline{3}$ repeats across the top and bottom and 4 repeats along the sides.

   If you were using a #18 canvas, more repeats would be needed to allow room for your central area.

   7" x 18 = 126 ÷ 24 = 5¼. You would need 5 repeats across the top and bottom.
   9" x 18 = 162 ÷ 24 = 6 3/4. You would need 7 repeats along the sides.

5. Before you cut your canvas, you must determine your outside dimensions. This is very easy. You know that your border will be Corner + 4 repeats + Corner across the top and bottom. Simply add the number of holes required to complete a corner (23) + the 4 repeats (96) + the next corner (23) = 142 holes wide. Divide this figure (142) by the size canvas you are using (14) to convert it back to inches = about 10" wide.

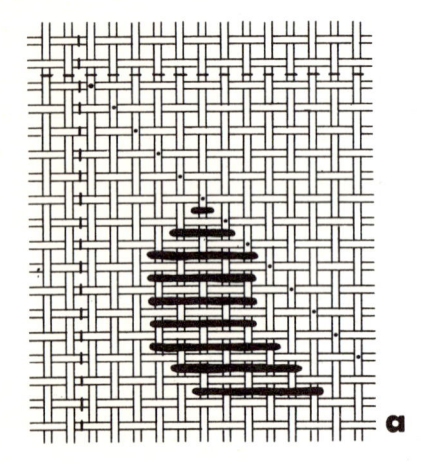

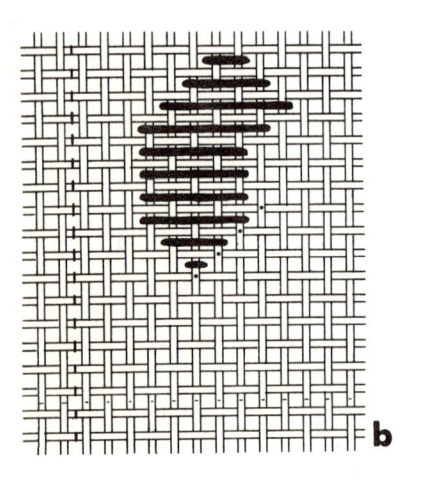

Do the same for height. 23 (Corner) + 120 (5 repeats) + 23 (Corner) = 166 holes high. Divide this by 14 (canvas size) = almost 12" high. Remember to add 2" all around for blank margin. You can safely cut your canvas 14" x 16".

6. Bind it and mark it as described in Marking for Borders.

7. Always start at a miter. Locate your first stitch on the canvas to correspond with the first stitch on the diagram (A). This enlarged "canvas" shows how you begin stitching along the Miter line. Count and stitch the dark line for the required number of repeats and miter it into the next corner. Your last three stitches fit into the next Miter Line. It has not yet been marked.

8. Look at these last three stitches (B). They show the direction and angle of the miter. Which thread is on top of the mesh along this diagonal line? In this diagram, a vertical thread is on top and your Miter Line can now be marked. Remember, just "dot" these mesh. The pale dotted line across the bottom shows the outline for the next side.

9. Go back and stitch the pale line from the first corner to the second corner. Continue working one line at a time around the canvas, mitering when necessary. Your border will eventually reconnect with itself.

46

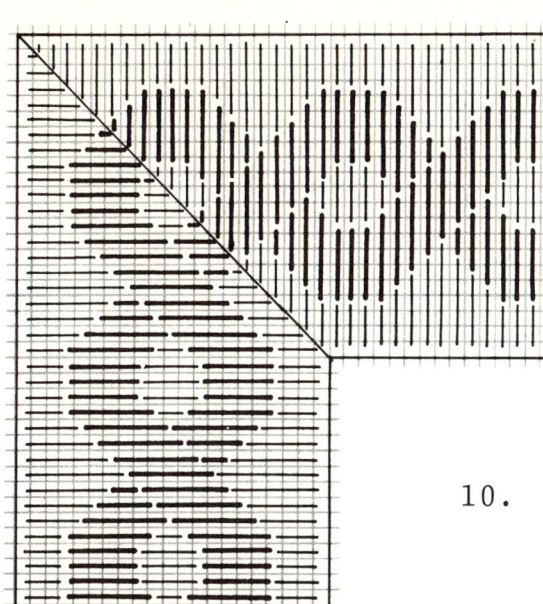

10. When both lines of your border pattern are complete, you can fill in the border background with vertical stitches. These background stitches share holes with the pattern stitches and square up the border area. The background is indicated on the diagram by an outline; the individual stitches are ordinarily not diagrammed as it would be too confusing.

11. Your border is complete and you may now trace on your central design. Tape the tracing onto a picture window or storm door. Place your canvas over it; move it until the design is properly centered; then tape it securely. Trace your motif with a marker, and use acrylics if you want a painted design.

12. Stitch your central motif, and then stitch the balance of the central area between the border and the motif.

13. Work two rows of Tent around the entire piece (outside the border). This acts as a seam allowance when you assemble your pillow. Finishing techniques are well explained in the last Chapter.

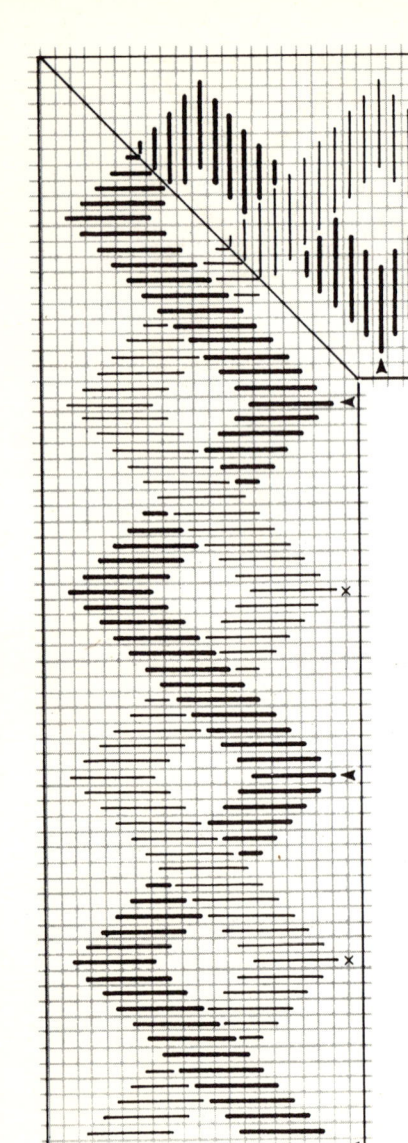

R - 24 (Repeat-arrow to arrow)
½ - 12 (½ Repeat-arrow to x)
C - 22 (Corner)
D - 21 (Depth)

Our intertwining borders make beautiful belts, curtain tie-backs, luggage rack straps and would be smashing as the boxing for a plain velvet pillow.

There are several ways to vary the width of the border to fit your needs. Our suggested background width has been indicated by an outline, or you may:
1. Extend the background width evenly on both sides.
2. Work flush with your Peak stitch.
3. Work on a #18 canvas if you need a thinner band. No matter what width you make your border, be sure you do the background in vertical stitches. This is what produces the depth and carved effect that make the borders so attractive. The introduction of Bias Tent in this area detracts from the final appearance.

Our borders have been diagrammed with bold and pale lines representing two different colors. If you wish, you may stitch all lines in the same color. On some of our borders this would reduce the repeat width. Any time you see a small x on the diagram, as above, you have the option of continuing the pattern into another repeat or turning a corner. The "x-stitch" is exactly the same as the arrow stitch and you would follow the stitch pattern for the bold line to turn a corner. This applies only if all pattern lines are stitched in the same color. If you are using more than one color, ignore the x's and stitch as diagrammed.

In color picture P-13, we see an easy border variation. Only the corner segment, and one repeat on each side was used. The four corners were then connected by straight Gobelin.

48

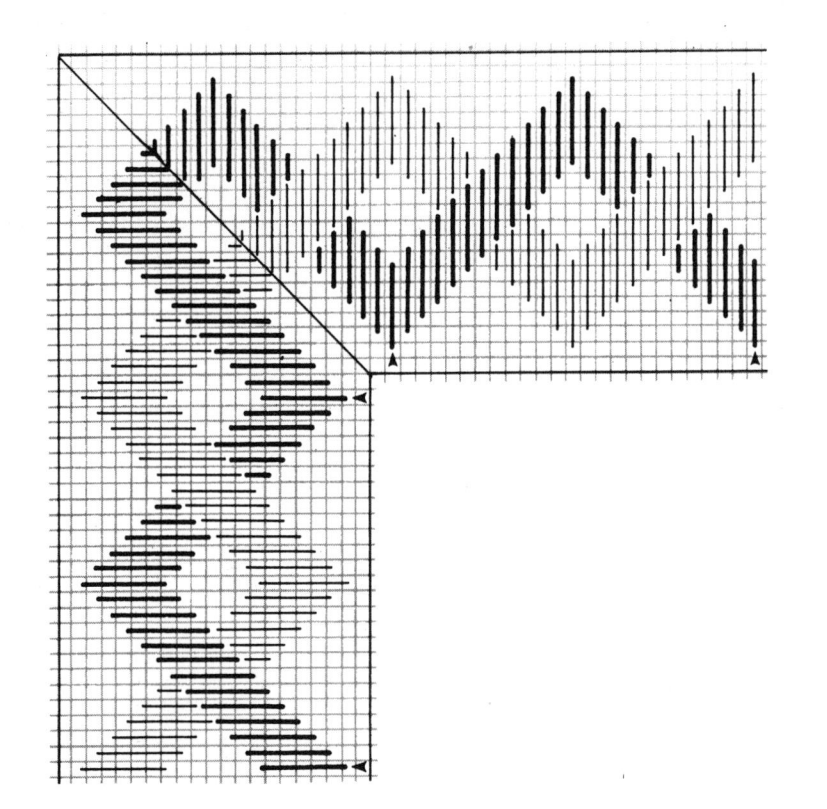

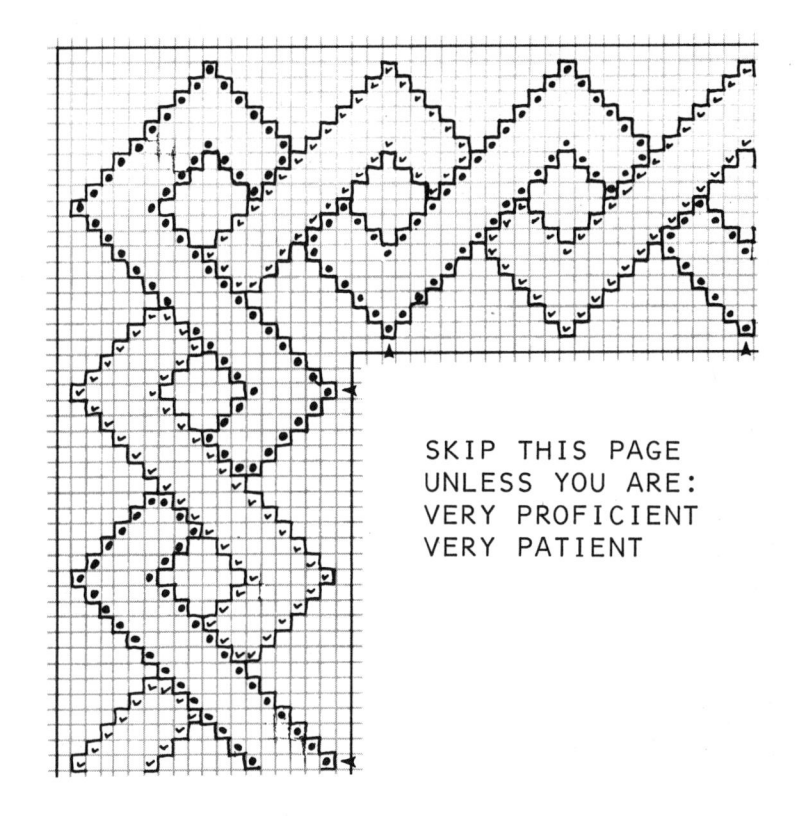

SKIP THIS PAGE
UNLESS YOU ARE:
VERY PROFICIENT
VERY PATIENT

The diagram on the left is the chart for an intertwining Bargello border. The diagram on the right is the conversion chart for Bias Tent. This is not an easy task but if you are "hung up" on Bias Tent you may convert any of our patterns. A rug border requires conversion; Bargello would be too snaggy underfoot.

Notice the stitches on the Bargello diagram are 7 holes high; only 6 mesh high on the conversion diagram. THERE IS ALWAYS ONE LESS MESH THAN HOLE WHEN YOU CONVERT TO BIAS TENT.

All border conversions must be planned on graph paper first and then transferred to the canvas. It is necessary to mark only the outer mesh for each line. Be sure to use different colored markers to eliminate confusion.

49

A slender Flame for small projects.

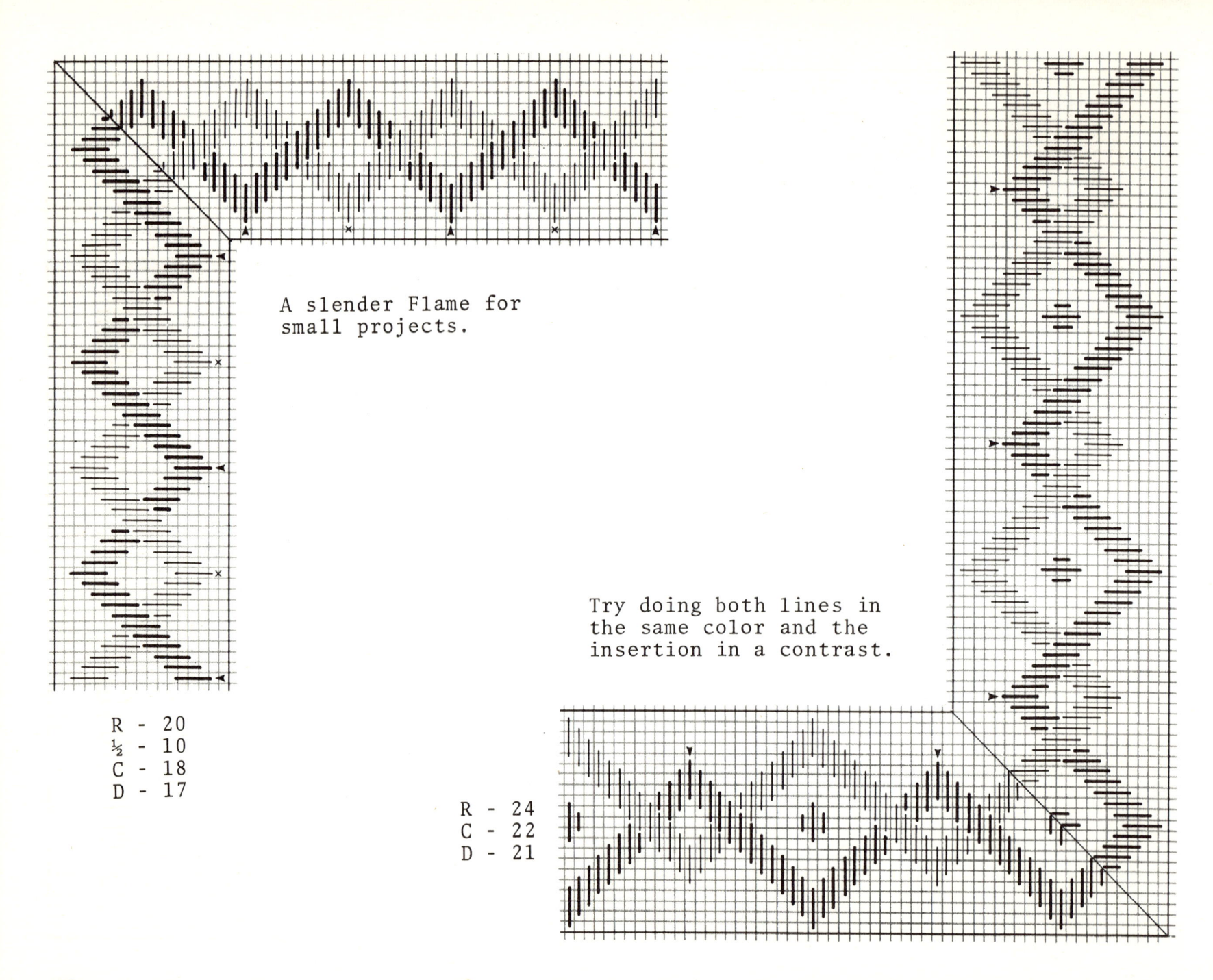

Try doing both lines in the same color and the insertion in a contrast.

R - 20
½ - 10
C - 18
D - 17

R - 24
C - 22
D - 21

50

R - 36
C - 35
D - 25

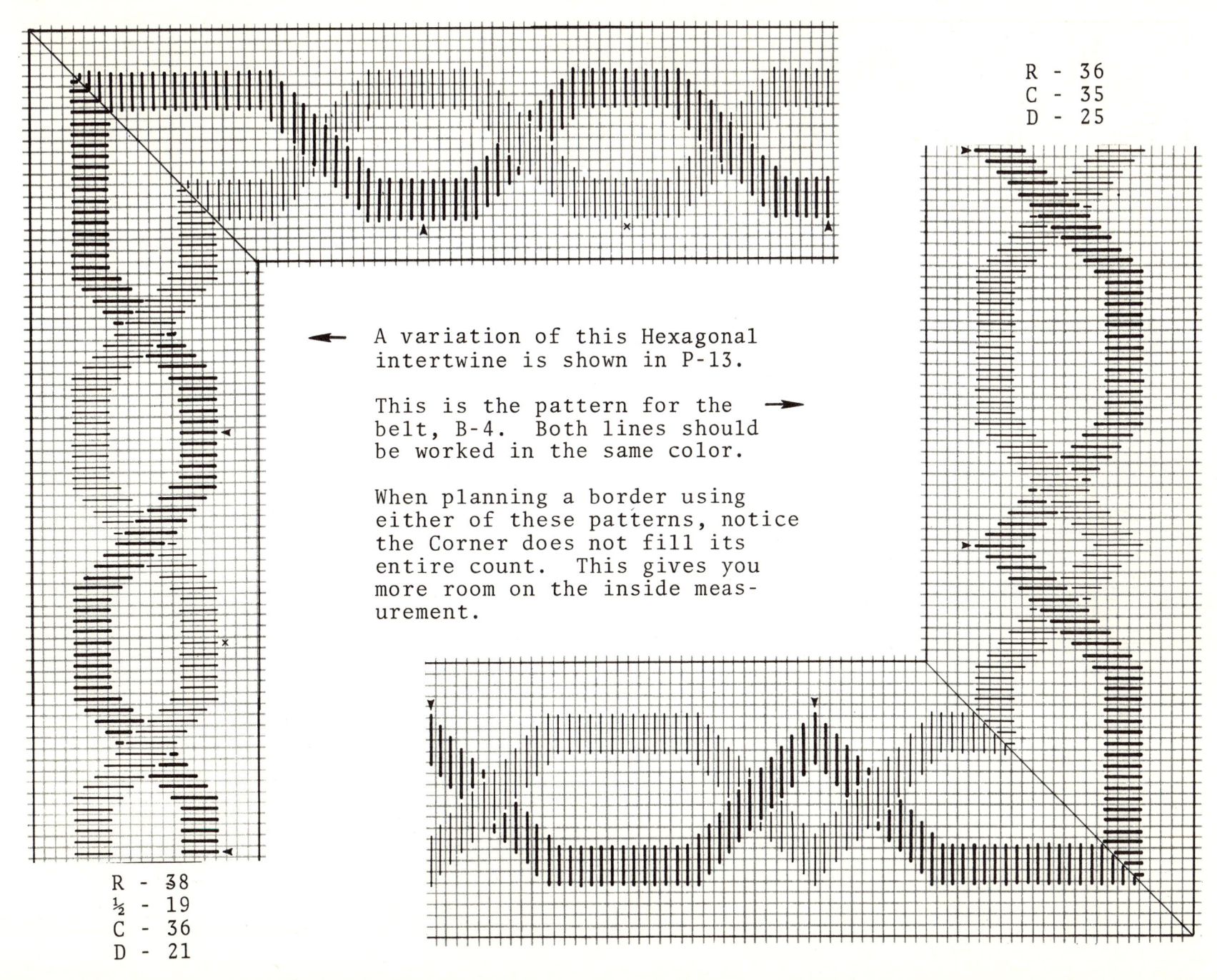

← A variation of this Hexagonal intertwine is shown in P-13.

This is the pattern for the → belt, B-4. Both lines should be worked in the same color.

When planning a border using either of these patterns, notice the Corner does not fill its entire count. This gives you more room on the inside measurement.

R - 38
½ - 19
C - 36
D - 21

51

This small twisted ribbon is a good choice when you need a border with a short Repeat.

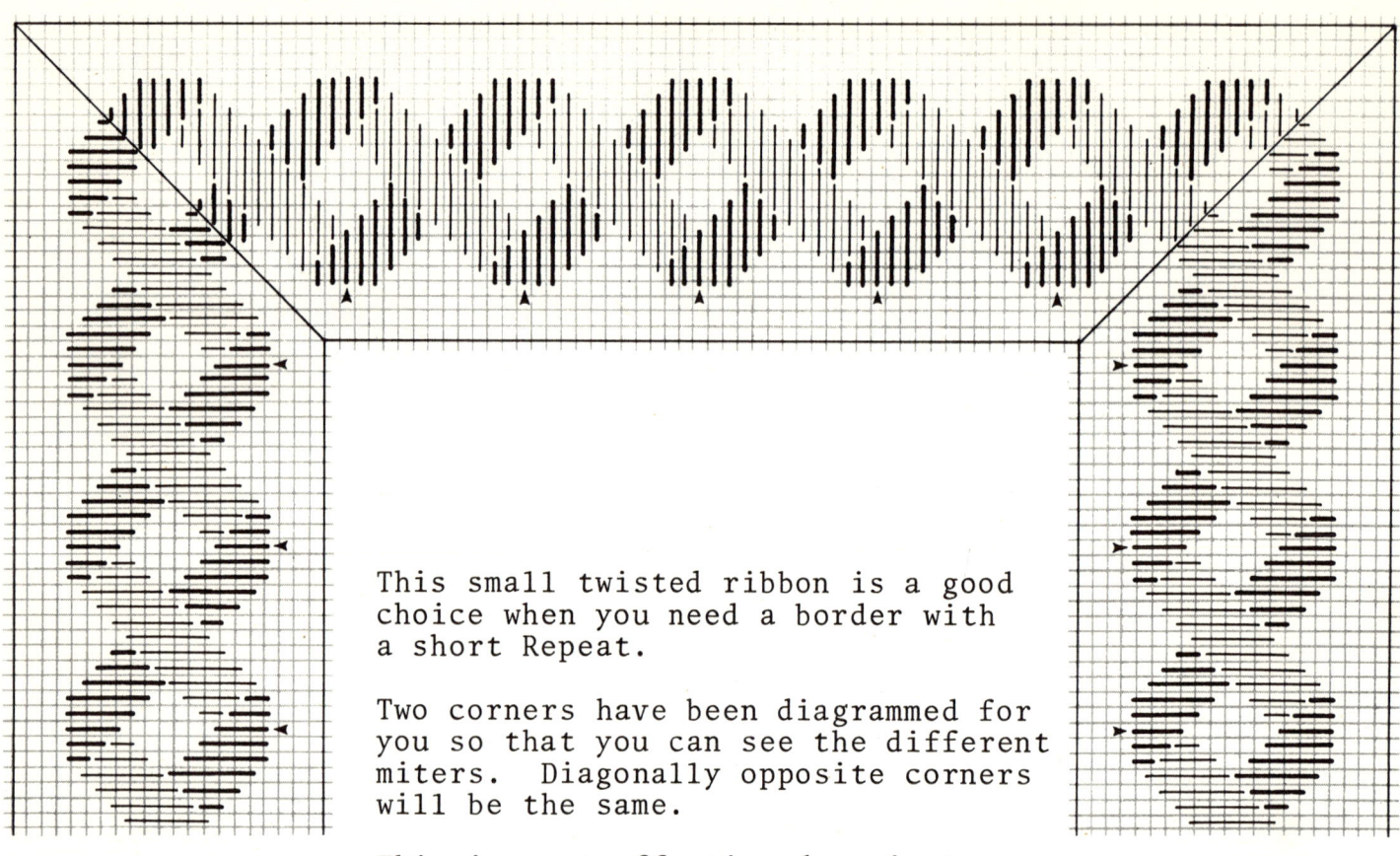

Two corners have been diagrammed for you so that you can see the different miters. Diagonally opposite corners will be the same.

R - 12
C - 22
D - 21

This is most effective done in two shades or two colors against a contrasting background. If you want both lines in a single color, the simple Scallop would be a better choice.

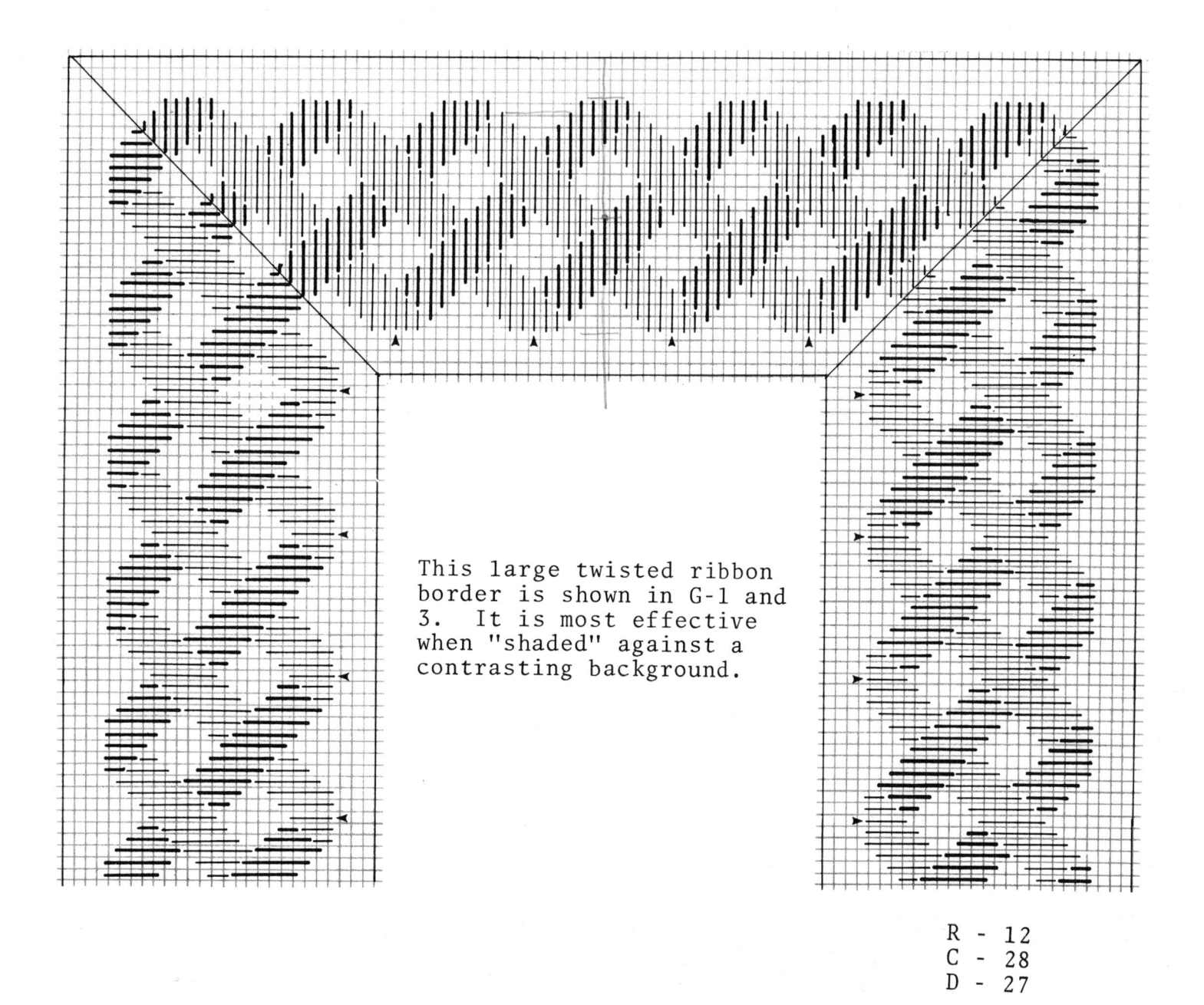

This large twisted ribbon border is shown in G-1 and 3. It is most effective when "shaded" against a contrasting background.

R - 12
C - 28
D - 27

The eye glass case on page 101, was done on a #18 canvas and used the small pattern. The large pattern has been used on the Zodiac pillow, P-8 (in the foreground). These two patterns do not intertwine. They are good choices because the Repeat is short and you can choose the depth most suited to your needs.

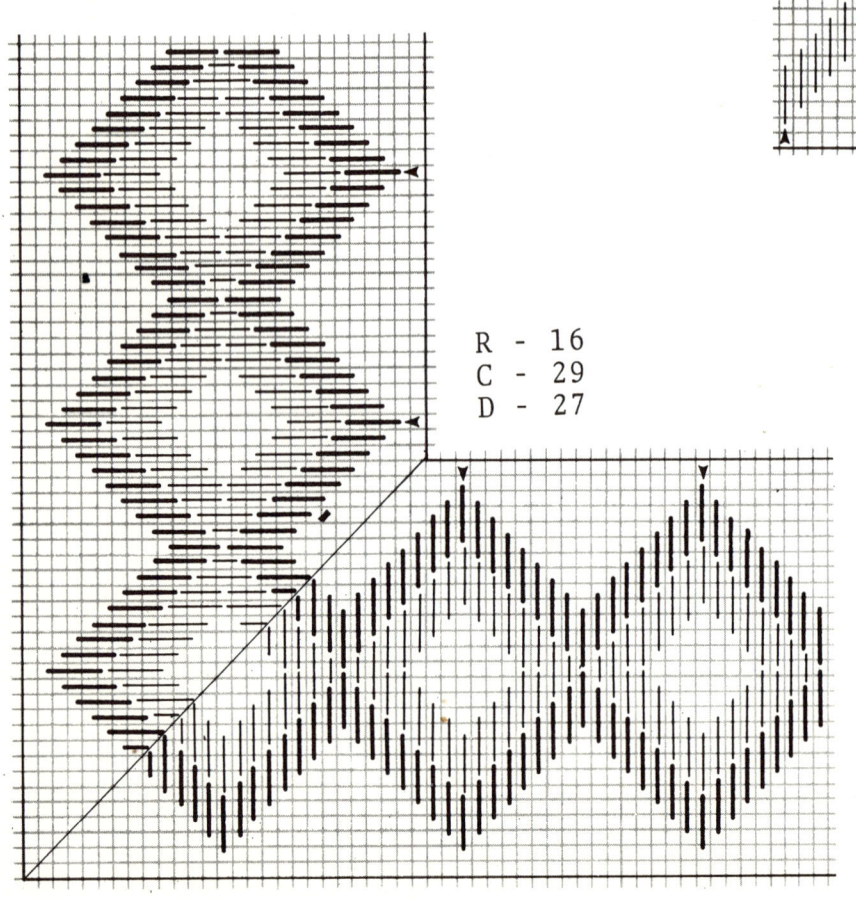

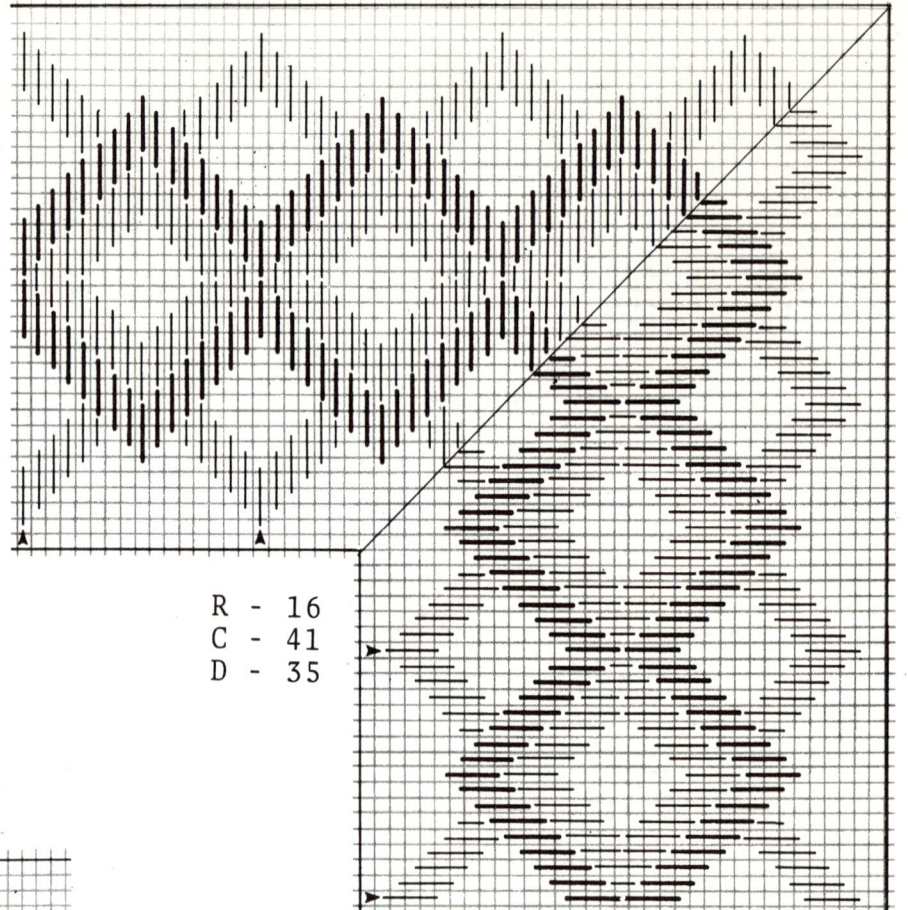

R - 16
C - 29
D - 27

R - 16
C - 41
D - 35

54

This is a wider version of the last two patterns. It has been used on the other Zodiac pillow, P-7.

R - 16
C - 45
D - 43

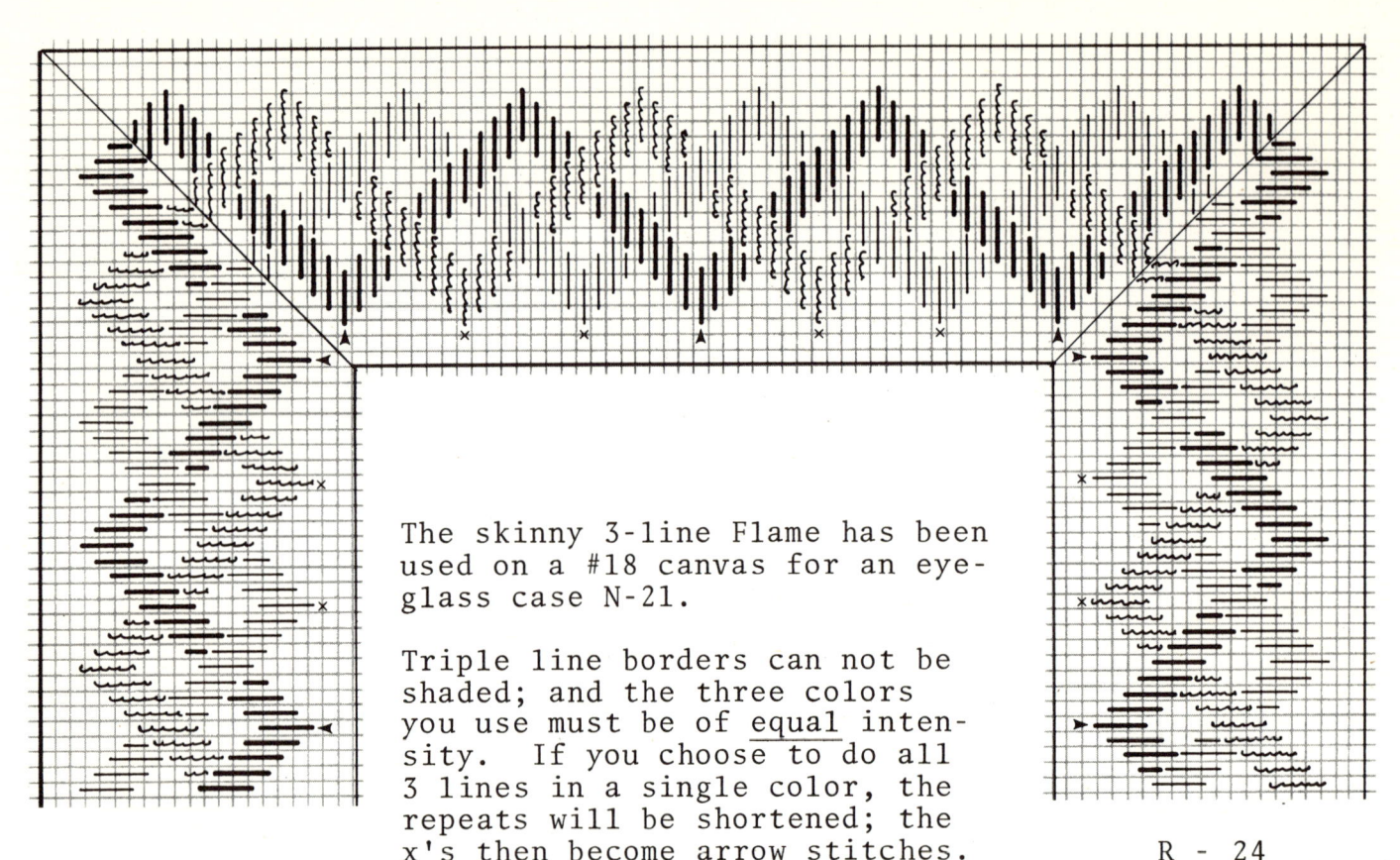

The skinny 3-line Flame has been used on a #18 canvas for an eyeglass case N-21.

Triple line borders can not be shaded; and the three colors you use must be of equal intensity. If you choose to do all 3 lines in a single color, the repeats will be shortened; the x's then become arrow stitches.

The diagram shows 2 corners so that you can see the alternating peaks. On the left corner, the squiggly line miters high at the corner; on the right, it miters low - the pale line is high. Because of this high-low miter, the border will appear off-balance if the colors are not of equal value. The triple borders on the next page follow the same principle. Let the bold line be your guide; it is the same at all corners.

R - 24
½ - 8
C - 20
D - 21

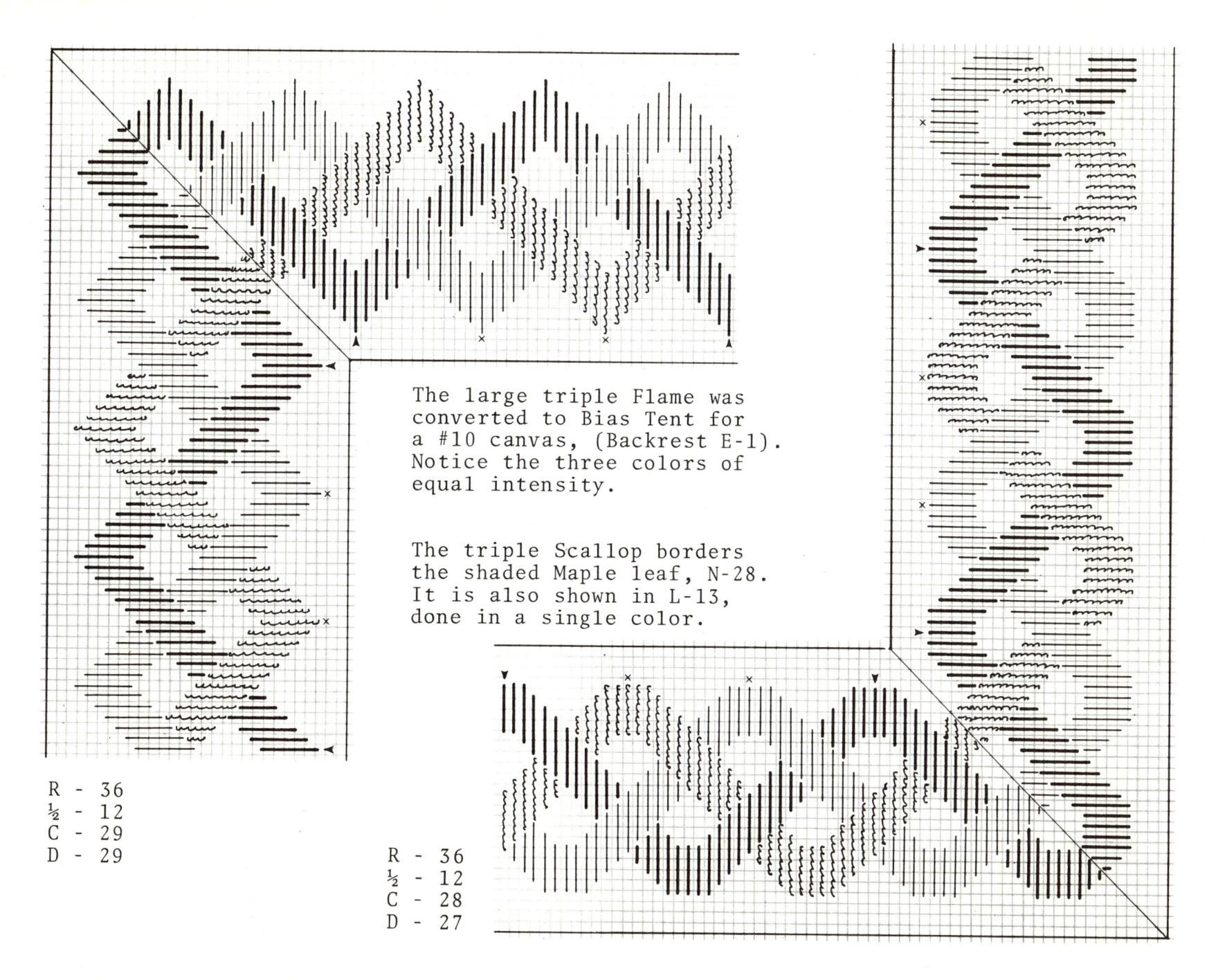

The large triple Flame was
converted to Bias Tent for
a #10 canvas, (Backrest E-1).
Notice the three colors of
equal intensity.

The triple Scallop borders
the shaded Maple leaf, N-28.
It is also shown in L-13,
done in a single color.

R - 36
½ - 12
C - 29
D - 29

R - 36
½ - 12
C - 28
D - 27

57

R - 16
C - 29
D - 27

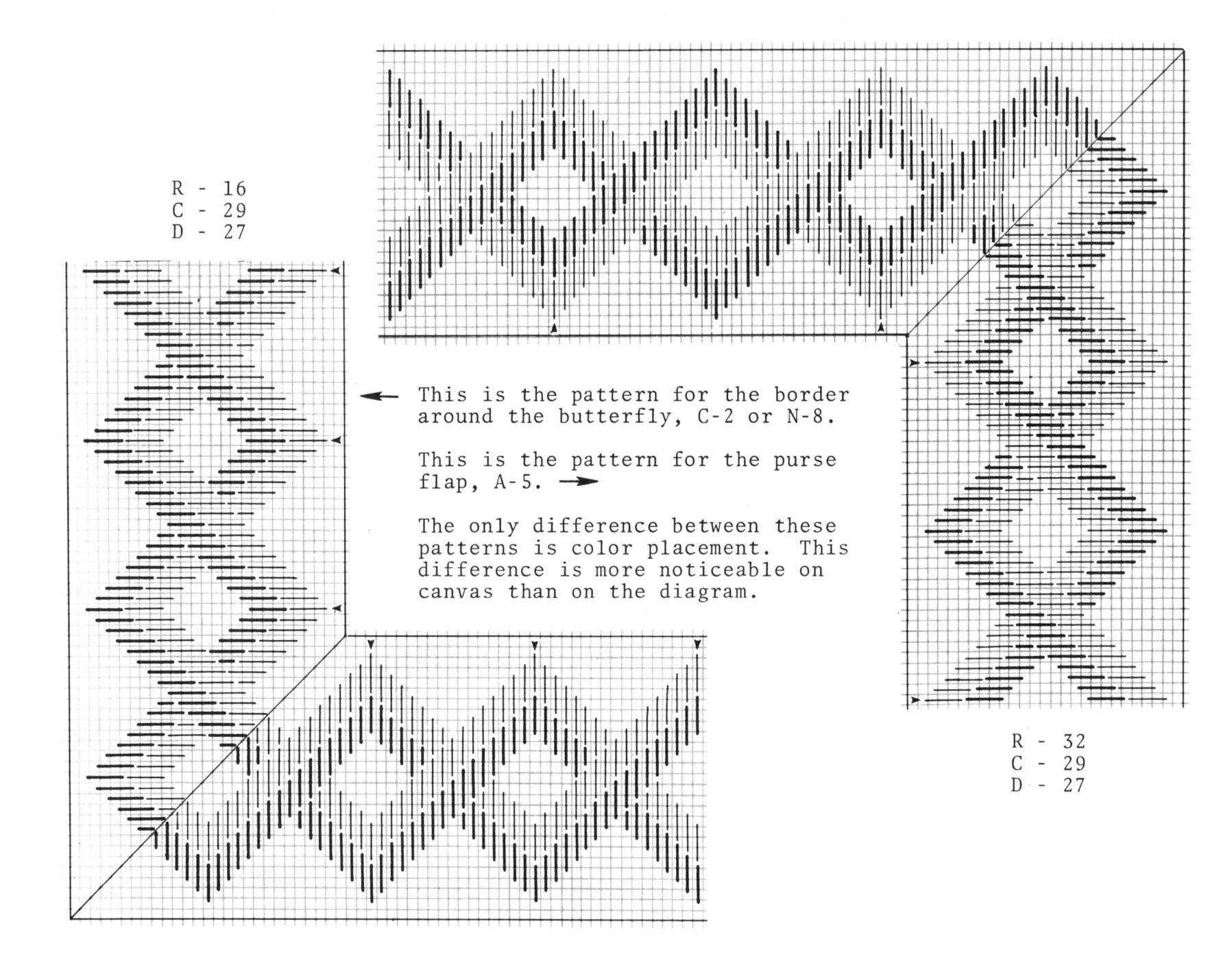

← This is the pattern for the border around the butterfly, C-2 or N-8.

This is the pattern for the purse flap, A-5. →

The only difference between these patterns is color placement. This difference is more noticeable on canvas than on the diagram.

R - 32
C - 29
D - 27

58

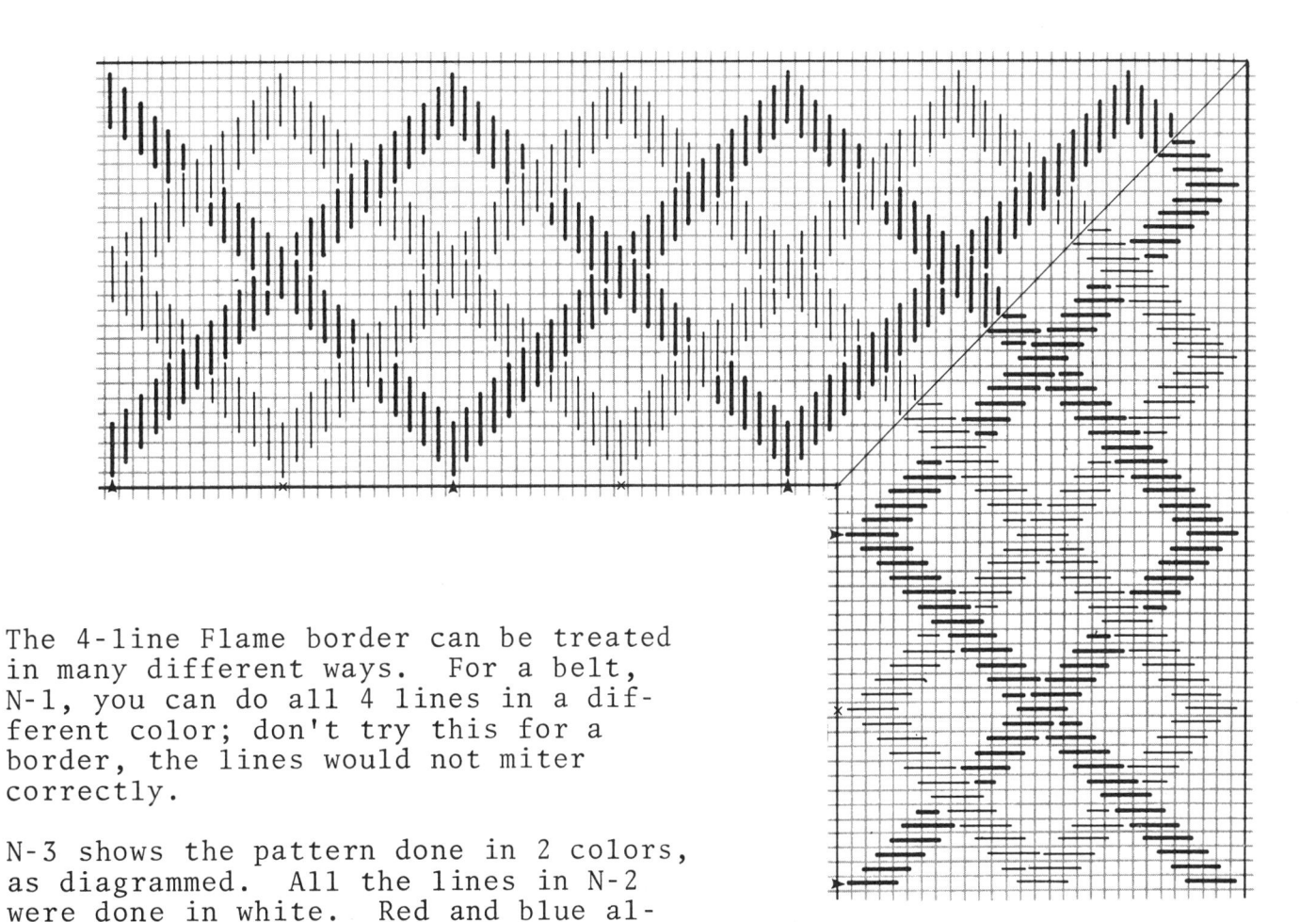

The 4-line Flame border can be treated in many different ways. For a belt, N-1, you can do all 4 lines in a different color; don't try this for a border, the lines would not miter correctly.

N-3 shows the pattern done in 2 colors, as diagrammed. All the lines in N-2 were done in white. Red and blue alternates in the background area.

The purse gusset, N-4, used brown for the pattern lines, gold for the outer background, and cream and rust for the inner background.

On a #14 canvas, this pattern is 2" wide; on a #18, it is not quite 1½" wide. The border background can be increased if you wish.

R - 24
½ - 12
C - 32
D - 29

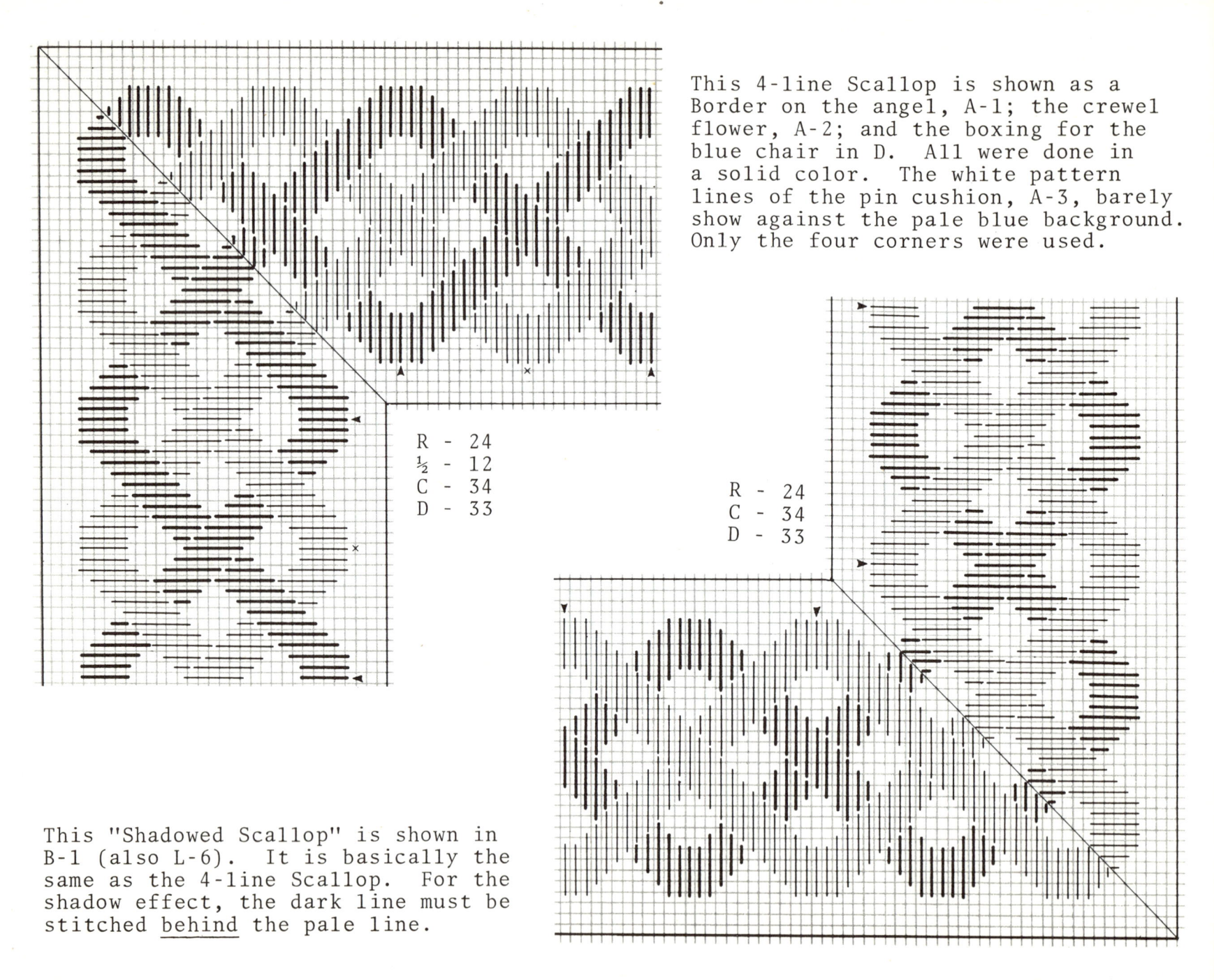

This 4-line Scallop is shown as a Border on the angel, A-1; the crewel flower, A-2; and the boxing for the blue chair in D. All were done in a solid color. The white pattern lines of the pin cushion, A-3, barely show against the pale blue background. Only the four corners were used.

R - 24
½ - 12
C - 34
D - 33

R - 24
C - 34
D - 33

This "Shadowed Scallop" is shown in B-1 (also L-6). It is basically the same as the 4-line Scallop. For the shadow effect, the dark line must be stitched <u>behind</u> the pale line.

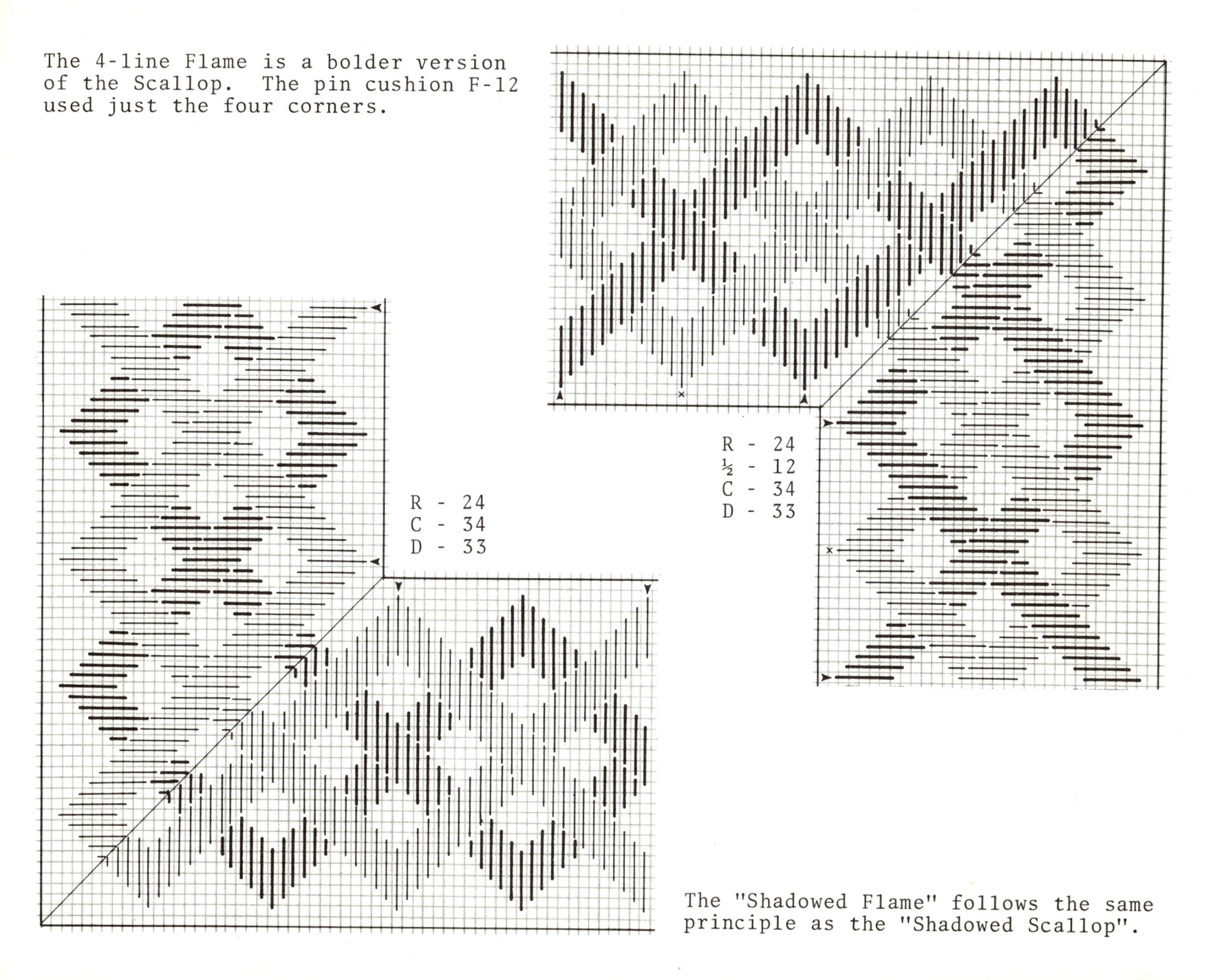

The 4-line Flame is a bolder version of the Scallop. The pin cushion F-12 used just the four corners.

R - 24
C - 34
D - 33

R - 24
½ - 12
C - 34
D - 33

The "Shadowed Flame" follows the same principle as the "Shadowed Scallop".

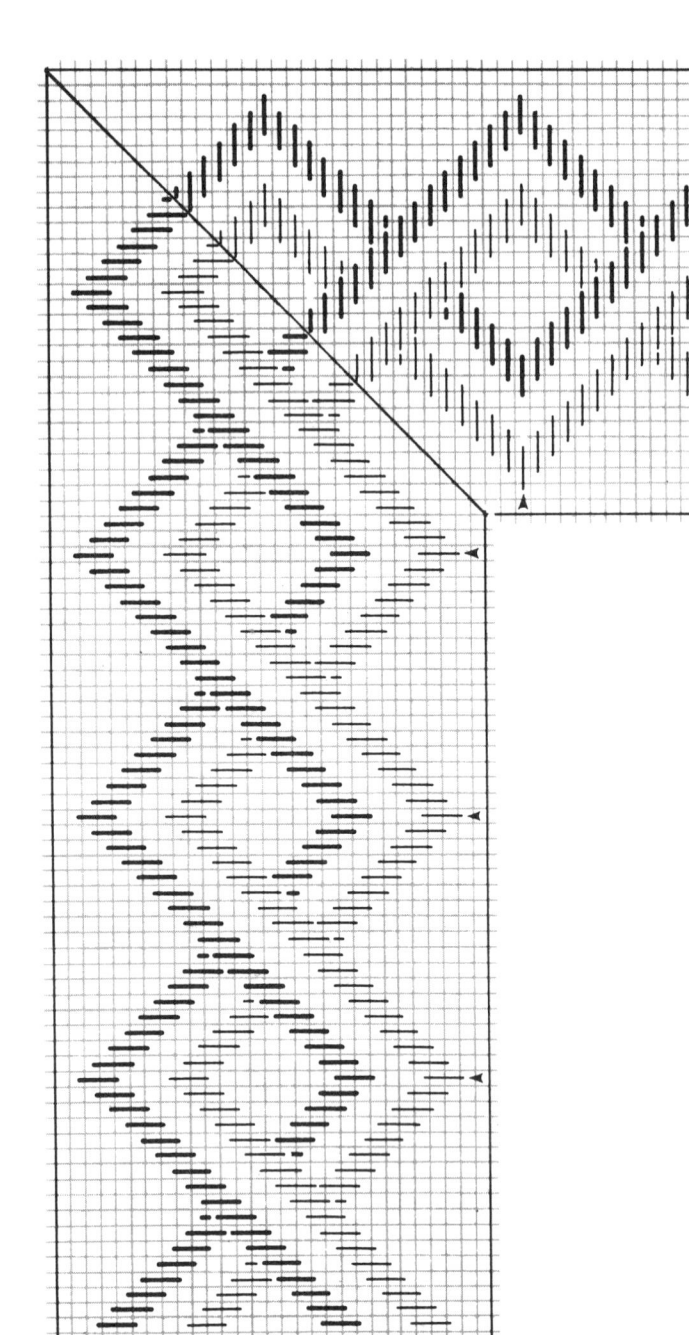

R - 17
C - 31
D - 29

This border and the one on the next page are 2-line intertwines. The unique feature is that each line is made up of three separate color areas; the bold, the pale, and the undiagrammed.

The small name tag F-10, was done on a #24 canvas. The diagrammed stitches, both bold and pale, were done in a medium blue embroidery floss. The background, including the undiagrammed stitches of the border lines, was done in a pale blue floss. The Binding stitch was used to finish the edges and the tag was backed with Pellon and matching felt.

The "Insanity" motto, F-9, used this pattern as a shaded border on a #18 canvas. The bold stitches were done with 2 ply dark green Persian. The pale stitches were done in a light green, and medium green was used for the undiagrammed stitches of each line.

R - 34
½ - 17
C - 31
D - 29

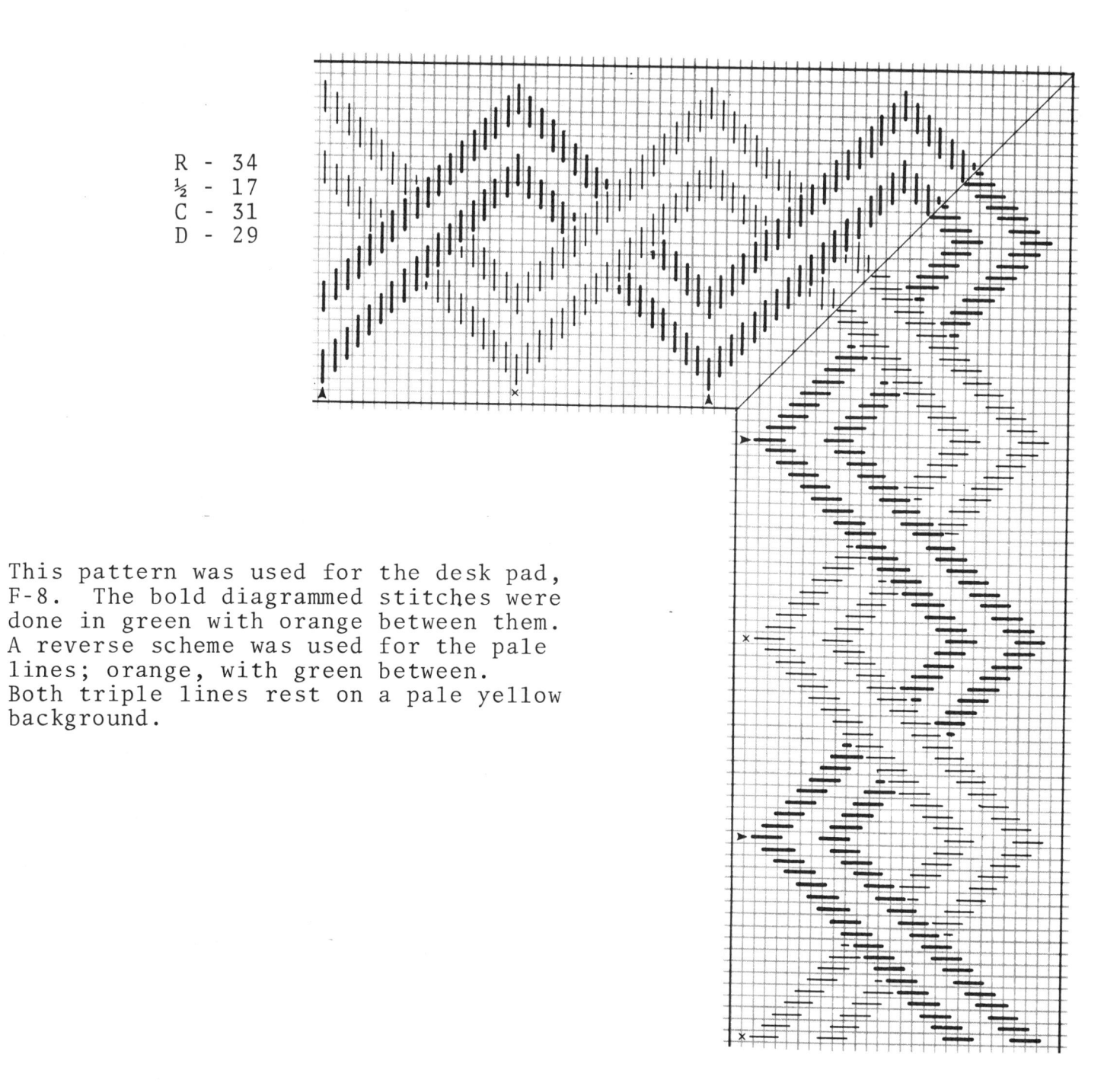

This pattern was used for the desk pad, F-8. The bold diagrammed stitches were done in green with orange between them. A reverse scheme was used for the pale lines; orange, with green between. Both triple lines rest on a pale yellow background.

63

R - 36
½ - 18
C - 32
D - 29

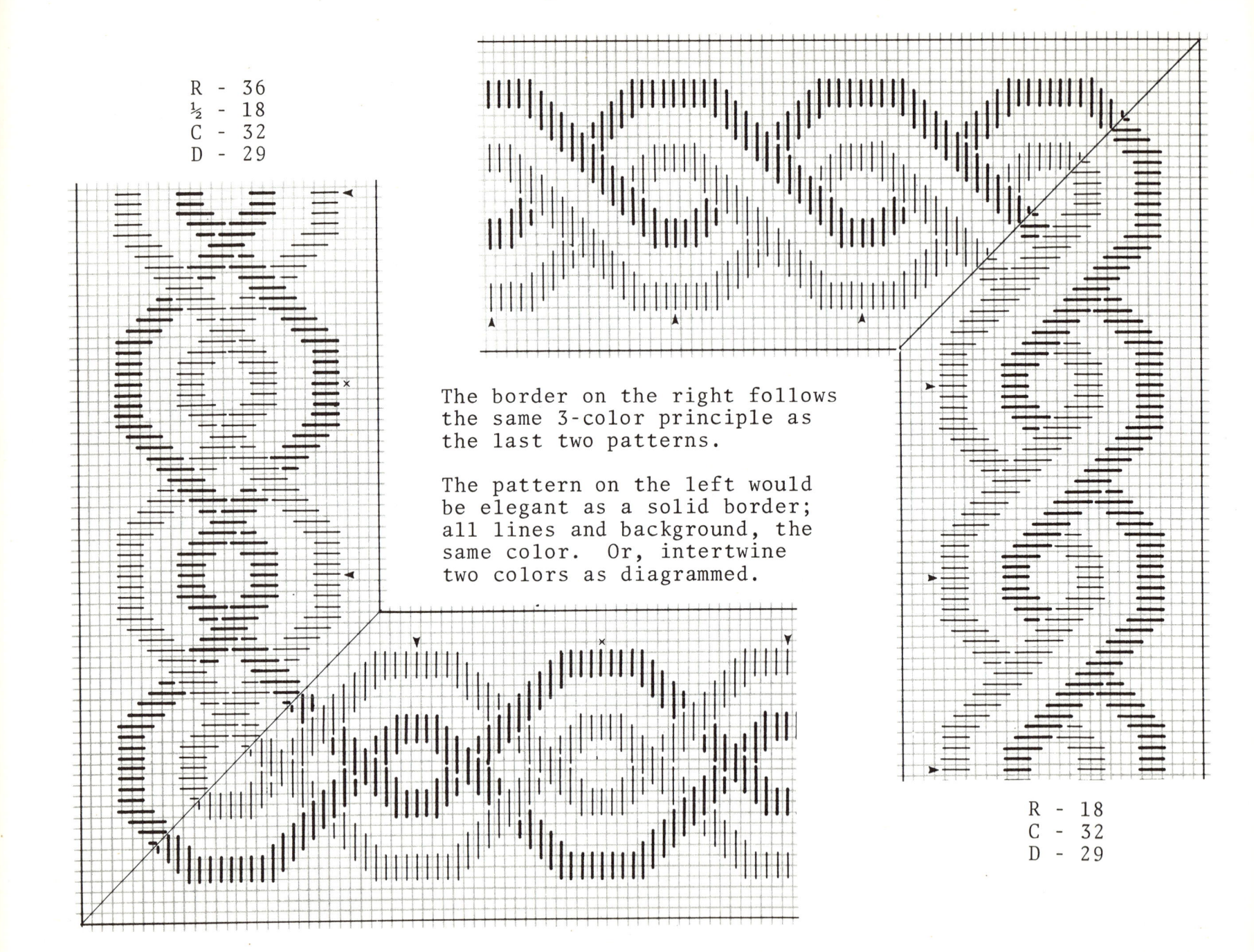

The border on the right follows the same 3-color principle as the last two patterns.

The pattern on the left would be elegant as a solid border; all lines and background, the same color. Or, intertwine two colors as diagrammed.

R - 18
C - 32
D - 29

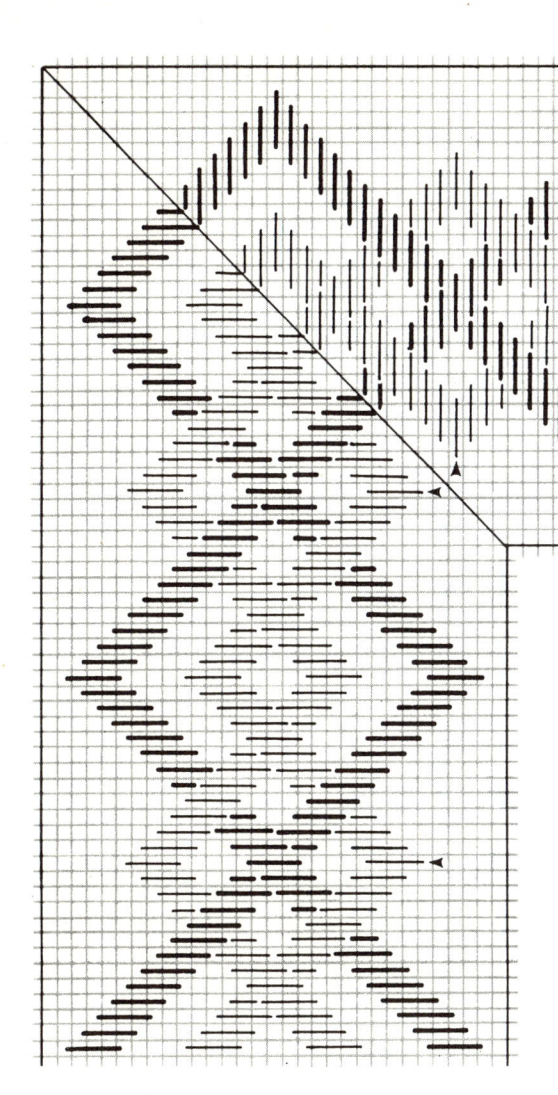

This is the pattern for the Border on the front cover.

The intertwining large and small Diamonds is one of our most versatile borders. It was used for the lamp base, N-24. The patterns were aligned at the top and bottom of the canvas. By following the pattern line, and working toward the center in a single color, a subsidiary pattern emerged. This was accented by the introduction of a deeper beige.

The interesting texture in the light beige area was created by alternating the stitch lengths for each row; one row, 5 holes high and the next row, 3 holes high.

R - 24
C - 28
D - 31

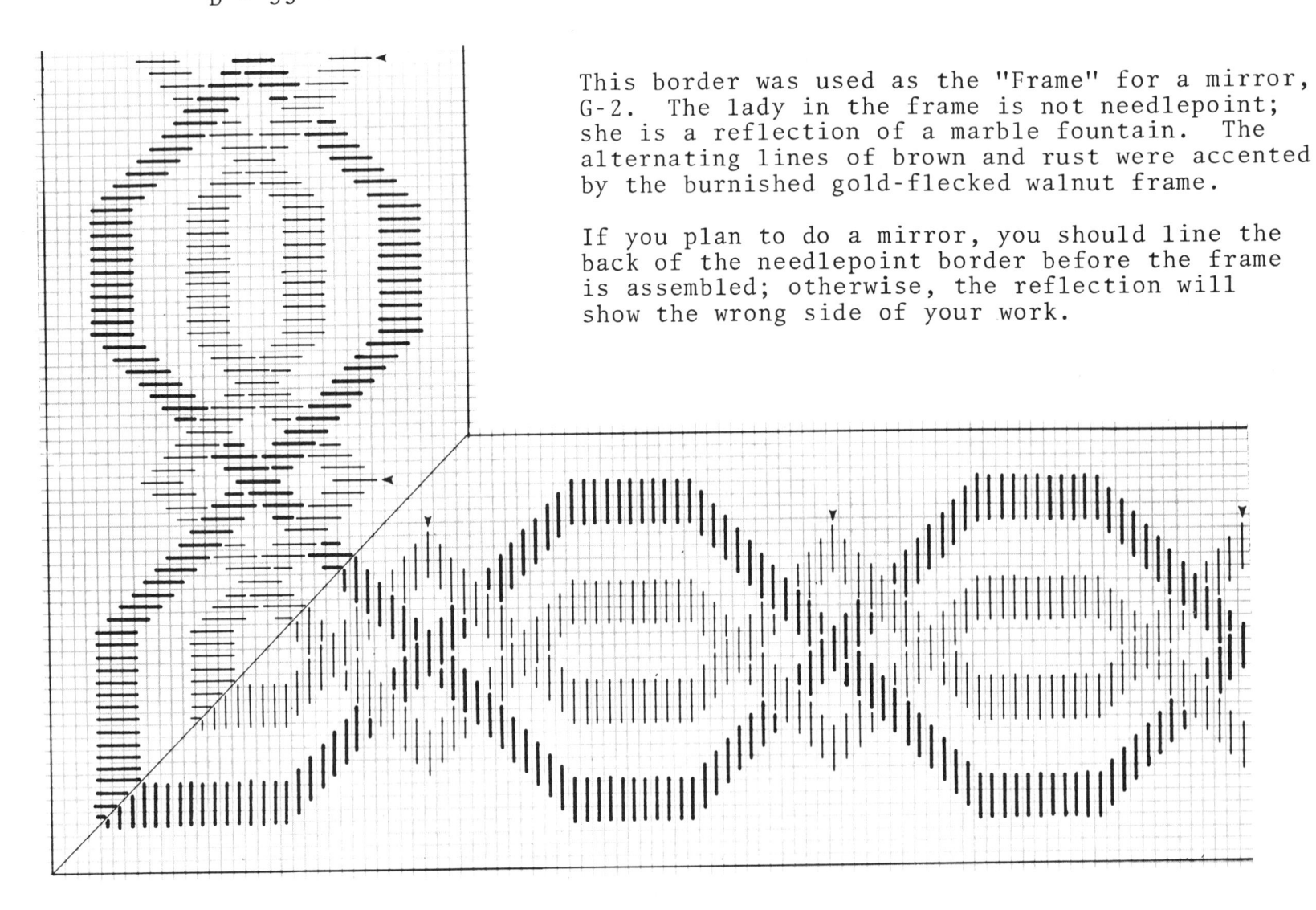

R - 34
C - 32
D - 35

This border was used as the "Frame" for a mirror, G-2. The lady in the frame is not needlepoint; she is a reflection of a marble fountain. The alternating lines of brown and rust were accented by the burnished gold-flecked walnut frame.

If you plan to do a mirror, you should line the back of the needlepoint border before the frame is assembled; otherwise, the reflection will show the wrong side of your work.

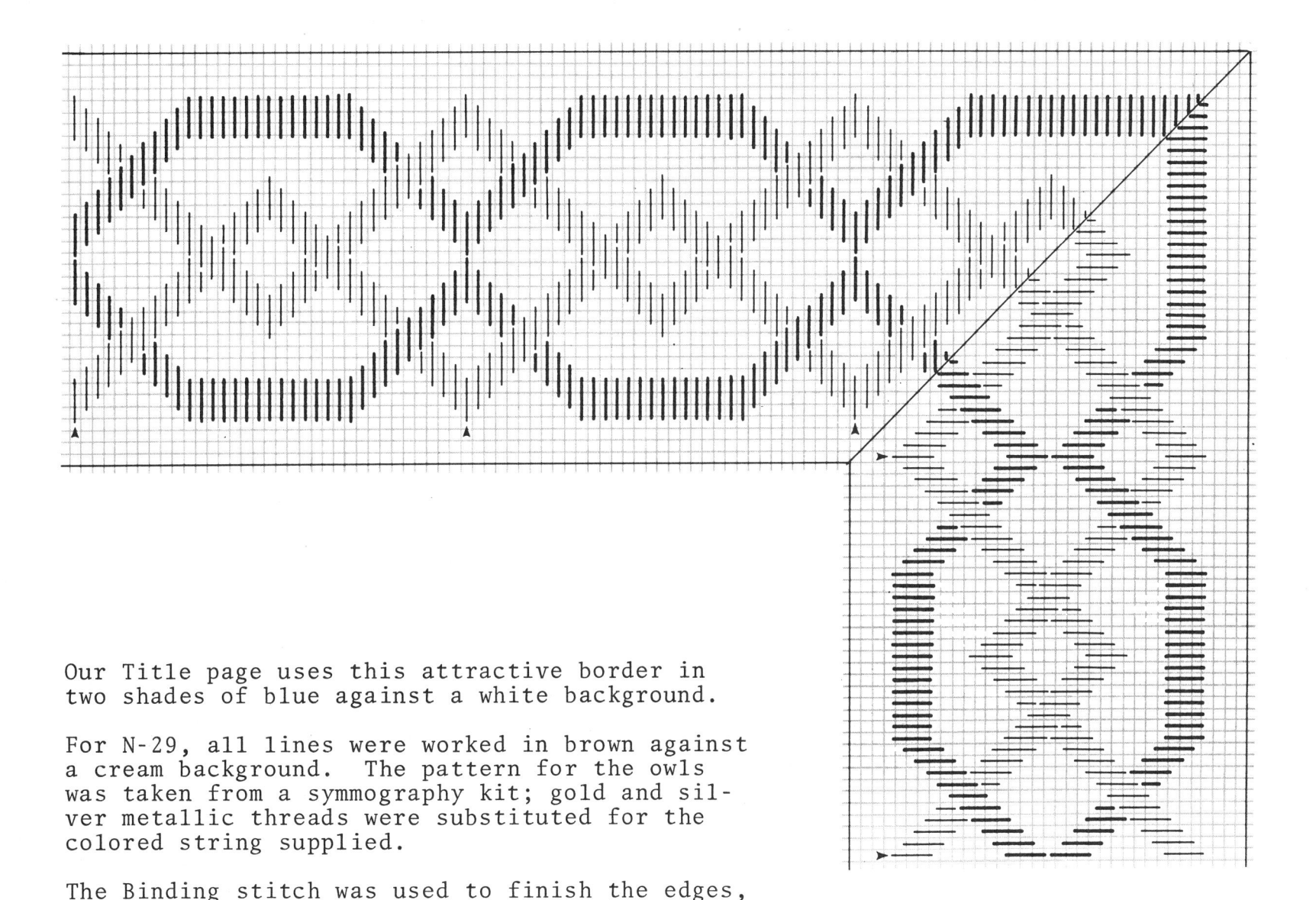

Our Title page uses this attractive border in two shades of blue against a white background.

For N-29, all lines were worked in brown against a cream background. The pattern for the owls was taken from a symmography kit; gold and silver metallic threads were substituted for the colored string supplied.

The Binding stitch was used to finish the edges, inside and out, and the border was glued to a brown flannel covered board.

R - 34
C - 34
D - 35

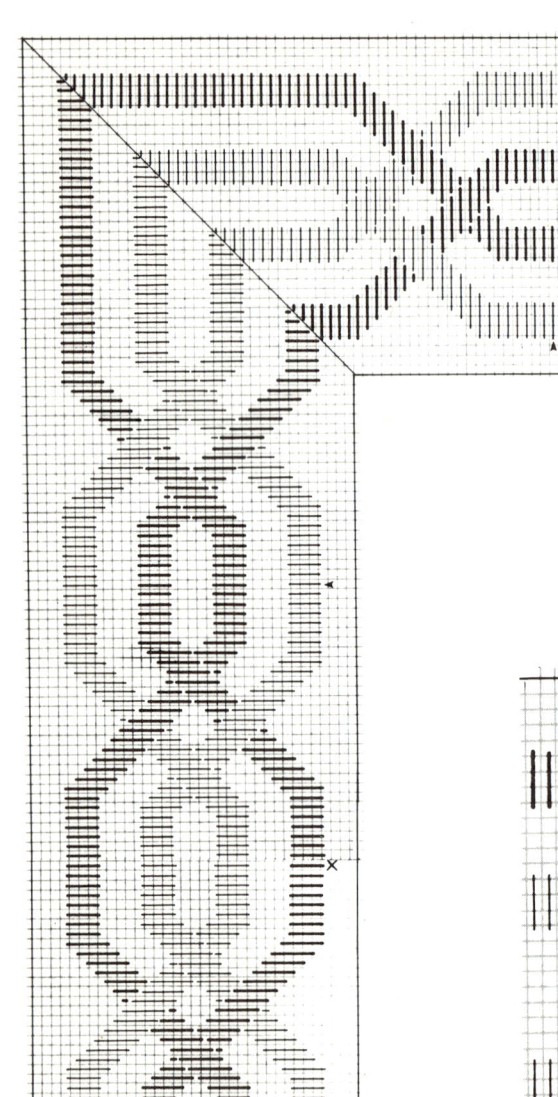

◄This border has a long repeat and a large Corner; perfect for a large project, the bench pad, P-10. The pattern was also used for the black and red belt, N-27. By making the x stitch the center of all four sides, you would have a 14" pillow with an 8" square design area.

▼This border does not follow our usual Border technique. The canvas is marked for a Kaleidoscopic and the arrow stitch is equivilent to a Pivot stitch. It would be helpful for you to read the step-by-step instructions for Kaleidoscopics before you attempt this border.

If you place the arrow stitch (Pivot) in holes 47-51 in the center row of holes, your border will be 12" square. If it (Pivot) is in holes 54-58, your border will be 13" square; in holes 61-65, 14" square.

Start at the arrow stitch and work to the right Miter line. Come back to the arrow and work to the left Miter

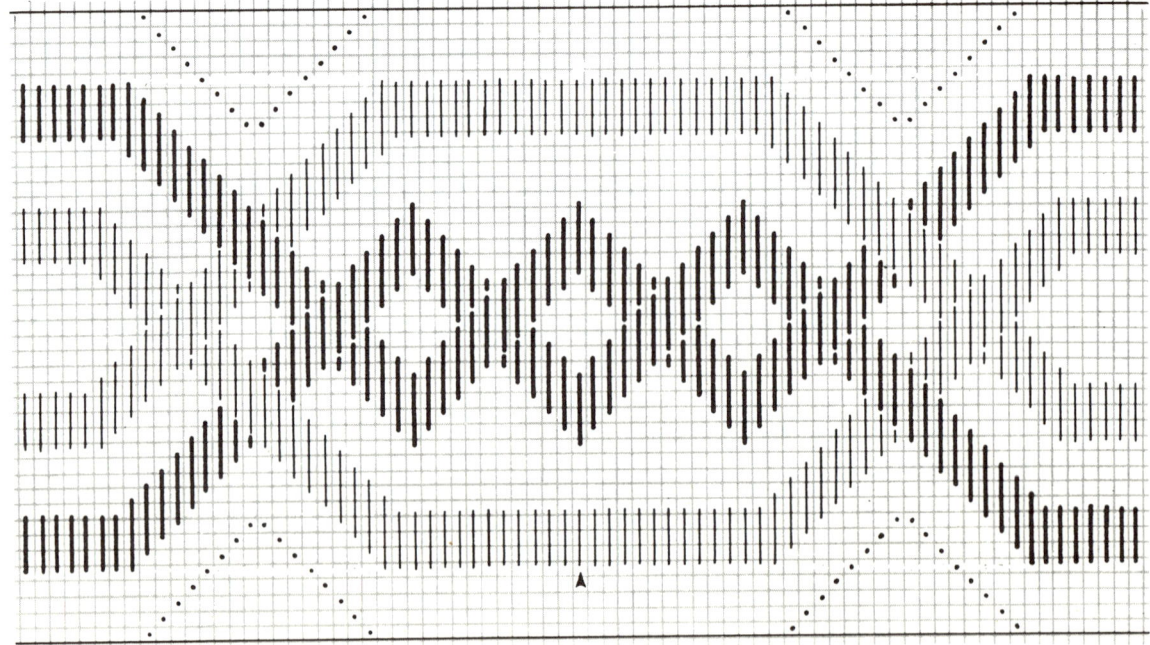

R - 58
½ - 29
C - 56
D - 35

68

line. Do the lower pale line for all four sides. Use these lines as guides for completing your border.

This border is the primary design for the piano bench pad, C-1. The pattern was aligned and started at the center of each long side and worked to the mitered corners (see Rectangular Kaleidoscopics). Five diamond filled patterns were used along each long side (or 1¼ repeats on each side of the center). One pattern was centered at each end and carried to the mitered corners.

The Border background was stitched next following the dotted lines. The Diamond stitch was used for the area within the border. By following the miter at the ends, the subtle texture was emphasized. The 3-stitch knitted cording gives a professional edge.

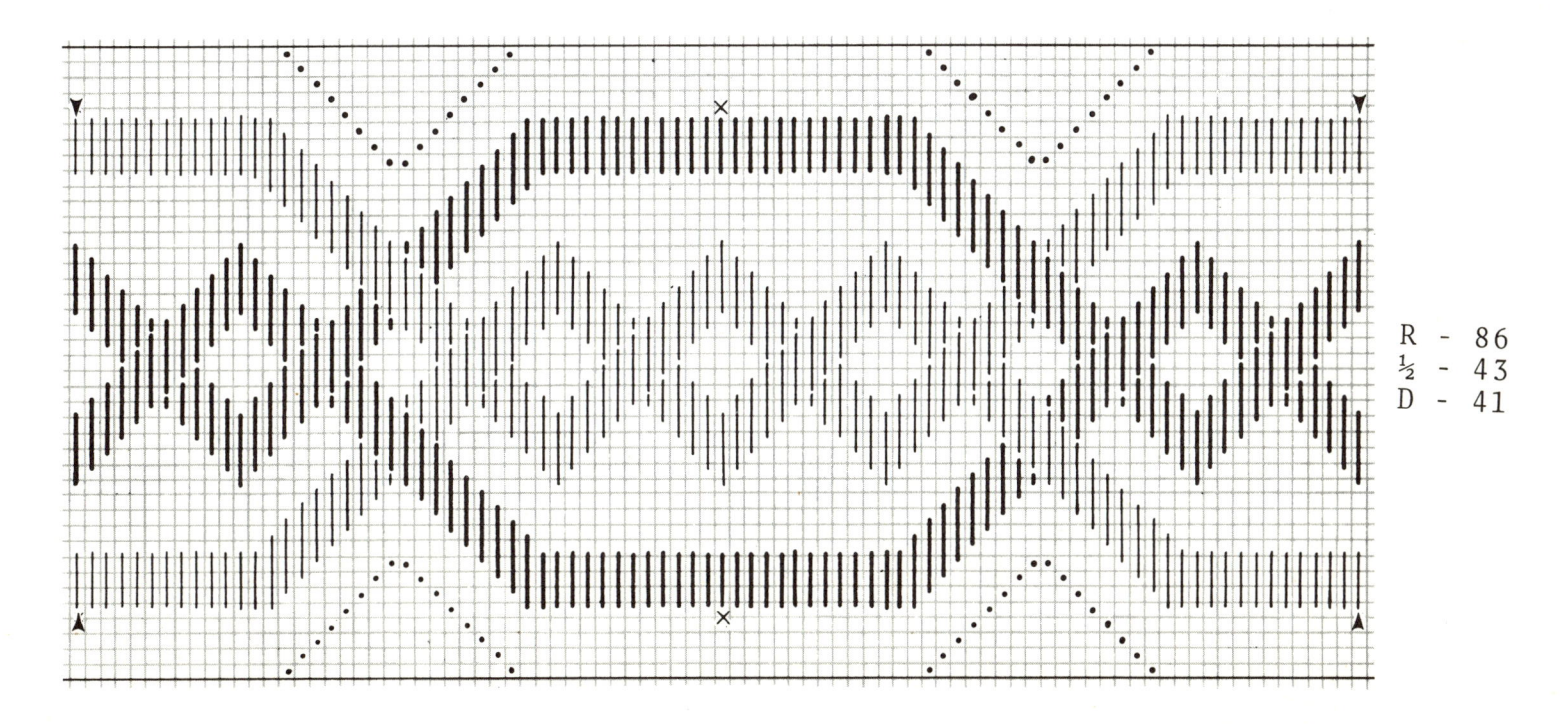

R - 86
½ - 43
D - 41

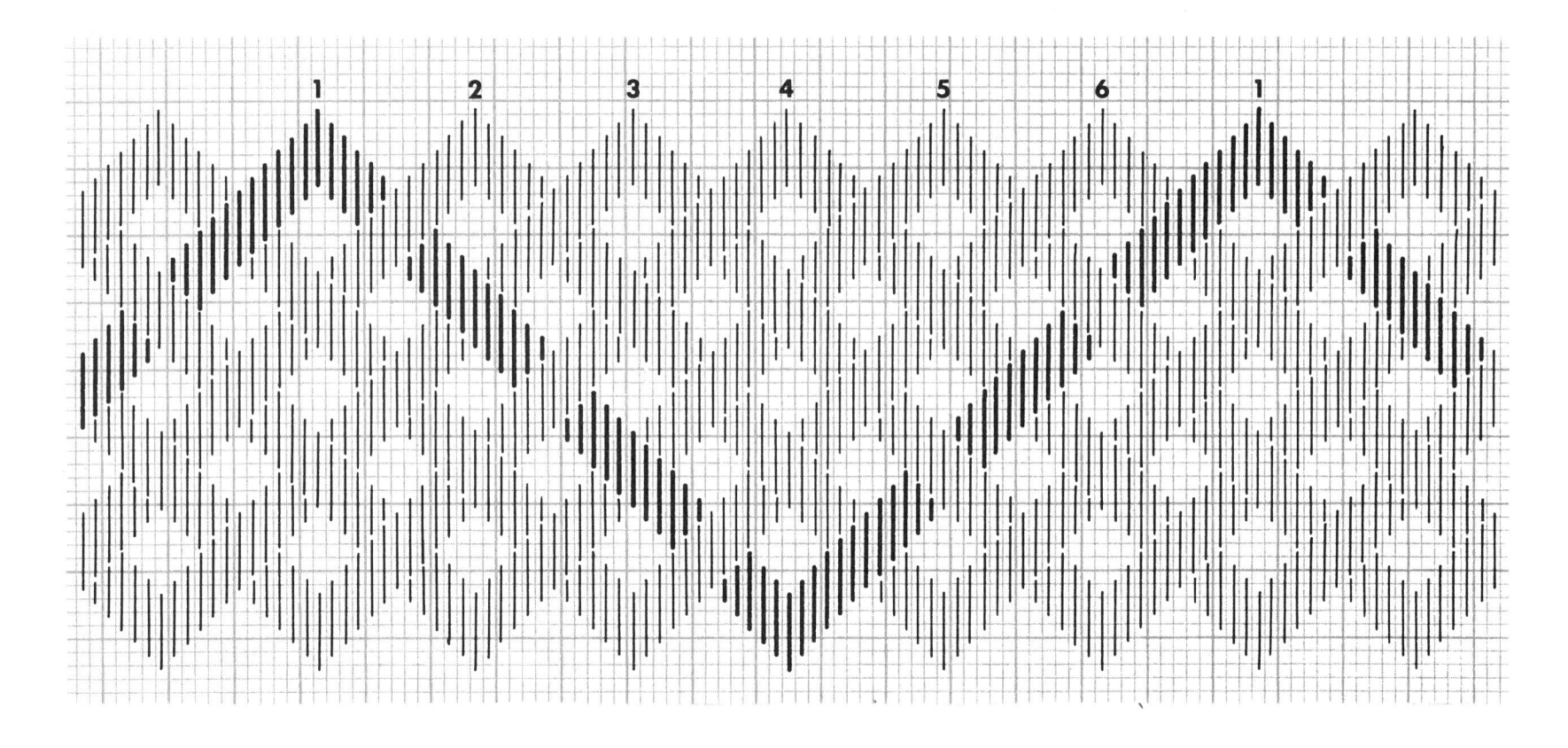

LATTICE

Our Lattice pattern works on the same principle as the borders - alternate lines weaving over and under each other. This pattern allows you to work a band of almost any width for an indeterminate length. No attempt should be made to miter the Lattice for a border. Too many lines would be involved in the corner, and it would be too heavy.

The Lattice is a good pattern if you want a finished look at the top and bottom of a piece. It is the perfect choice for covering any cylindrical item that has the same circumference measurement top and bottom. The canvas can be wrapped around and the ends hidden in a seam. We have used it as the covering for a pencil cup, a letter basket, lamp base, ice bucket, and as the upholstery for an antique gout stool. It could also be used to cover a waste basket or a cornice board.

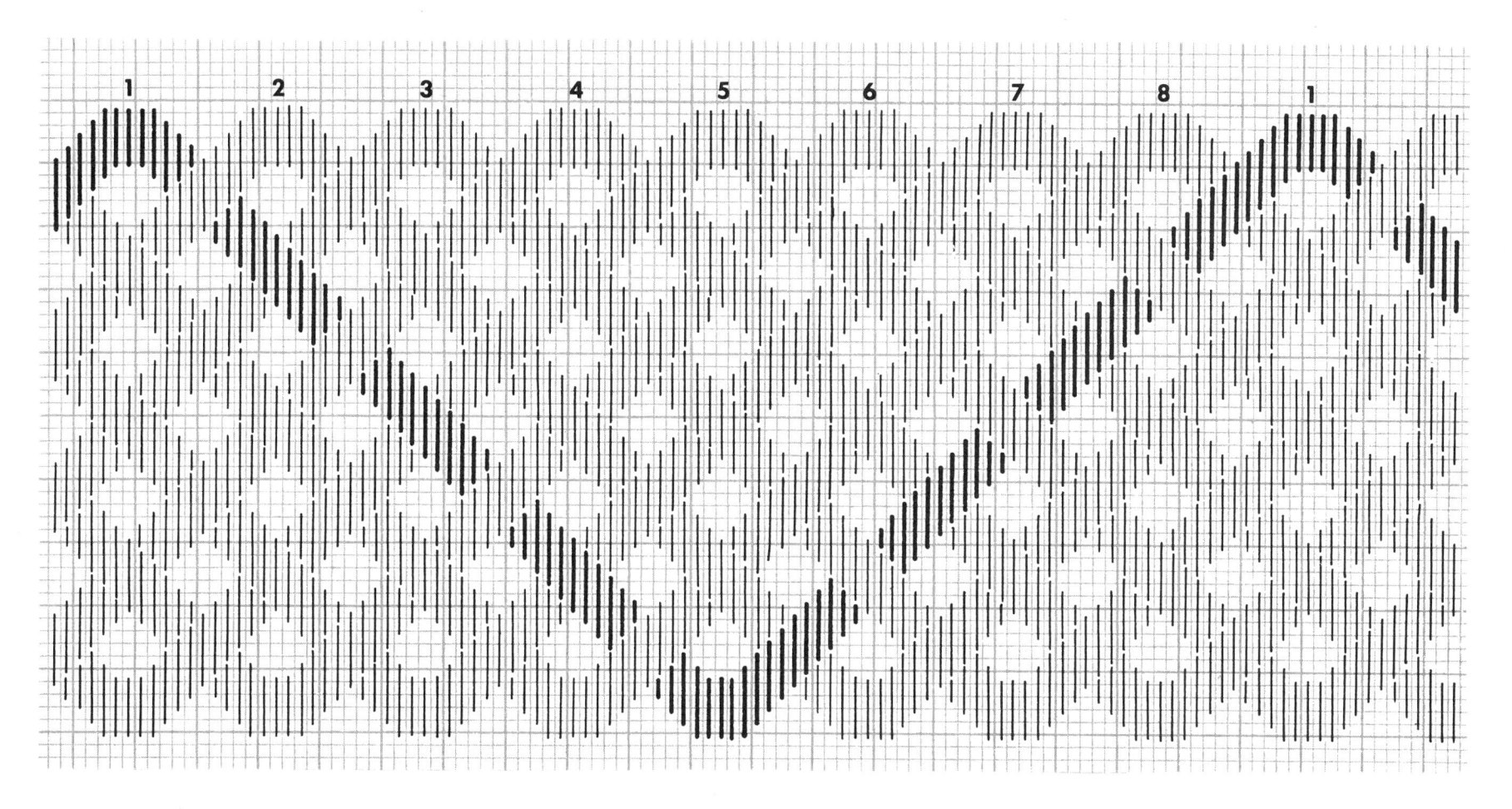

The bold lines on these diagrams show how each row is worked diagonally down and up. These patterns consist of four parts: a top finial, the repeats for working down, the bottom finial, and the repeats for working up. The top and bottom finials are identical - but reversed. As diagrammed, the Flame is a 6 line repeat. Count the top finial as 1 - there will be a total of 6 Peaks before this same row reaches the top again.

The Scallop pattern on this page is an 8 line repeat. Again the top and bottom finials are the same, only here we offer a Scallop in place of a Flame. The repeats in both patterns are identical. The only difference is that we have added one more repeat in both directions to take us to the next size. IT IS THE NUMBER OF REPEATS USED THAT DETERMINES THE SIZE OF THE PATTERN.

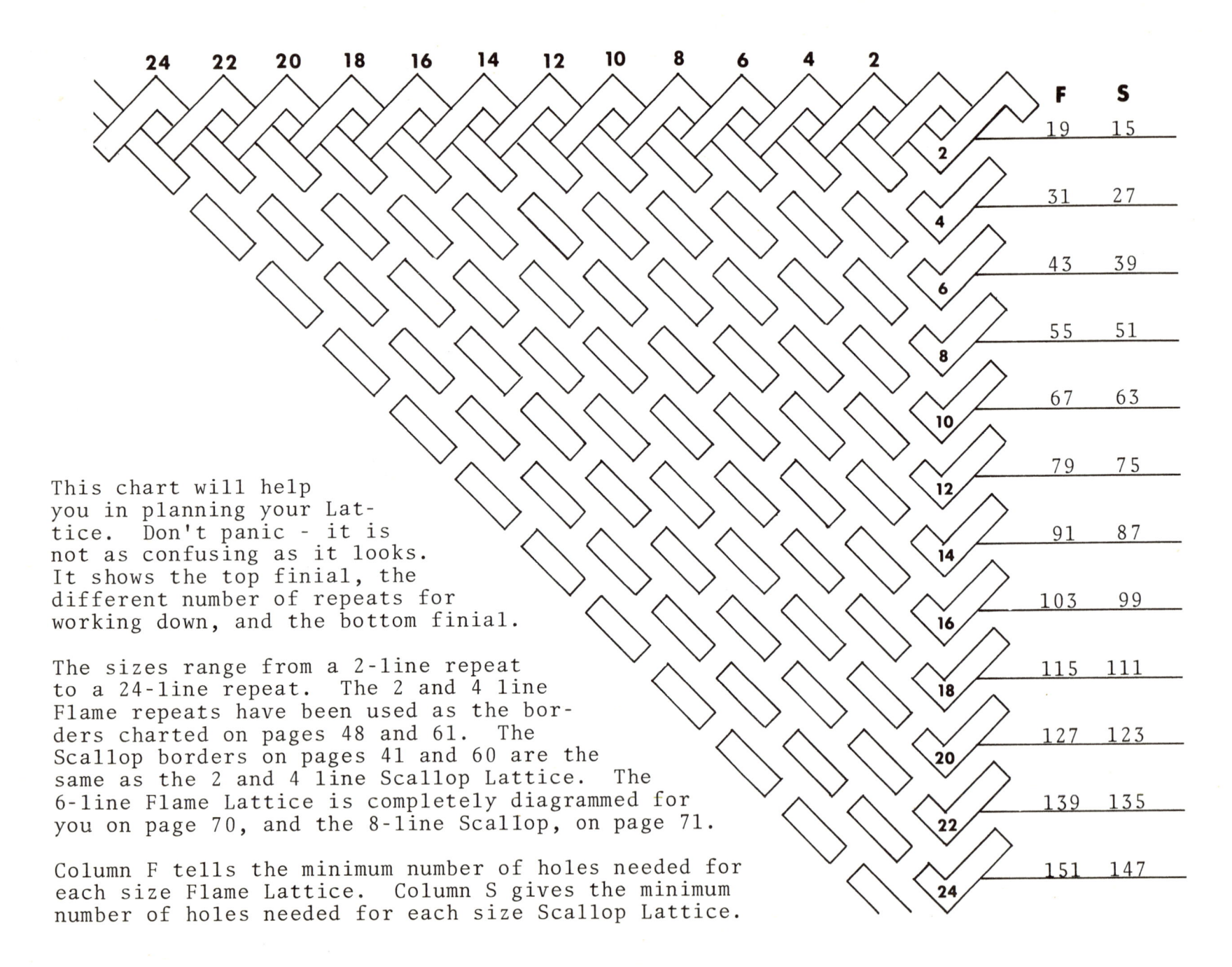

	F	S
2	19	15
4	31	27
6	43	39
8	55	51
10	67	63
12	79	75
14	91	87
16	103	99
18	115	111
20	127	123
22	139	135
24	151	147

This chart will help you in planning your Lattice. Don't panic - it is not as confusing as it looks. It shows the top finial, the different number of repeats for working down, and the bottom finial.

The sizes range from a 2-line repeat to a 24-line repeat. The 2 and 4 line Flame repeats have been used as the borders charted on pages 48 and 61. The Scallop borders on pages 41 and 60 are the same as the 2 and 4 line Scallop Lattice. The 6-line Flame Lattice is completely diagrammed for you on page 70, and the 8-line Scallop, on page 71.

Column F tells the minimum number of holes needed for each size Flame Lattice. Column S gives the minimum number of holes needed for each size Scallop Lattice.

We will take you step-by-step to show you how the chart works.

1. Measure the height of what you want to cover; let's say it is 6" high.

2. Measure the circumference and add 2" on all four sides for blocking and finishing. You may now cut the canvas 10" x as long as you need.

3. Multiply the height (6") x the size canvas you are using (14) to give you the number of holes from top to bottom. (6" x 14 = 84 holes) (6" x 18 = 108) (6" x 10 = 60)

4. Decide which Lattice you want to use - Flame or Scallop. Find the number closest to 84 or less. The 12 line Flame Lattice uses 79 holes; the 12 line Scallop uses 75 holes. Either pattern could be used (on an 18 canvas, you would use the 16 line pattern; on a 10 you would use an 8 line). The length of the background stitches at the top and bottom can be adjusted to fill out the required height. They may be flush with the Peak of the pattern line or extended to as many as 6 holes above the Peak.

5. The Lattice offers many color variations. You may:
    a. Do all the rows in the same color with the same color background. (Gout stool)
    b. Do all the rows in the same color with a contrasting background. (Lamp)
    c. Alternate 2 colors against a contrasting background. (Pencil cup, and letter basket)
    d. Do each row in a different color.
    e. Use as many colors as can be evenly divided into the size Lattice you are using. The 12 line is evenly divided by 2,3,4,or 6; the 20 line is evenly divided by 2,4,5,or 10; whereas the 14 is divisable by only 2 or 7. The Ice-bucket uses 6 colors in the 12 line Flame.

    A little pre-planning and care in keeping the colors in their proper order will insure you an interesting design.

6. Start at the top finial of the 12 line Flame. How many repeat patterns are there between the top and bottom finial? There are 5. Your first stitch will be the Peak of the top finial. Complete the short end of the finial - the 5 repeats down and the bottom finial. When working the Lattice back up to the top, there will be 4 repeats and the next top finial. THERE IS ALWAYS ONE LESS REPEAT WHEN WORKING FROM THE BOTTOM FINIAL TO THE TOP. The detailed stitch diagrams show how the lines fit together and that the stitch count for each row is identical. To begin your second row, count from Peak to Peak. Your second row would begin in the 12th hole from your 1st Peak. Your canvas will look a little weird until all the lines have been completed.

7. Do the background <u>between</u> the pattern rows, filling in with vertical stitches (the same as Borders). Before you start stitching the <u>outer</u> background, wrap the worked canvas around the item.

8. The Binding stitch is used for finishing the edges. It requires 2 threads along each edge, or a total of 4 threads in both height and width. There should be a gap of no more than 4 threads in the circumference. Any stitch adjustments should be made now.

9. With the circumference adjusted, determine how much outer background you will need. Remember to allow 2 threads at the top and bottom for the Binding stitch. Fill in the outer background to the required height.

10. Block and allow to dry thoroughly. Apply the Binding stitch around the entire piece. The lucite ice bucket required a white felt lining. This is not necessary when covering any opaque object. Wrap the needlepoint around the object and whip the ends together. These stitches will be almost invisible if you use thread that matches the Binding stitch.

Geometrics have always appealed to one's sense of balance and order. There is something very satisfying about the planned symmetry of lines and angles. Throughout the centuries much ornamental design has been based on geometric principles. Or is it possible, that the science of Geometry was formulated from examples of primitive art?

Many geometric shapes are a "natural" for needlepoint canvas because of its even weave construction. Squares and rectangles are the most obvious. Diamonds, octagons, eight-pointed stars, and modern patchwork patterns are a simple alternative to the overworked checkerboard samplers. By following our diagrams, these geometric shapes can be used to subdivide your canvas into smaller, more workable units.

The basic shape is your focal point and main design area. Although our examples show monograms, any simple motif would be appropriate. The Bias Tent is the perfect stitch to use to achieve the detail needed in the design area. For variety, textured stitches in the outer sections are fun and work up quickly.

By working within Geometric subdivisions, it is easy to incorporate color and texture into a simple, un-cluttered design. By combining different shapes, even more interesting areas can be created.

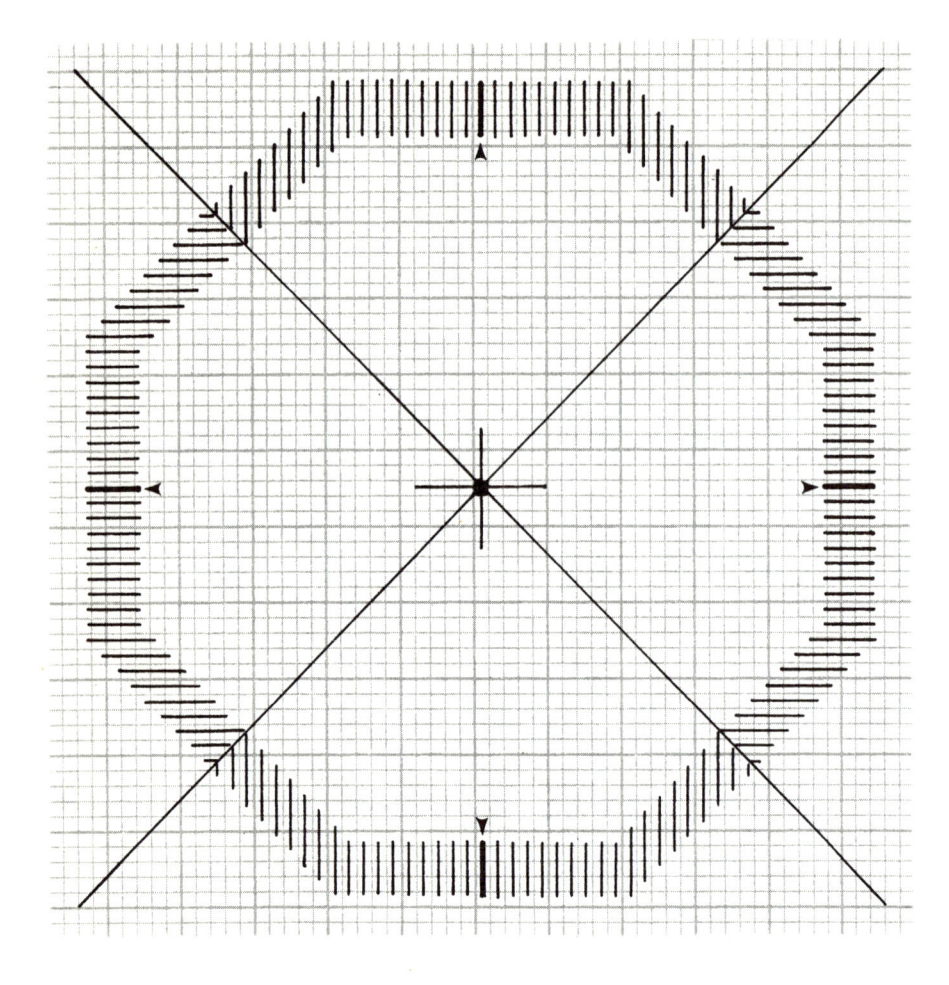

This diagram shows a 4" Octagon. The canvas has been divided into 8 equal segments. In order to understand our procedure and explanations it would be helpful to review Marking for Geometrics.

The Pivot stitch (bold) is your starting point. It is the central stitch of the pattern and fits into the center row of holes both vertically and horizontally. Look at the diagram. How many holes are there from the Center Hole (black) to the bottom of the Pivot (inclusive)? 24? Right! Now find the same spot on your canvas. Count the Center Hole as #1 - continue counting up the center row of holes. Bring your needle up in the 24th hole and down in the 28th hole. The Pivot is now properly positioned and you can work from the Pivot to the left Miter line or from the Pivot to the right Miter line. The pattern is identical on either side of the Pivot. Across the "flat" the stitches are 5 holes high. There are 9 stitches on either side of the Pivot for a total of 19. Along the diagonal line, the stitches are 6 holes high. The first stitch of the diagonals is level with the top of the "flat" but has been increased by 1 hole at the bottom. Work a total of 7 stitches (6 more). The bottom of the 7th stitch will fit into the Miter line. Decrease to complete your miter. Turn your canvas and work from the Miter line to the next Pivot which will fit into the next center row of holes.

The following table lists the formulas for Octagons ranging in size from 3"-30" on #14 canvas.

Column 1 gives the outside dimension of the Octagon.

Column 2 tells the position of the Pivot stitch in relation to the Center Hole. Bring the needle up for the first number and down for the second number.

Column 3 shows the Pivot as #1 plus the number of stitches on either side of it. Remember, across the "flat" the stitches are 5 holes high.

Column 4 tells you how many stitches along the diagonal (6 holes high). The + merely indicates the completion of the miter.

Look at the formula for the 4" Octagon and compare it to the diagram on the preceding page. As long as you understand the procedure, it is just as easy to stitch from the formula as from a diagram.

Let's look at the 12". You would bring your needle up in the 80th hole and down in the 84th. Add 33 stitches across the "flat" (5 holes high), do 23 stitches (6 holes high) along the diagonal to the Miter line. Complete your miter, turn your canvas and begin the next segment. Miter out, do 23 along the diagonal (6 holes high), do 33 + 1 + 33 for a total of 67 across the flat (5 holes high). The Pivot stitch (+1) should fit into the marked center line. Continue around the canvas.

1	2	3	4
3"	17-21	1+6	5+
4"	24-28	1+9	7+
5"	31-35	1+12	9+
6"	38-42	1+15	11+
7"	45-49	1+18	13+
8"	52-56	1+21	15+
9"	59-63	1+24	17+
10"	66-70	1+27	19+
11"	73-77	1+30	21+
12"	80-84	1+33	23+
13"	87-91	1+36	25+
14"	94-98	1+39	27+
15"	101-105	1+42	29+
16"	108-112	1+45	31+
17"	115-119	1+48	33+
18"	122-126	1+51	35+
19"	129-133	1+54	37+
20"	136-140	1+57	39+
21"	143-147	1+60	41+
22"	150-154	1+63	43+
23"	157-161	1+66	45+
24"	164-168	1+69	47+
25"	171-175	1+72	49+
26"	178-182	1+75	51+
27"	185-189	1+78	53+
28"	192-196	1+81	55+
29"	199-203	1+84	57+
30"	206-210	1+87	59+

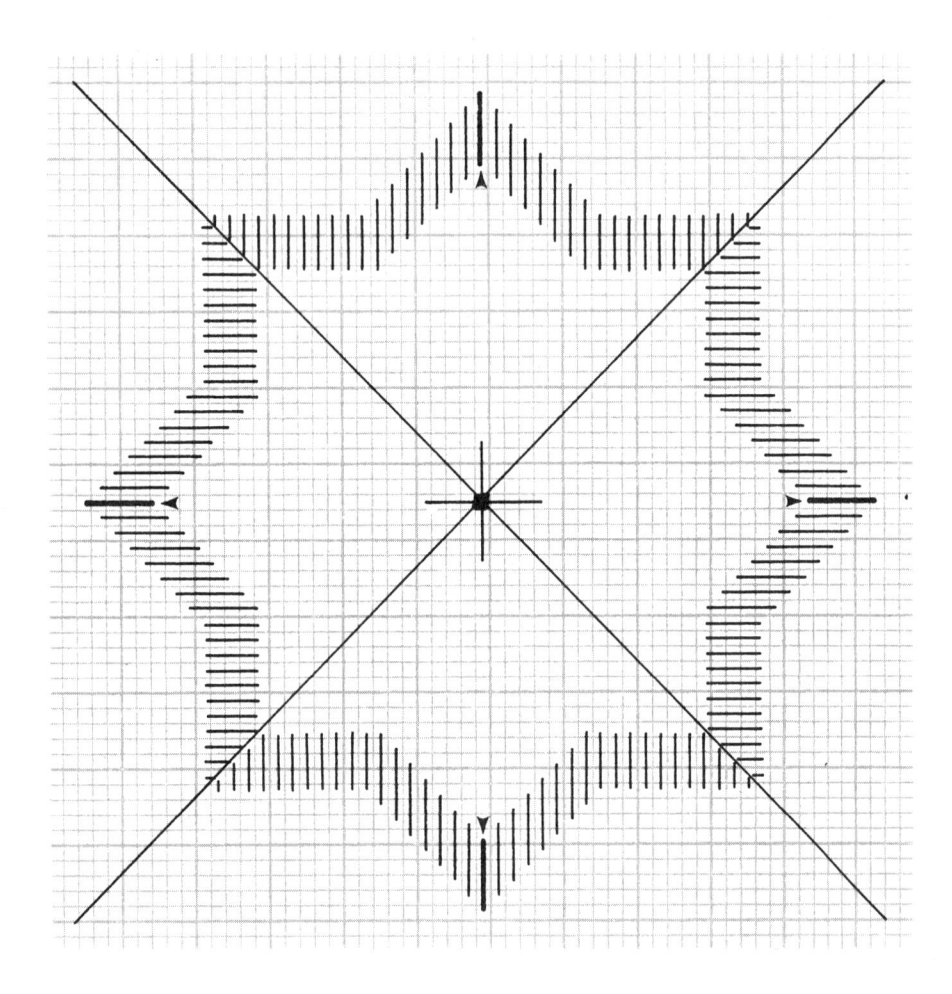

The procedure for the 8-pointed star is similar to that of the Octagon. Again the stitches across the "flat" are 5 holes high, and along the diagonal are 6 holes high. Here, the Pivot stitch is at the peak of the diagonals. You locate your Pivot as before by counting from the Center Hole.

Bring your needle up in the 23rd and down in the 28th hole. Your Pivot is now properly placed and you may work toward either Miter line. There will be a total of 8 stitches down the diagonal line (Pivot plus 7 more). The first stitch along the "flat" (5 holes high) is level with the bottom of the last diagonal but is one hole shorter at the top. Work across the "flat" until the bottom of the 7th stitch fits into the Miter line. Complete your miter and turn the canvas. Miter out and work a total of 7 stitches (5 holes high). The first stitch of the diagonal will be level with the bottom of the stitches along the "flat" but will be increased by one at the top. Work up to your next Pivot.

The chart for the 8-pointed star has been arranged in the same manner as for the Octagon.

Column 1 gives the outside dimension of the star from point to point.

Column 2 tells the location of the Pivot in relation to the Center Hole.

Column 3 shows the Pivot (#1) plus the number of stitches along the diagonal.

Column 4 shows the number of 5's across the "flat". The + again means to complete the miter.

1	2	3	4
3"	16-21	1+5	5+
4"	23-28	1+7	8+
5"	30-35	1+9	11+
6"	37-42	1+11	14+
7"	44-49	1+13	17+
8"	51-56	1+15	20+
9"	58-63	1+17	23+
10"	65-70	1+19	26+
11"	72-77	1+21	29+
12"	79-84	1+23	32+
13"	86-91	1+25	35+
14"	93-98	1+27	38+
15"	100-105	1+29	41+
16"	107-112	1+31	44+
17"	114-119	1+33	47+
18"	121-126	1+35	50+
19"	128-133	1+37	53+
20"	135-140	1+39	56+
21"	142-147	1+41	59+
22"	149-154	1+43	62+
23"	156-161	1+45	65+
24"	163-168	1+47	68+
25"	170-175	1+49	71+
26"	177-182	1+51	74+
27"	184-189	1+53	77+
28"	191-196	1+55	80+
29"	198-203	1+57	83+
30"	205-210	1+59	86+

VARIATION OF THE 8-POINTED STAR

Color pictures M-1 and M-3 illustrate an easy variation of the 8-pointed Star and the interesting effects you can create. The basic shape is still an 8-pointed Star but by using different colors you create the illusion of a Diamond-interlaced-Square. This variation can be planned for any size Star on the chart.

79

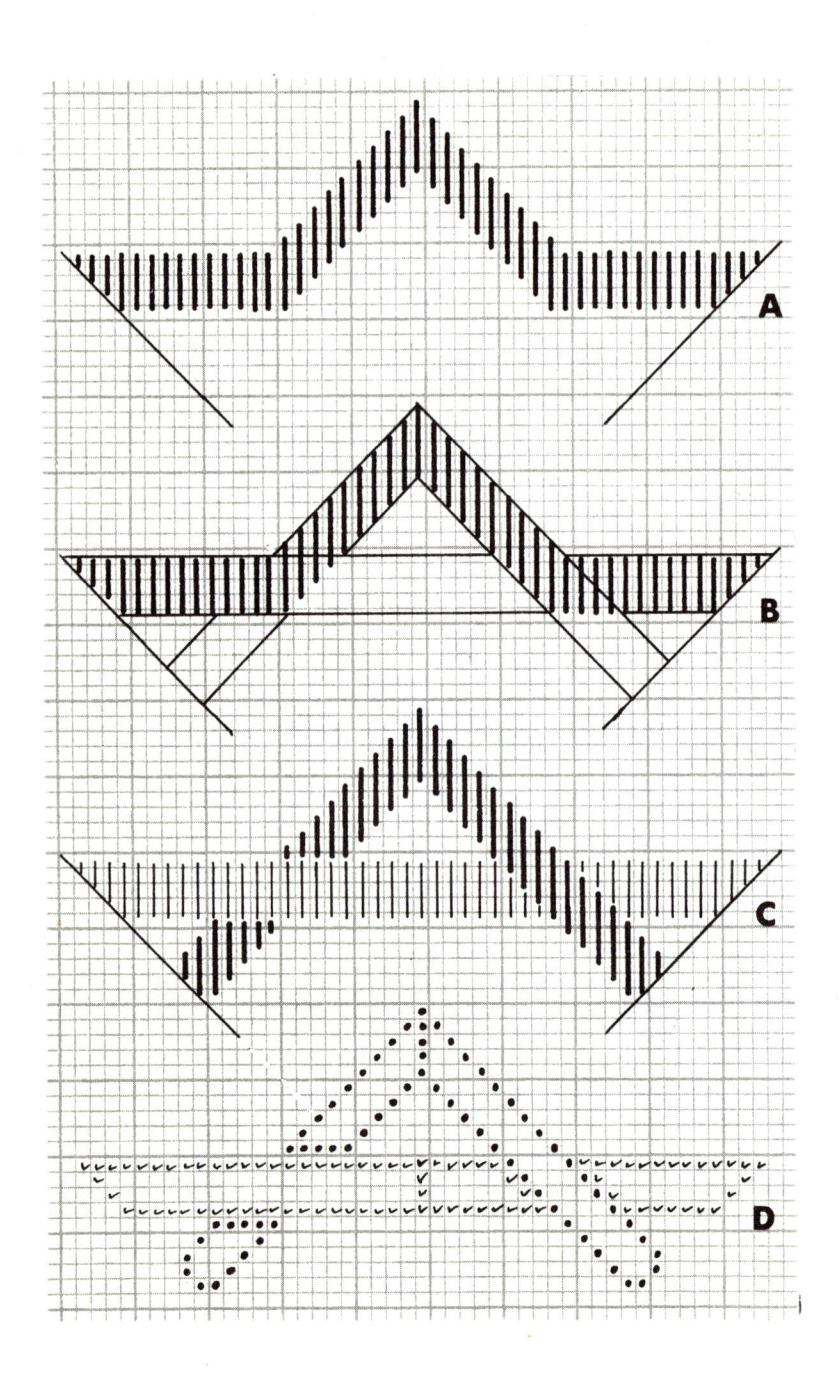

Diagram A shows the 5" Star pattern charted from Miter line to Miter line as bold stitches. Diagram B shows the same charted stitches plus the overlaid lines which will help you in constructing the new pattern (Diamond and Square). In order to create a new pattern, these few lines must be drawn to show how the 2 shapes fit together.

The line drawing on the previous page shows the Diamond pattern underneath the Square on the left side and over the Square on the right side. This holds true for all four sides of this interlaced pattern.

Because this pattern is most effective in two colors, Diagram C shows the bold line for the Diamond and the pale line for the Square. On this diagram it is easy to see where the stitch lengths have been shortened to allow the other line to "pass over". The overlaid lines on Diagram B show you where to make these adjustments, and where to increase the length of the stitches to fill in between the lines.

Color picture M-3 shows this 5" Star variation done in Tent stitch on #5 Quickpoint canvas.

If you wish to convert any of these patterns to Bias Tent, remember one very important rule. You must think MESH instead of holes. Look at the Pivot stitch of the Diamond on Diagram C. It is 6 holes high - crosses 5 threads. The Pivot stitch on Diagram D is 5 mesh high. THERE IS ALWAYS ONE LESS MESH THAN HOLE WHEN YOU CONVERT TO BIAS TENT.

The Octagon and Star are charted for #14 canvas. If you use a different gauge, the dimensions will change. The stitch formula for the 5" Star uses 70 holes. 5" x #14 = 70

For an approximate measurement, divide by the size canvas you wish to use: 70 ÷ #18 = 4"
  70 ÷ #12 = 6"
  70 ÷ #10 = 7"
  70 ÷ # 5 = 14"

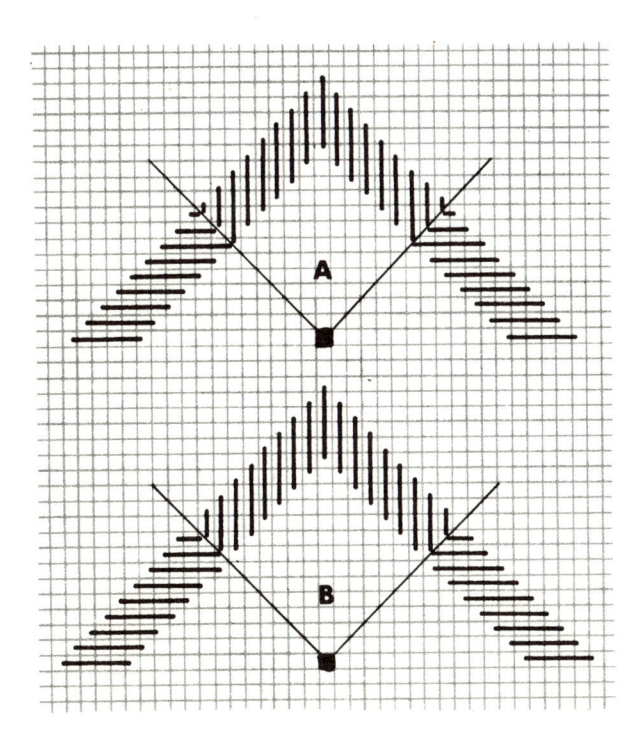

The stitches of the Square are 5 holes high in Diagram C and 4 mesh high in Diagram D. It is not necessary to mark all the mesh, the outlines are enough. Be sure and use two different colored markers.

The purse flap (M-1) was based on the 6" Star and an additional Square of Mitered Gobelin was worked all around the pattern. IN ORDER TO CONSTRUCT THIS VARIATION FOR ANY SIZE 8-POINTED STAR, YOU MUST FOLLOW STEPS A, B AND C.

DIAMOND

There is no set formula for a diamond shape. As long as your canvas is properly prepared for Geometrics, you can do a diamond of any size. All stitches are 6 holes high and the Pivot will be the Peak of the diamond. It must fit into the center row of holes. It may be placed as close to, or as far away from the Center Hole as you want. Work from the Pivot to the Miter line. There are two different Miters possible. In Diagram A, the bottom of the 6 hole stitch fits into the Miter line and you complete the Miter with a 4 and a 2. In Diagram B, the bottom of the 6 hole stitch is one hole away from the Miter line and you must complete your Miter with a 5 and a 3. Either is correct; just remember, in working around the canvas to be consistent.

Interesting new areas can be created by combining shapes.
1. When an Octagon is set outside an 8-pointed Star it must be at least one size larger than the Star. The patch pocket for the skirt (N-12) used the 5" 8-pointed Star and the 6" Octagon.
2. An 8-pointed Star set outside an Octagon must be 3 sizes larger. The shapes that result are a bit awkward to work with.
3. When similiar shapes of different sizes are used, there should be a difference of 3 sizes between

81

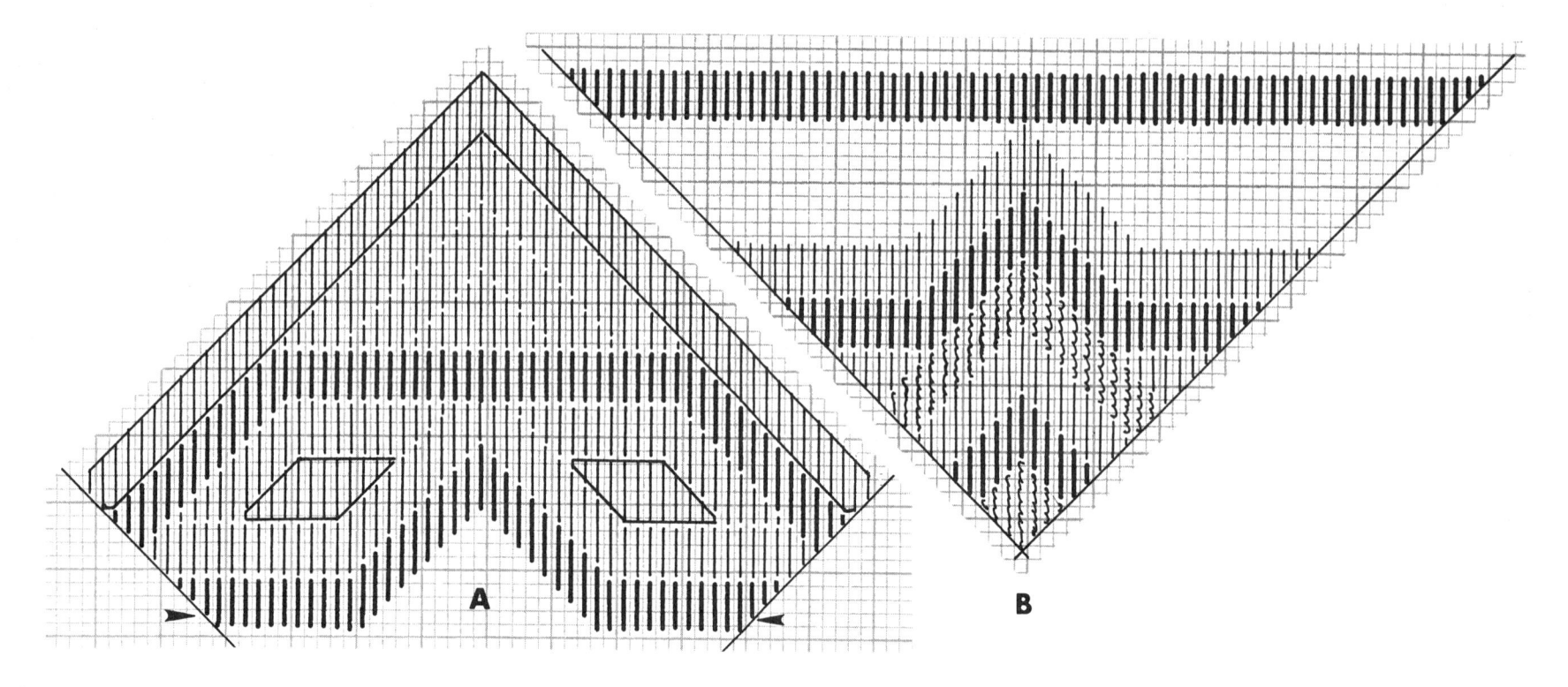

them. The green sampler pillow (N-9) used 4",7",10" and 13" Octagons. Twelve different textured stitches were used and each section was worked from Miter line to Miter line. I-7 shows a double Octagon (12" and 15") used as the border for a Kaleidoscopic.

A good example of combining shapes is the JR tennis racquet (M-5). The arrows on Diagram A show the primary pattern (5" 8-pointed Star) which was stitched first. The 6" Octagon was applied next and finally the white Diamond was stitched all around the Octagon. The diagonal of the Octagon was the guide for the Diamond and here the stitches were worked from the Miter upward to the Peak. The stitch that fit into the center row of holes became the Pivot. The pale lines on the diagram show how these new areas were treated.

Diagram B shows the stitch pattern for the pin cushion in front of the tray in color picture F. The 4" Star (bold lines) was stitched first in green. Another Star (pale lines) was added outside in orange. Inside the primary pattern were successive rows of yellow, orange, green and yellow Diamonds. A row of green Mitered Gobelin was stitched around the entire piece and the open areas were filled with Scotch stitch.

82

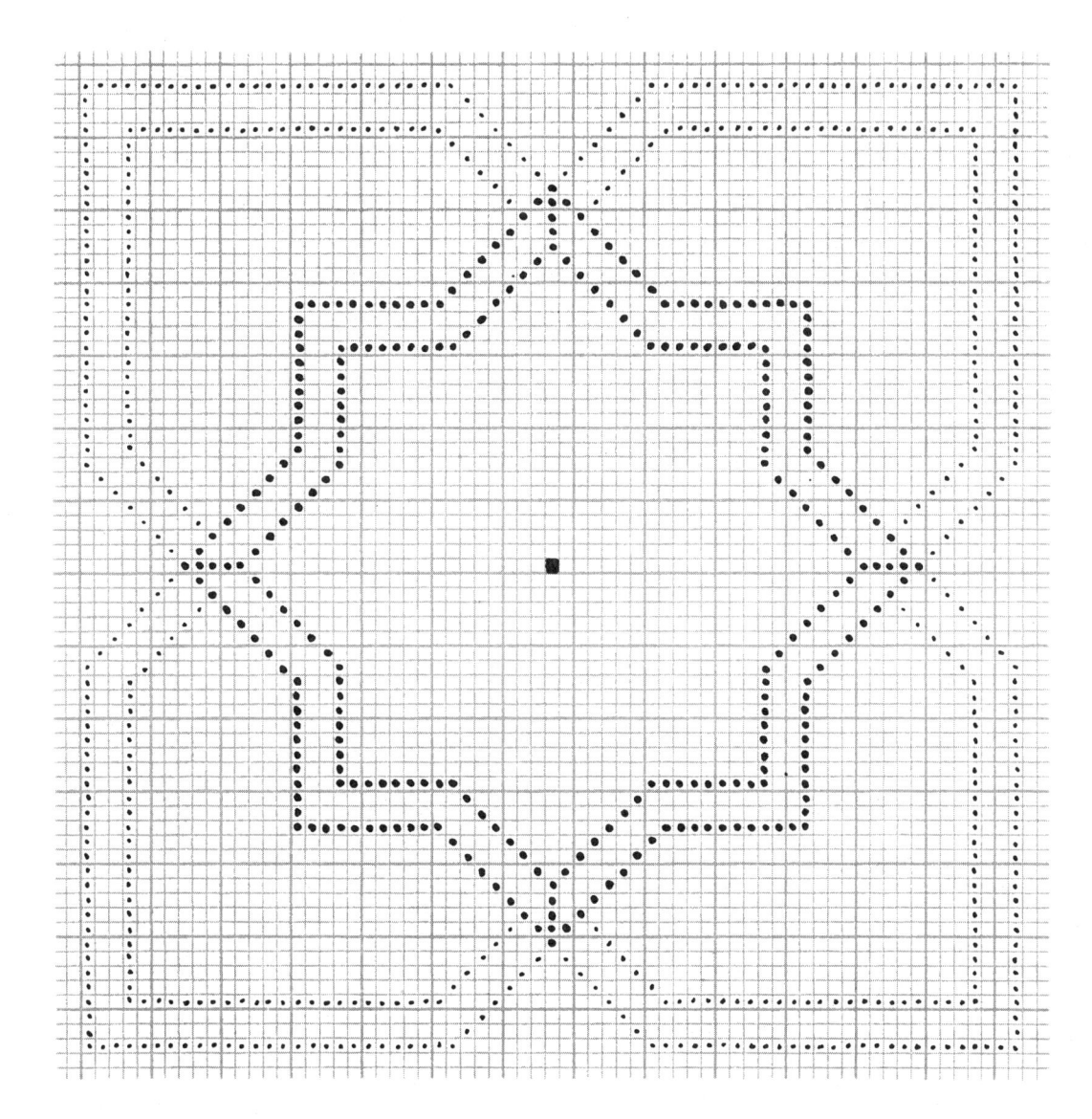

Color pictures M-2 and M-4 have both been done in Tent stitch on a #5 Quick-point canvas. Using the basic 4" Star, the bold dots show the pattern for the red star on the camp stool.

The black square in the center of this diagram indicates the CENTER MESH. Each square on the graph paper represents a mesh on your canvas - not a hole. When working a pattern of this kind on canvas, it is only necessary to mark the outer and inner line of the pattern. If you wish, you may go back and "dot" the mesh in between.

This same 4" Star was carried into a Square (M-2) and all of the dots (bold and light) were marked on the canvas and stitched in green.

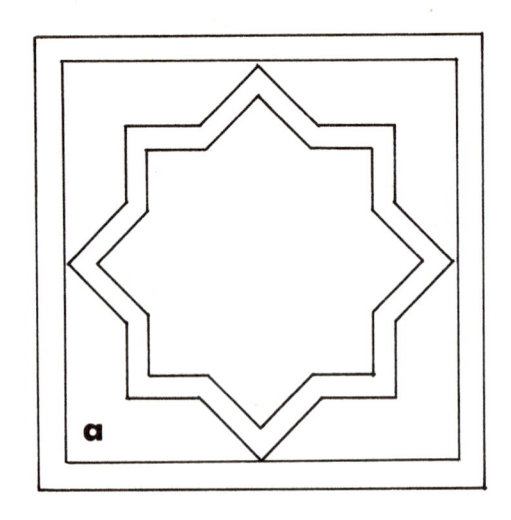

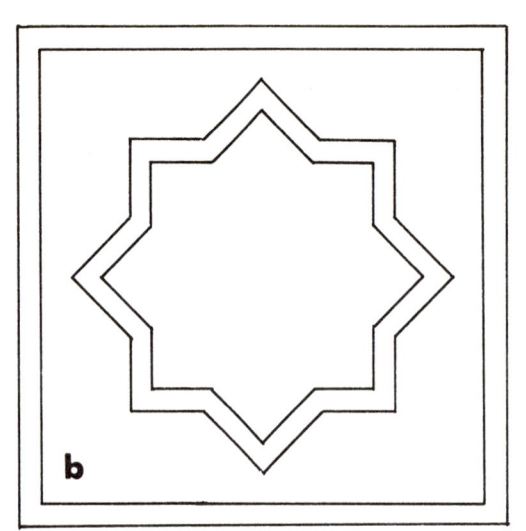

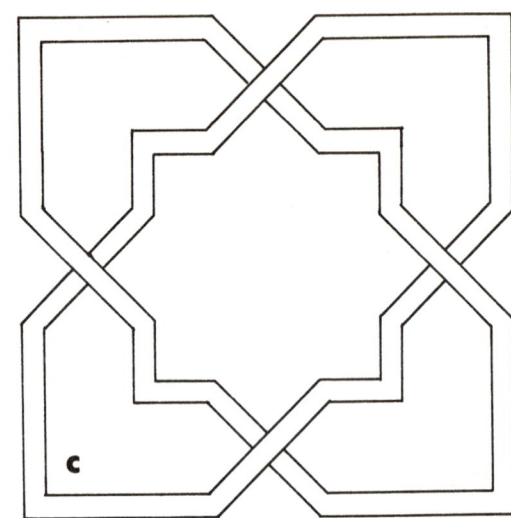

The row of Mitered Gobelin at the Peak of the Star squares up the pattern for the pin cushion (Diagram A). This creates new areas for the use of textured stitches. The row of Mitered Gobelin in Diagram B has been placed considerably outside the Peak of the Star creating a larger secondary area.

Another way to use this versatile 8-pointed Star is to allow the lines to flow into the Square. This creates four separate new areas and 4 V's at the perimeter. This new type of pattern can also be planned for any size Star. All you have to do is chart the Star you wish to use from the Pivot stitch to the left Miter line. Notice in the diagram on the next page that the Pivot is very bold and is not only the Pivot for the Star but for the Square as well.

The clock (P-1) carries a 9" Star into a Square. The Pivot stitch is your starting point (hole #58-63). The pattern lines were stitched in white; and a red Star was added inside by following the established pattern. It is not the next size smaller on the chart. You can always repeat a pattern for one or two rows inside or outside of an established line. Notice where the diagonal line (6 holes high) changes to 5 holes for the "flat".

The clock face and numerals were done in Bias Tent and the 7-step Scotch stitch was checkerboarded (diagonal rows in alternating colors) in the L-shaped corners. The V's were filled in with vertical stitches as diagrammed. A row of Mitered Gobelin and 2 rows of Tent were worked around the entire piece prior to blocking.

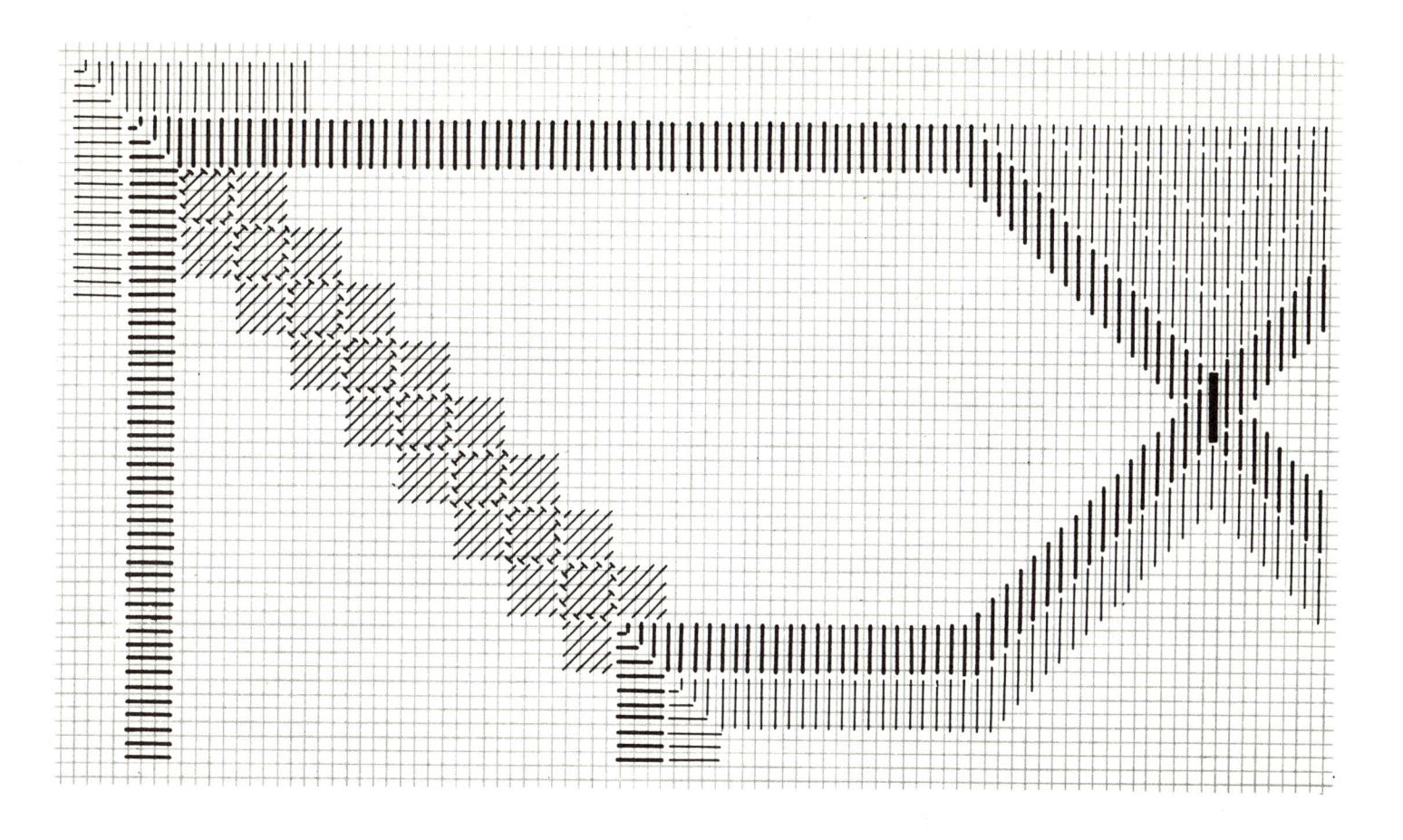

The hands and battery operated works were purchased from a clocksmith. On his suggestion, a ¼" square (4 mesh) was left unstitched in the very center of the canvas to accommodate the shaft of the clockworks. This area was reinforced by machine stitching prior to cutting the canvas threads and gluing them to the back. The needlepoint was glued to a piece of ¼" masonite, taking care to align the center holes in both. The excess canvas was folded to the back and taped (See Finishing - Pictures). A custom frame was made to allow for the depth of the battery and clockworks.

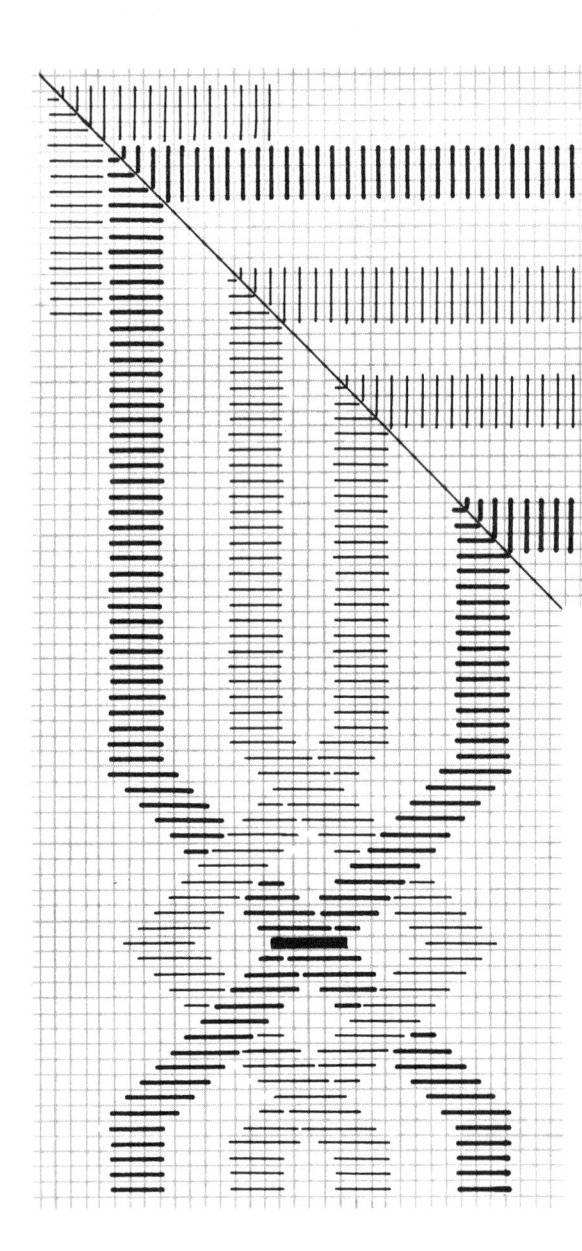

The 6" Star was the basis for this border. The Pivot stitch (very bold) of the Star is the center of the auxiliary pattern and is positioned in holes 37-42 of the vertical center row of holes. If you have trouble visualizing it from this diagram, look at color picture P-6. The orange lines show the 8-pointed Star carried into a Square and the yellow lines are the auxiliary pattern that forms a Diamond on each side.

If you prefer a heavier, bolder look, our patterns can be worked on a #10 canvas as was this piece. The finished size was a bit more than 11" square. If it had been worked on a #14 canvas it would have been 8" square.

It doesn't matter what size canvas you work on, the hole and stitch count remain the same. Just remember, when using a #10, Bargello requires 4-6 ply Persian and Bias Tent uses 3 ply. A row of Mitered Gobelin around the entire piece gives it a finished look and two rows of Bias Tent will act as a seam allowance.

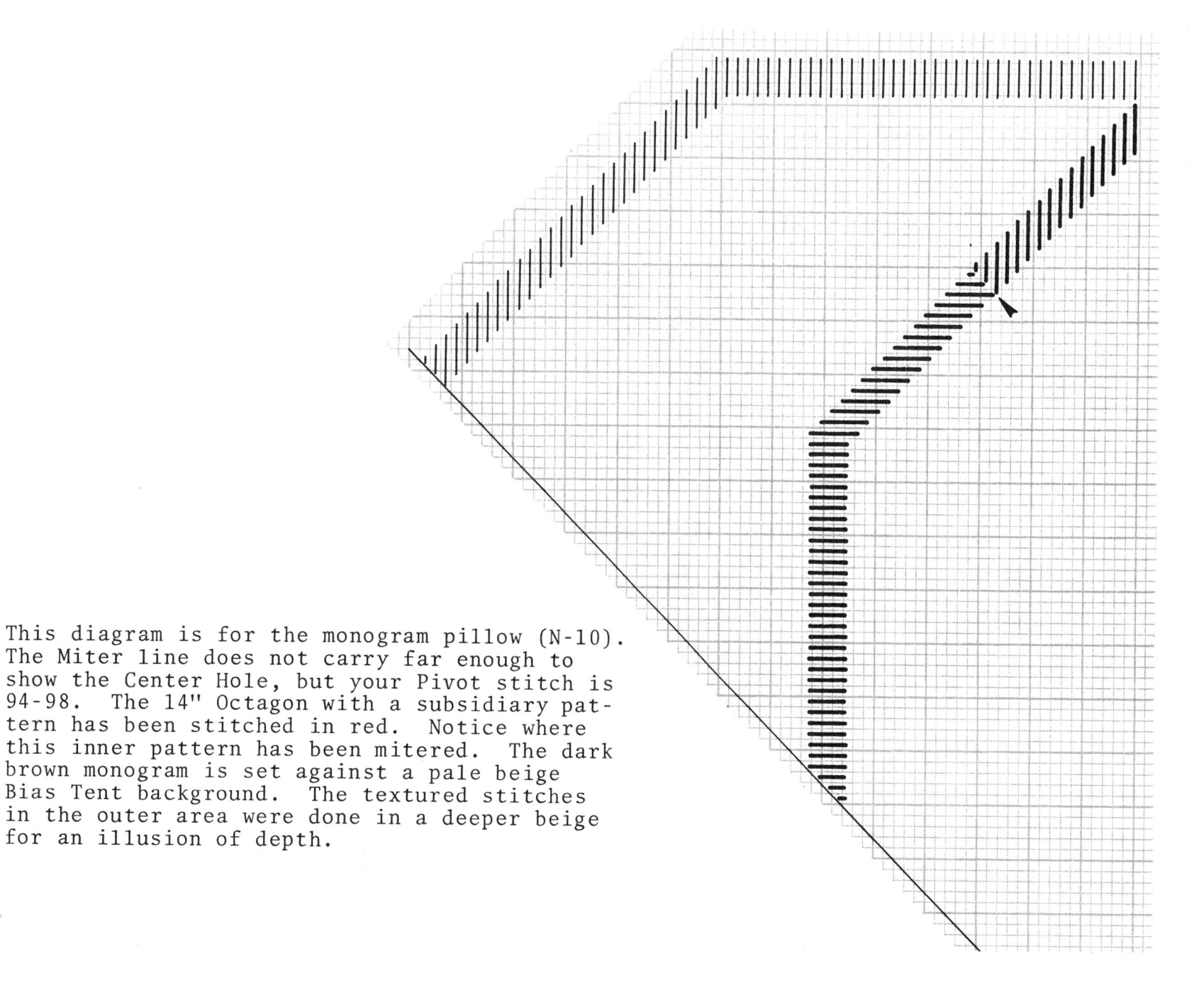

This diagram is for the monogram pillow (N-10). The Miter line does not carry far enough to show the Center Hole, but your Pivot stitch is 94-98. The 14" Octagon with a subsidiary pattern has been stitched in red. Notice where this inner pattern has been mitered. The dark brown monogram is set against a pale beige Bias Tent background. The textured stitches in the outer area were done in a deeper beige for an illusion of depth.

Sincere thanks to our many friends and students who stitched our designs and allowed us to photograph them. We gave them Borders, Corners, and Geometrics; they designed or adapted their own central motifs. We gave them stitch diagrams; they gave us the colorful Kaleidoscopics you see.

To make it easier for you to locate a particular pattern, we have provided these legends to correspond to the color photographs. Beginning on page 157, is an index for every pattern photographed, the name of the person who worked it, and the page on which it can be found.

On our stitch diagrams, we refer you to the proper legend so you can see the pattern photographed!

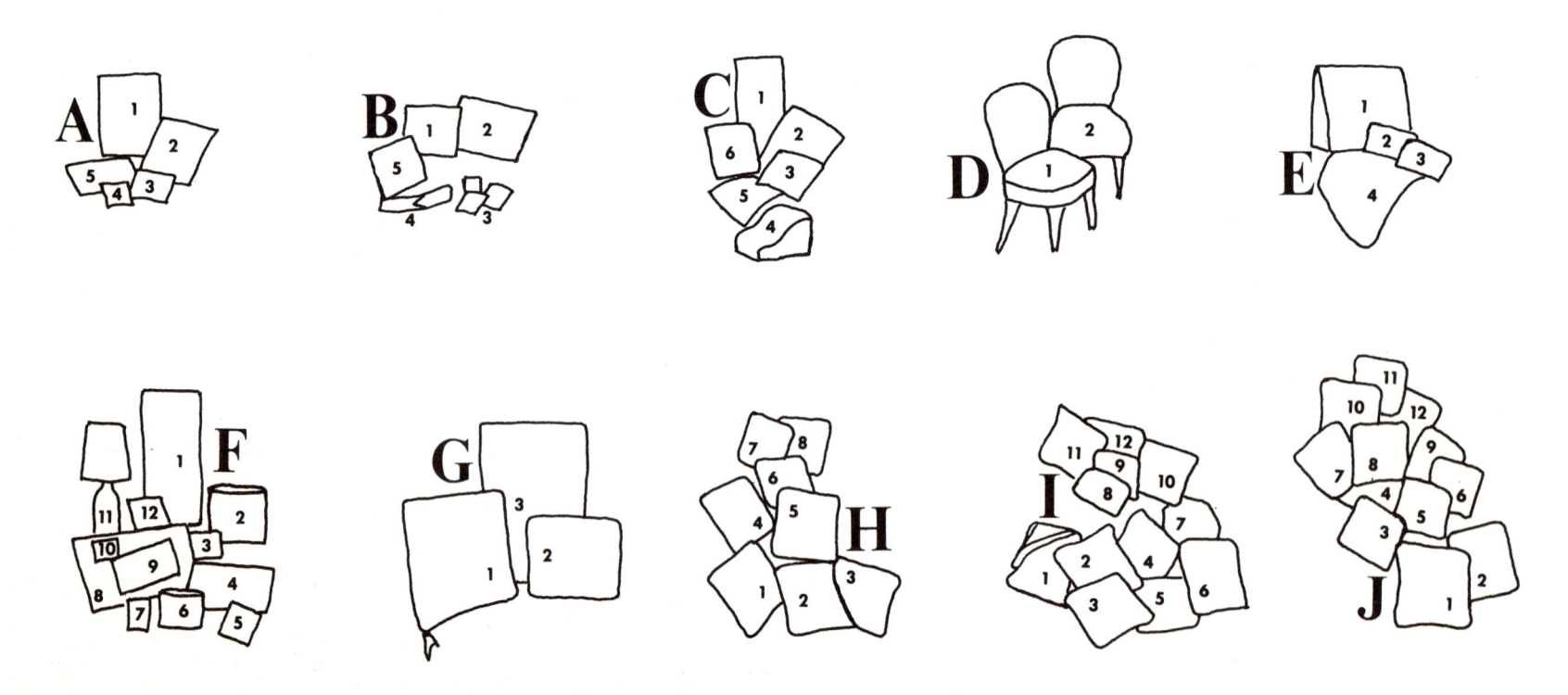

A

B

C

D

E

F

G

H

I

J

K

L

M

N

O

P

97

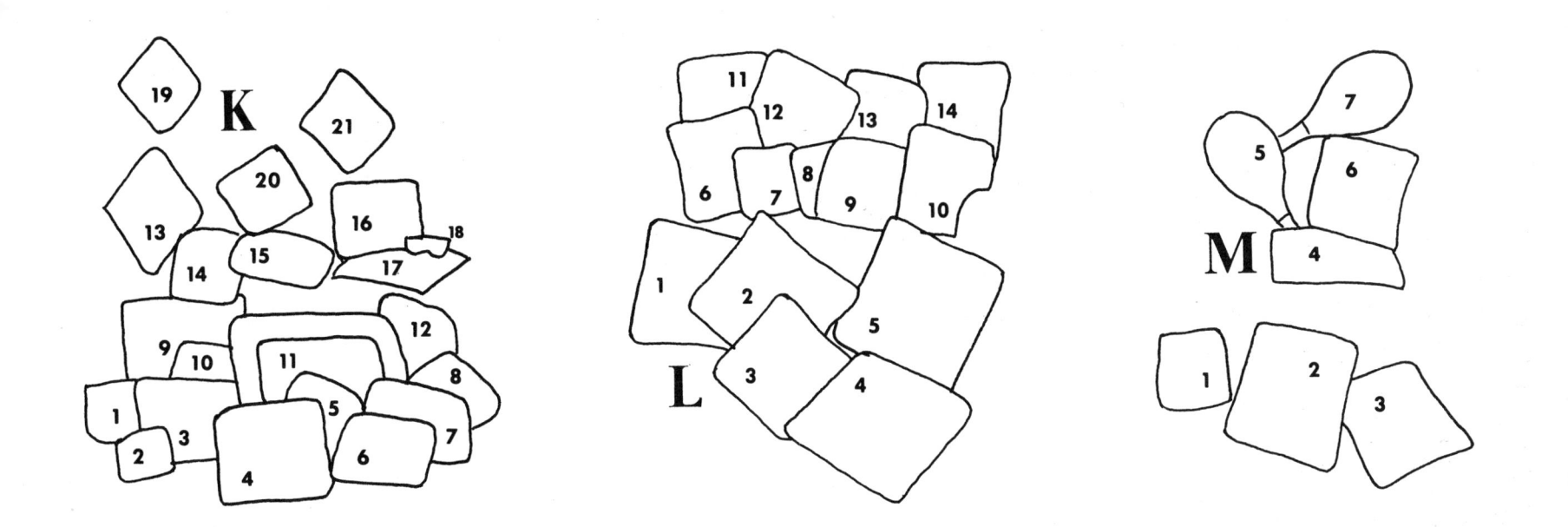

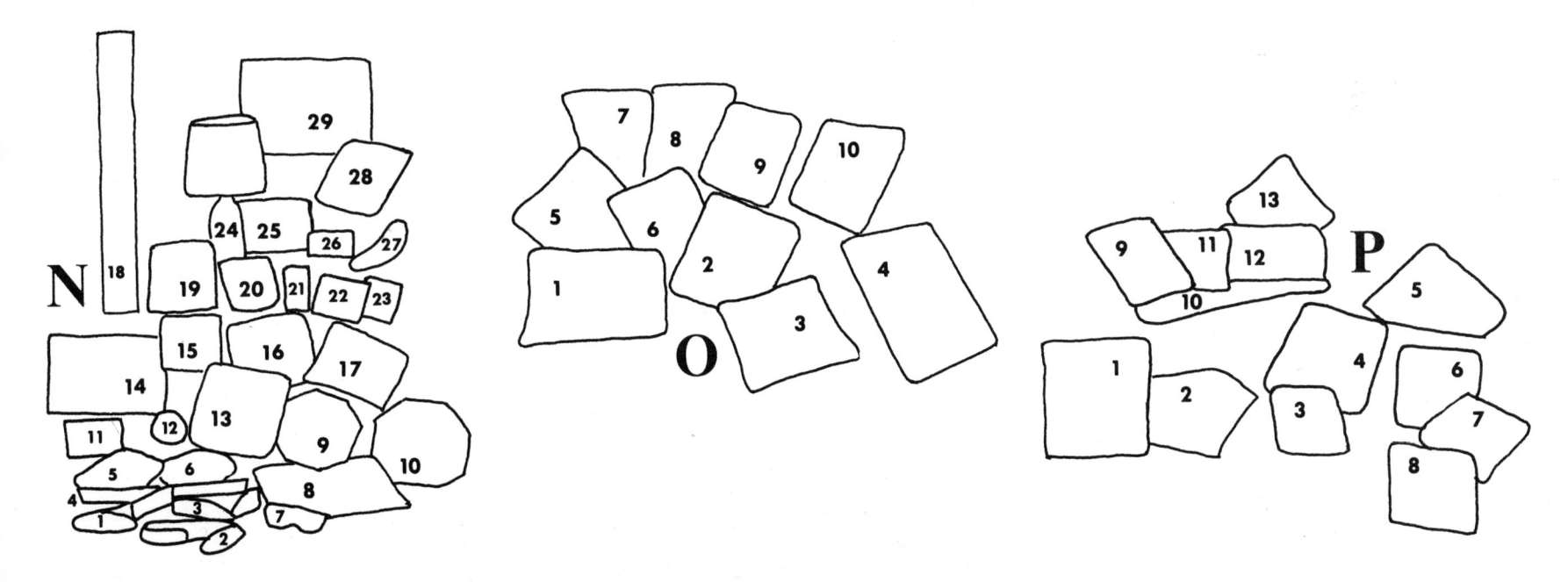

PATCHWORK designs are enjoying a rebirth of interest. They appeal to all ages and are compatible with any decor. Done in soft color combinations, they blend with formal settings; using strong, bold colors, they can "go modern".

The following chart shows just a few of the many possibilities for patchwork samplers. Notice that all the division lines are either vertical, horizontal, or on a true diagonal. They are based on a sub-structure of 64 equal divisions - eight squares in each direction (a). The grids serve as reference points in constructing your pattern. The bold lines (b) show pattern 5A superimposed over the pale grid lines.

You can use as many colors as you want for a "wild" patchwork. If you want a controlled form to emerge, limit yourself to 3 or 4 colors and pre-plan their positions (c).

As an example, we have chosen the following color scheme for 5A.

A - Royal Blue	or	A - Dark Blue
B - Bright Avocado		B - Medium Blue
C - White		C - Ecru (neutral)
D - Yellow		D - (1) - Light Blue, or
		(2) - Red (bright), or
		(3) - Camel (deep neutral)

The 20 patchwork patterns offered can be handled in many different ways. By experimenting with color and texture, there is no end to the variety of effects you can achieve.

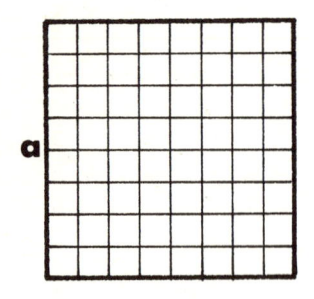

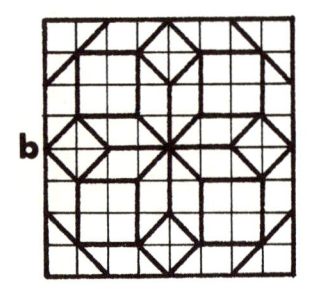

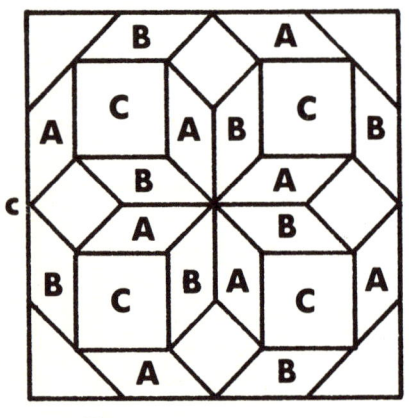

D = blank areas

	1	2	3	4	5
A					
B					
C					
D					

1. Before you can construct any of these designs, you must draw your own gridwork over our patterns. The guide lines along the border are the division points. Lay a ruler over the pattern and draw 7 lines in each direction with a hard #4 pencil. As diagrammed, each of these patterns would be a 14" pillow on a #14 canvas. If you want a larger pillow, use a #10 canvas; the finished size will be 19"

2. Cut your canvas 18" square (23 " square if you are using a #10 canvas) and bind with masking tape.

3. To find the horizontal center row of holes, fold the canvas so the taped edges meet. Make a mark on the fold. Open it and run a #4 pencil in the channel of holes between two threads. Fold the canvas the other way and mark the vertical center row of holes in the same manner. Your canvas is now divided into four parts.

4. Begin constructing the gridwork on your canvas. There are 24 threads <u>between</u> each grid line. Start at the center row of holes, <u>count 24</u> threads, and put the next grid line in the 25th channel of holes. Most diagonal stitches are based on crossing 2,3,or 4 mesh (Scotch, Mosaic, Byzantine, etc.). These same numbers (2,3,and 4) can be evenly divided into 24 so there will be little need for "fillers". You may choose to use vertical stitches; they miter well and the "fillers" are no problem. THE GRID LINES IN ANY DIRECTION FROM THE CENTER HOLE ARE IN ROWS 25, 49, 73, 97. Row 97 is the outline of your working area.

5. Use your marker to lay on the pattern over the grid lines. You will have no trouble marking the horizontal and vertical lines. Wherever a horizontal grid crosses a vertical grid, you will have a Center Hole. Your pattern lines, vertical, horizontal, and diagonal, all begin and end at a Center Hole. For a more complete explanation, refer to Marking for Geometrics and Kaleidoscopics.

6. Work within the pattern lines when stitching - ignore the grids.

The three Kaleidoscopics on the left were all worked from the same pattern and are shown in color picture I. The two on the right are variations and are shown in color picture N. Many different effects can be achieved from the same basic pattern by your choice and use of color.

All you need for blocking is: a gingham covered board, aluminum push pins, and a spray bottle. The polyester fiberfill is inexpensive, easy to work with, and a perfect pillow stuffing. The 3-stitch knitted cording and the 5-stitch knitted "gimp" are the perfect finishing touches.

101

Bargello has always been a popular form of needlepoint, though somewhat monotonous. Once your pattern row has been counted and stitched, you merely fill in below, row after row in varying colors.

Kaleidoscopic Bargello cannot possibly be boring because the pattern changes with each succeeding row and the center is always a surprise. Although these designs appear quite complex; in reality, the procedure is very simple.

A single pattern row worked at the perimeter creates a medallion. Once the size and shape of your design has been established, the only hard part is behind you. Put away your diagram, sit back, relax, and stitch. Before you know it, your medallion will be complete.

Both pillows in the photograph were worked from the same pattern Only a portion of the original Bargello line (bold stitches) was used in converting it to a Kaleidoscopic. What a startling difference! Once you understand our procedures, you will be able to create your own Kaleidoscopics.

103

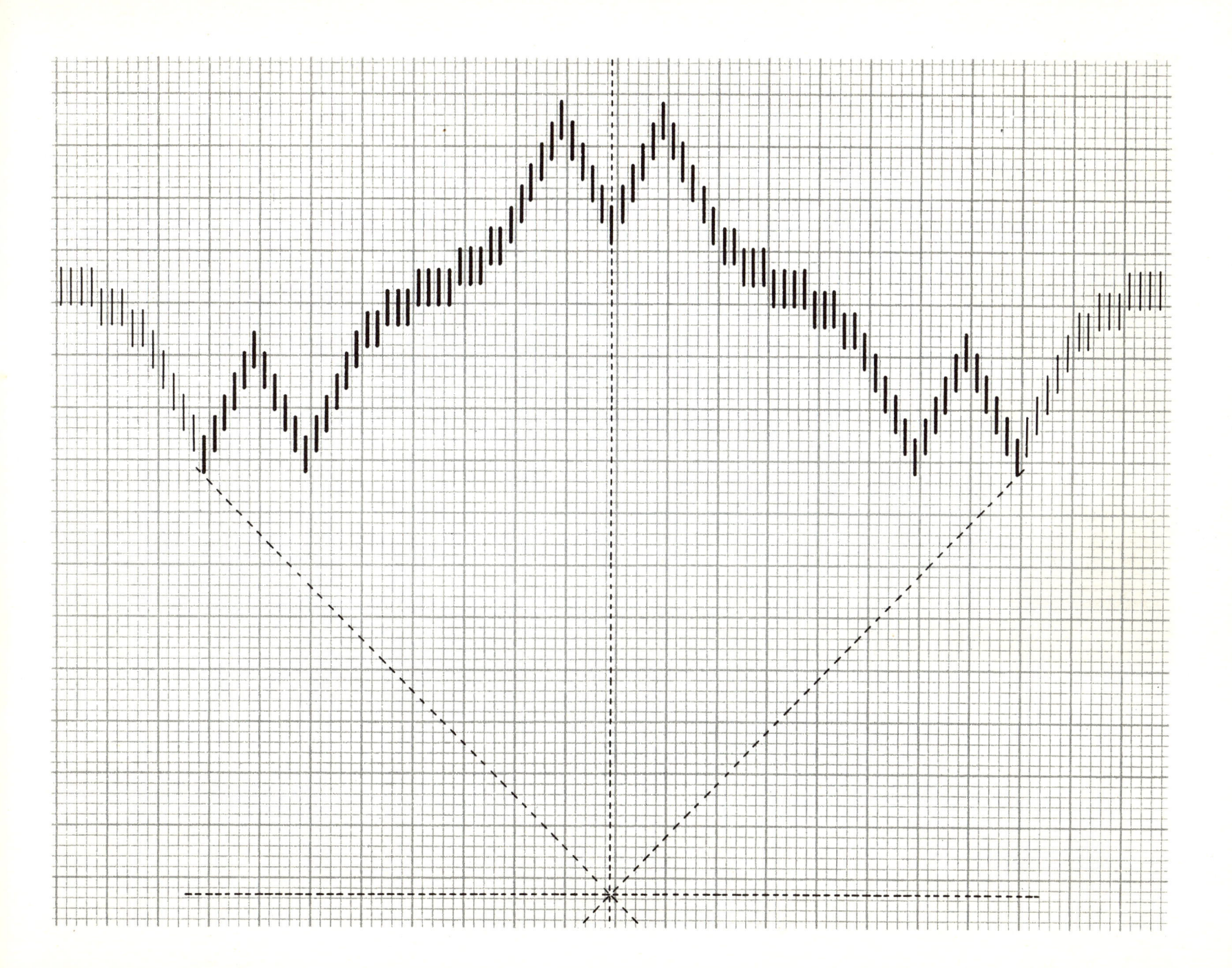

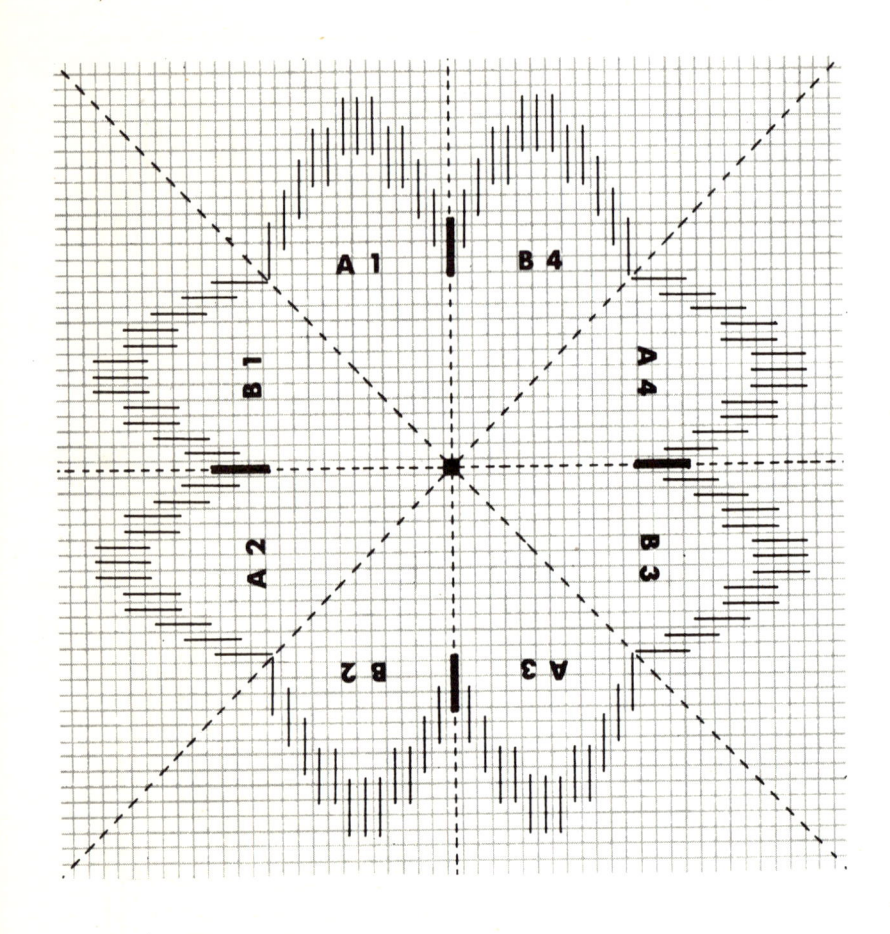

This diagram shows a properly marked 'canvas' (Marking for Kaleidoscopics) with the pattern line applied. The pattern segments have been numbered and it is easy to see that all the A's are the same. All the B's are the same and are nothing more than a 'flip' or mirror image of A.

The Pivot stitches (bold) are the central stitches of the pattern and are very important. They fit into the center row of holes, both vertically and horizontally. The Pivot may be a single stitch, or the center stitch of a group of 3,5,or 7. In order for your pattern line to fit into the canvas segments correctly, the Pivot stitch must be properly positioned in the center row of holes.

How many holes are there from the Center Hole to the bottom of the Pivot (inclusive)? In this case, there are 13. If you were stitching this pattern, you would locate the same spot on your canvas (13 holes from the center). Bring your needle up at this point, and down at 17. Notice that all stitches are 5 holes high - cover 4 threads. They move up or down the canvas by 3 holes - skip 2 threads. Very carefully lay in the first portion (A-1) of your base row. The bottom of your last stitch will fit into the Miter line.

Now turn your canvas ¼ turn clockwise and lay in the next segment (B-1) of your base row. The stitches in this segment are at right angles to the stitches of the first segment (A-1). Your Pivot stitch should fit into the next center row of holes. Continue working each segment around the canvas. The base line must be very carefully counted and stitched.

Our charts will show 1/8 of the pattern (A). From this one segment, you will be able to work the entire pattern. To see what it will look like across the top (from miter to miter), hold a small frameless mirror next to the center stitch (Pivot). The mirror image (B-4) will show the 'flip' of A-1. To see how the pattern will look around a corner, (B-1), place the mirror along the Miter line.

Our Kaleidoscopics are worked from the base row to the center. Work each row all the way around - do not try and complete just one segment at a time.

To begin row #2 - remember that all stitches are 5 holes high. The top of these stitches fit into the same holes as the bottom of the preceding row.

NEVER USE MORE THAN 5 HOLES FOR A STITCH AND NEVER CROSS THE MITER LINE INTO THE NEXT SEGMENT. This is the only place where your stitch length will vary; it may be only 2,3,or 4 holes high along the Miter line.

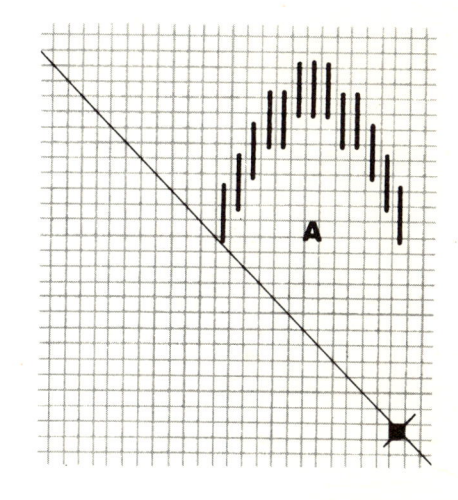

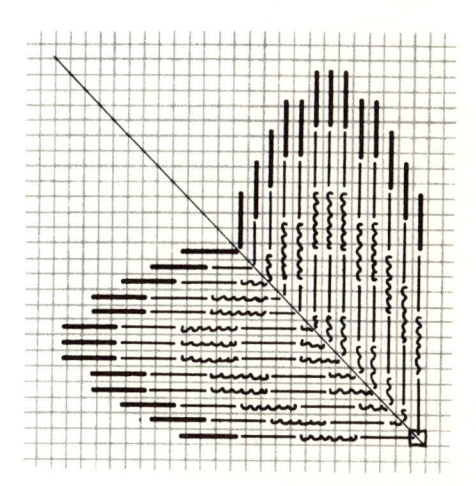

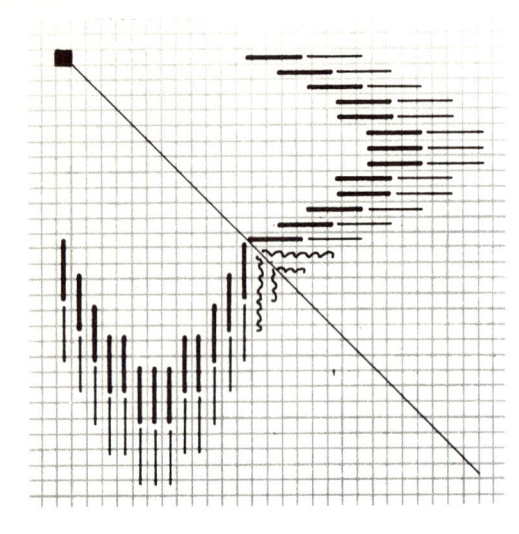

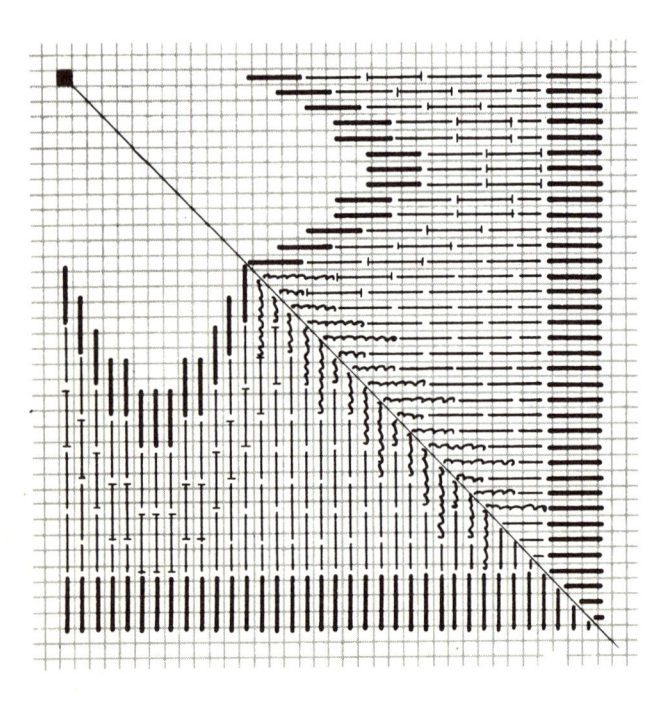

Your BACKGROUND is stitched in a single color which allows your medallion to remain the focal point. A subtle texture will emerge by using your base line as your stitch guide. Your stitches will fit perfectly and there will be no need for 'fillers'.

Hold your canvas so that the medallion is above the working area and stitch your background around it. Always bring your needle up in an empty hole and down in a hole with yarn in it.

You will have no problem following the pattern where there are groups of stitches to guide you. The doubles are placed in a line with doubles, and triples with triples. The balance of the background is nothing more than singles.

Look at the Miter line carefully. You will see how we have compensated (in the background only). If a stitch falls one hole short of the Miter line, enlarge it to 6. This gives a smoother line for the background. A row of Mitered Gobelin around the entire piece squares it off for a finished look.

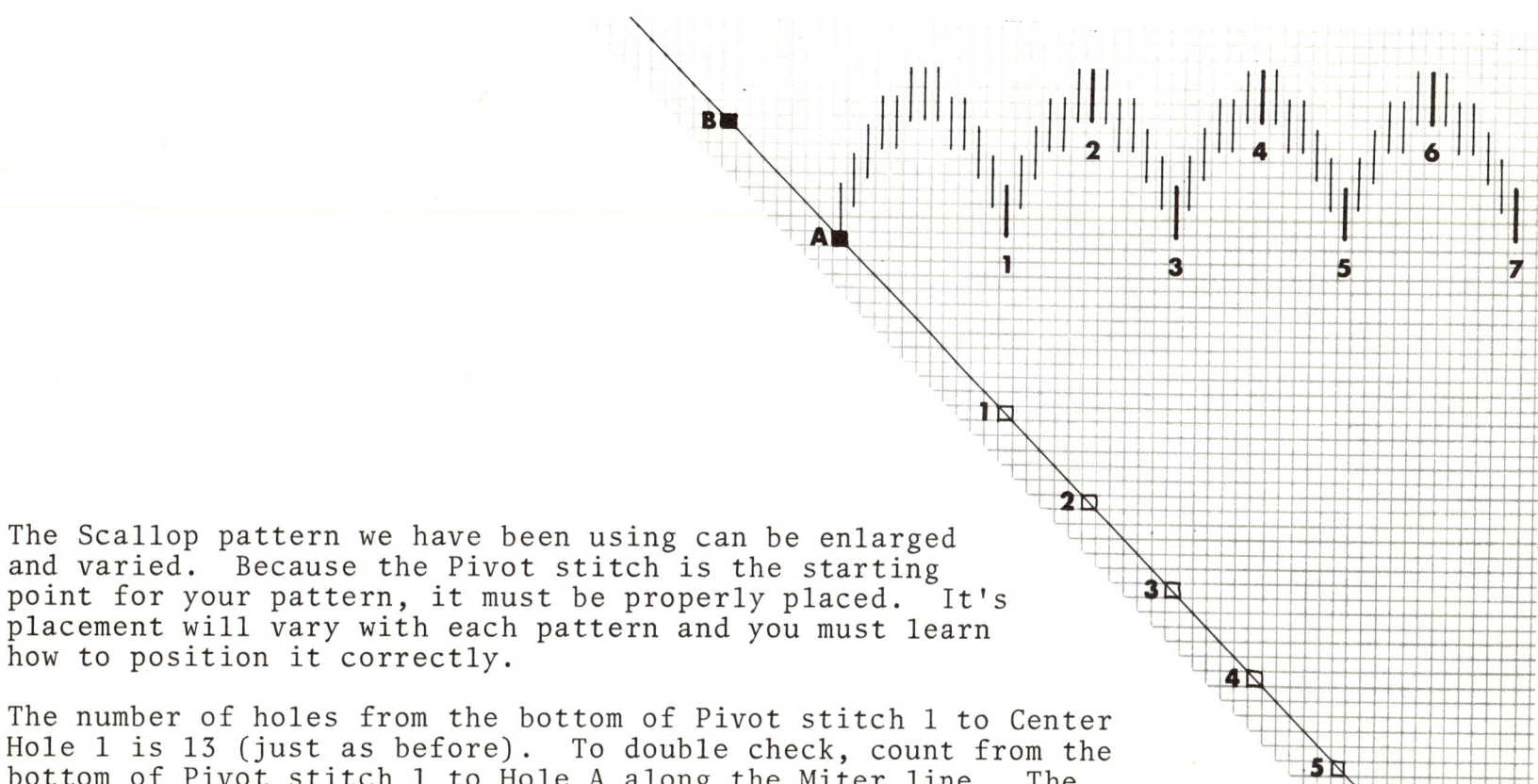

The Scallop pattern we have been using can be enlarged and varied. Because the Pivot stitch is the starting point for your pattern, it must be properly placed. It's placement will vary with each pattern and you must learn how to position it correctly.

The number of holes from the bottom of Pivot stitch 1 to Center Hole 1 is 13 (just as before). To double check, count from the bottom of Pivot stitch 1 to Hole A along the Miter line. The figure is also 13. The number of holes from Pivot stitches 3, 5, and 7 to their respective Center Holes will be the same as from these Pivot stitches to Hole A along the Miter line.

The count from the bottom of Pivot stitch 2 to Center Hole 2 is 27; from Pivot stitch 2 to Hole B along the miter is also 27. THESE TWO NUMBERS WILL ALWAYS BE THE SAME.

Our diagrams will not always show a Center Hole, but they will all have the Miter line. You know the count for both is identical. Count from the bottom of the Pivot stitch to the black hole along the Miter line on your diagram. Use this figure to count from the Center Hole (always #1) to the bottom of the Pivot stitch on your canvas.

107

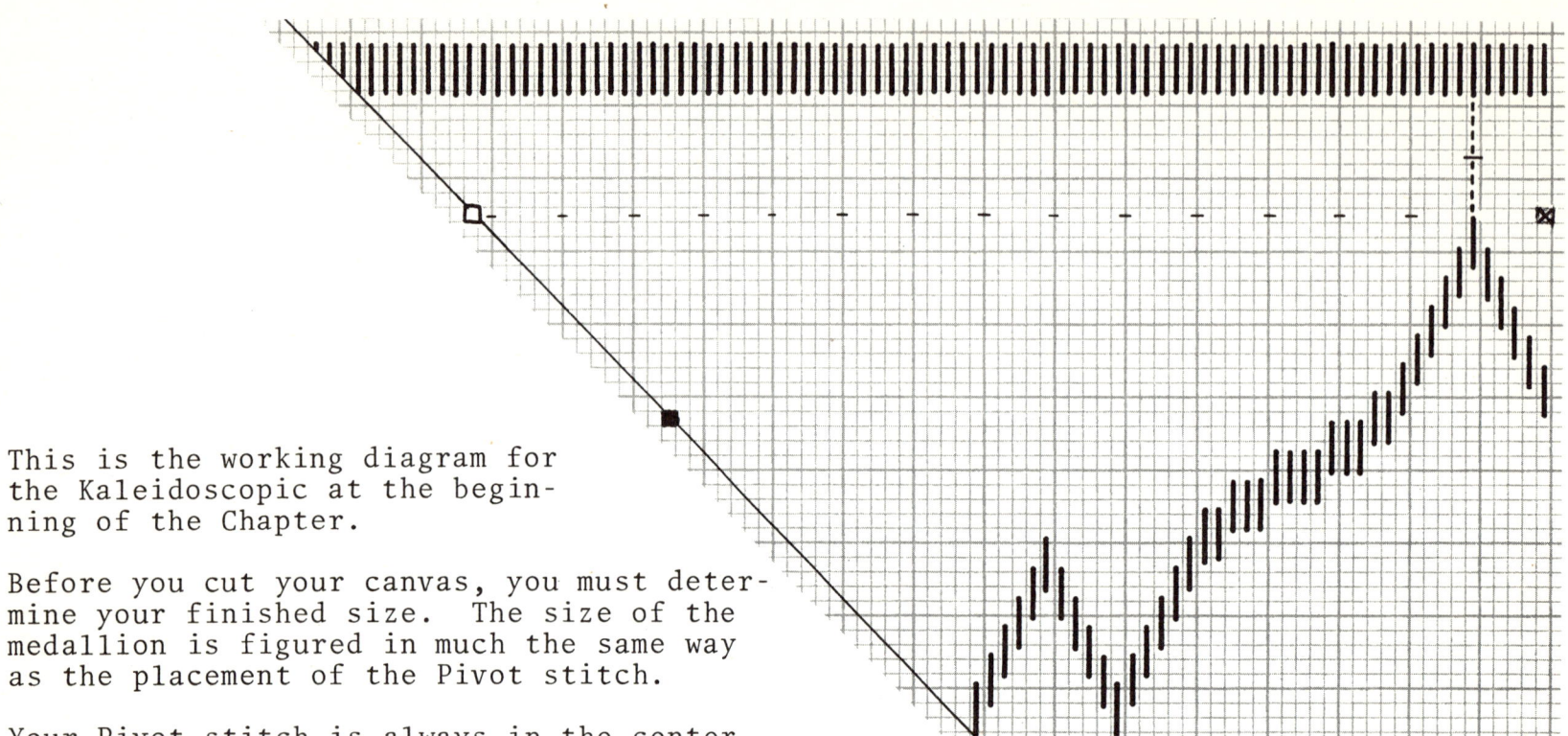

This is the working diagram for the Kaleidoscopic at the beginning of the Chapter.

Before you cut your canvas, you must determine your finished size. The size of the medallion is figured in much the same way as the placement of the Pivot stitch.

Your Pivot stitch is always in the center row of holes. Sometimes your Pivot is the highest or Peak stitch of the pattern. To establish its size, you would count from the top of the Peak stitch to the open square on the Miter line. On this diagram, the Pivot is lower than the Peak stitch. Count from the hole that is directly above the Pivot and in line with the Peak stitch (indicated here by an X). Count the number of holes from the X to the open square; the count is 77 holes.

Because you have already counted the Center Hole, add 76 holes for the other half to give you the total hole count.
   77 + 76 = 153 holes

To give you the inch size of the medallion, divide this figure (153 holes) by the size canvas you are using (14). 153 ÷ 14 = 11" approximately. On a #10 canvas, it would be more than 15". On a #18 canvas, it would be only 8½".

Allow at least 1" all the way around for background. This will give you room for three rows of background above the Peak stitch or two rows of background and one row of Mitered Gobelin.

1. Allow 1½"-2" blank margin on all sides and cut your canvas 16" x 16". Bind and mark it for Kaleidoscopics.

2. Refer to your diagram and locate your Pivot stitch. Count from the bottom of the Pivot to the Center Hole or to the black dot on the Miter line. These counts are both 63.

3. Count the Center Hole on your canvas as #1. Bring your needle up in the 63rd hole and down in the 67th hole. Your Pivot stitch is now properly placed. Very carefully stitch on your base line. Stitch the balance of your medallion.

4. Work 1 or 2 rows of background from the base line outward. There should always be some background above your Peak stitch.

5. Outline your working area (#4 hard pencil). There are three options open to you.

   a. If you want to square off level with the Peak stitch of the background, draw your outline in the channel of holes at the top of the Peak.

   b. If you want to add a row of Mitered Gobelin or a single line Corner, draw your outline in the 5th hole outside your Peak stitch. You must count the hole that already has yarn in it as #1. The circular or diamond shaped Kaleidoscopics are the only ones that will accommodate a Corner pattern (*).

   c. You may want to add one of the more complicated Corners. Refer to the diagram for that Corner to see how many holes it requires.

6. Finish the balance of the background.

7. Add two rows of Tent outside your Gobelin to be used as a seam allowance.

Look at color picture K. Would you believe that everything was worked from the same basic pattern? In some cases, different Pivot stitches and auxiliary base lines were used. This accounts for the variety of central effects. The most startling difference, however, is in the use of color. K-5,8,19,20 and 21 all used the same Pivot stitch; yet, each is unique. Why?

COLOR IS THE KEY FACTOR IN THE DEVELOPMENT OF INDIVIDUAL KALEIDO-SCOPICS. By using 'your' colors, you are really designing your own. Yes, we are giving you the stitch patterns but the final effect depends on what colors you choose and how you use them.

Unlike straight Bargello where there is room to flow through a wide range of colors, Kaleidoscopics are self-contained. As you work toward the center, each row gets smaller. By limiting yourself to 3 or 4 well chosen colors, you are able to control the development of the medallion. The repetition of a limited color sequence is much more effective than the introduction of too many colors.

Choosing your colors for a Kaleidoscopic requires some planning. What effect do you want to create? What will be your background color? Do you like the medallion set against a light or a dark background? Which color will you use for your base row? There should be sufficient contrast between the background and the base row so that the medallion remains the focal point.

For a monochromatic effect, you would choose a dark, a medium, and a light from one color family. In most cases, the background color should be used somewhere in the medallion for continuity. J-8,11 and 12; K-7,15 and 17; L-5 and 11 all used this type of color plan.

Several different color sequences can be arranged.

```
        LIGHT BACKGROUND                    DARK BACKGROUND
        1. d,m,l - d,m,l -                  1. l,m,d,m - l,m,d,m -
        2. d,m,l,m - d,m,l,m -              2. l,m,l,d - l,m,l,d -
        3. d,l,m - d,l,m -                  3. m,l,m,d - m,l,m,d -
```

By adding a BRIGHT, many new and more dramatic sequences are possible. The Bright sparks a monochromatic scheme for a bolder look. Basically, a dark, a medium, a light and a bright work well together. If you wish to use only three colors, the bright can be substituted for the medium or light value.

LIGHT BACKGROUND
1. d,m,l,b - d,m,l,b -
2. d,m,l,b,l,m - d,m,l,b,l,m -
3. b,l,m,d - b,l,m,d -
4. b,l,m,d,m,l - b,l,m,d,m,l -
5. b,m,l,m - b,m,l,m -
6. d,m,d,b,l,b - d,m,d,b,l,b -
7. b,d,m,l - b,d,m,l -

DARK BACKGROUND
1. l,m,b,m,l,d - l,m,b,m,l,d -
2. b,m,l,m,d - b,m,l,m,d -
3. b,l,d,l - b,l,d,l -
4. b,l,d - b,l,d -

BRIGHT BACKGROUND
1. d,m,l,m,d,b - d,m,l,m,d,b -
2. d,m,l,b - d,m,l,b -
3. l,m,d,m,b - l,m,d,m,b -
4. d,l,b,l,d - d,l,b,l,d -
5. m,l,m,b - m,l,m,b -

All of these combinations can be altered even further by doing a double row of one of your colors. Color pictures J-2,11; K-13 and L-5 all make liberal use of double rows.

I-6 uses 4 shades of blue, graduating from dark to light - bright (white) and light to dark. Notice how the background color has been carried into the medallion. After completing the first color sequence, two rows of the bright (background) introduce the next sequence.

I-4 has used double and triple rows. Can you see them?

O-8 and O-10 look entirely different. O-8 uses a double base row of white, and follows a longer color sequence (black, brown, rust, brown, black and white). O-10 uses a shorter sequence and no double rows.

We have given you just a few suggestions for color sequences; no doubt, you can think of many more. Experiment with your yarns. It is not necessary to stitch a portion of the pattern to see what it will look like, just lay your colors out in different orders. The ever-changing rows of pattern and color are what make Kaleidoscopics so much fun.

Using the same pattern and the same four colors, we have shown you the many different effects that can be achieved by:
1. changing the background color
2. changing the color sequence
3. doubling rows
4. Another easy, but very effective way to alter the pattern is by adding an auxiliary base line.

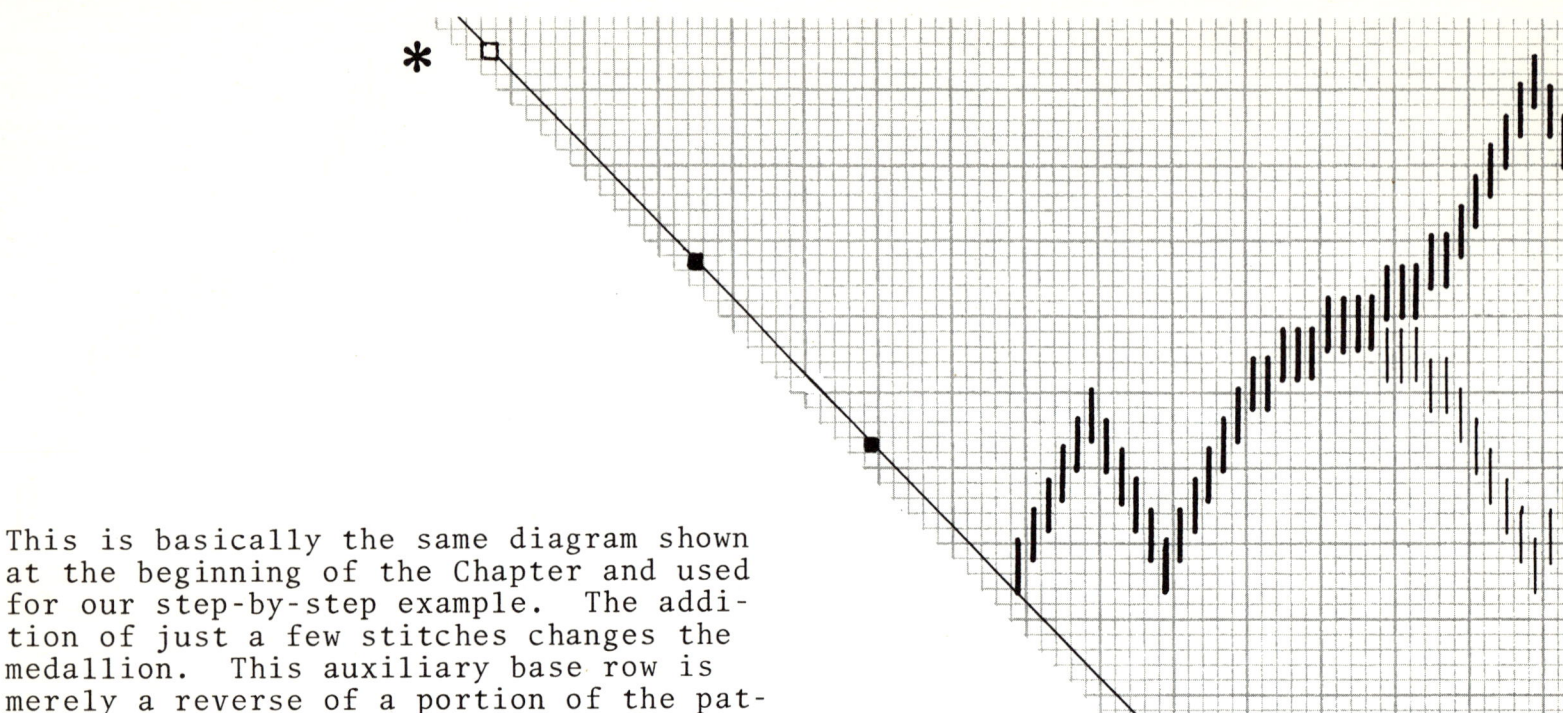

This is basically the same diagram shown at the beginning of the Chapter and used for our step-by-step example. The addition of just a few stitches changes the medallion. This auxiliary base row is merely a reverse of a portion of the pattern and has been planned as a controlled variation.

Although the outside of the medallion remains the same, the center of the pattern will look entirely different. It is the lower base row that controls the central effects. In some cases we have added an auxiliary base row _above_ the primary base row. Although the central effects remain the same, the basic shape of the medallion will change.

The basic pattern is always diagrammed _bold_; the auxiliary base rows are optional and are diagrammed _light_. Be sure that you stitch _all_ base rows (bold and/or light) in the same color.

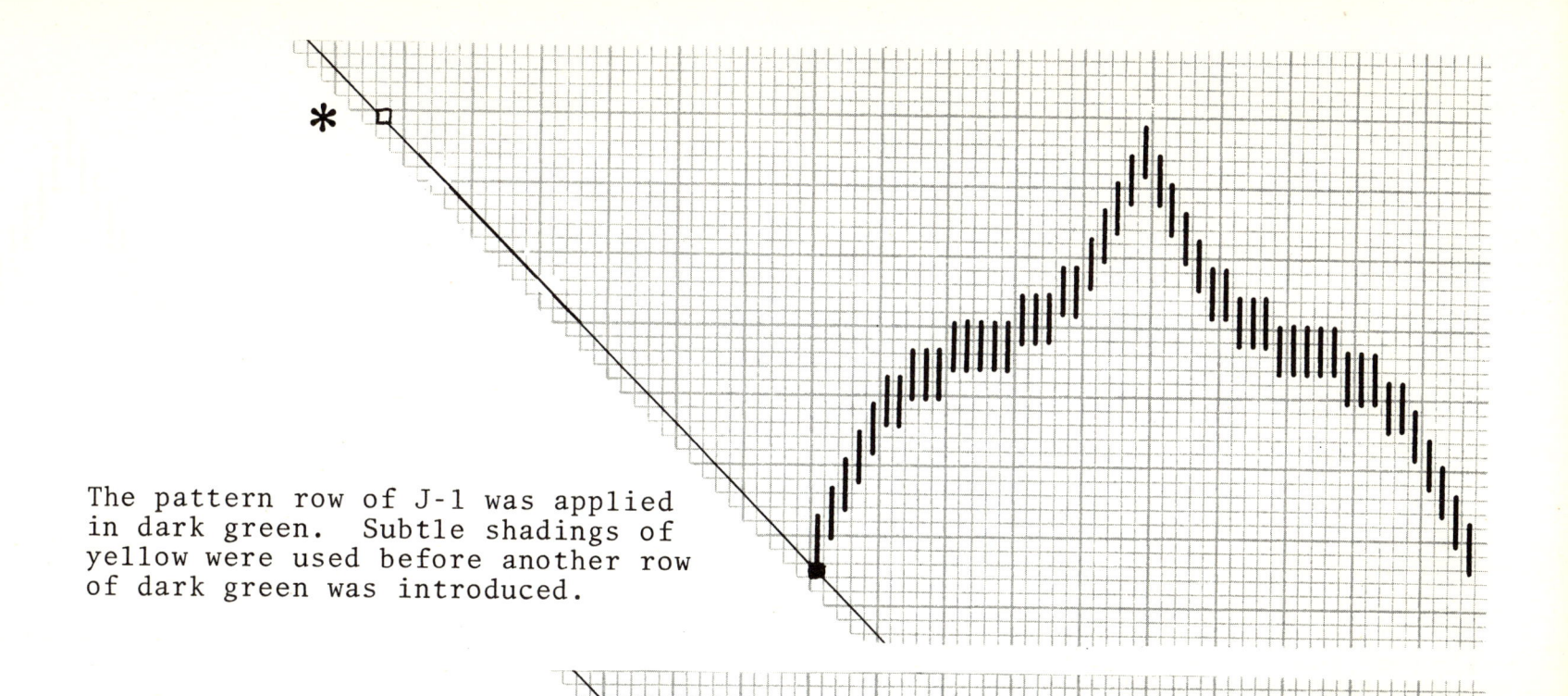

The pattern row of J-1 was applied in dark green. Subtle shadings of yellow were used before another row of dark green was introduced.

N-5 used Pivot stitch 1 and only the bold line.

J-5 and 6 used Pivot stitch 2 and only the bold line. The only difference is in the use of color.

J-3 used the auxiliary base line and Pivot stitch 2.

By using different Pivot stitches and colors, each variation is unique.

113

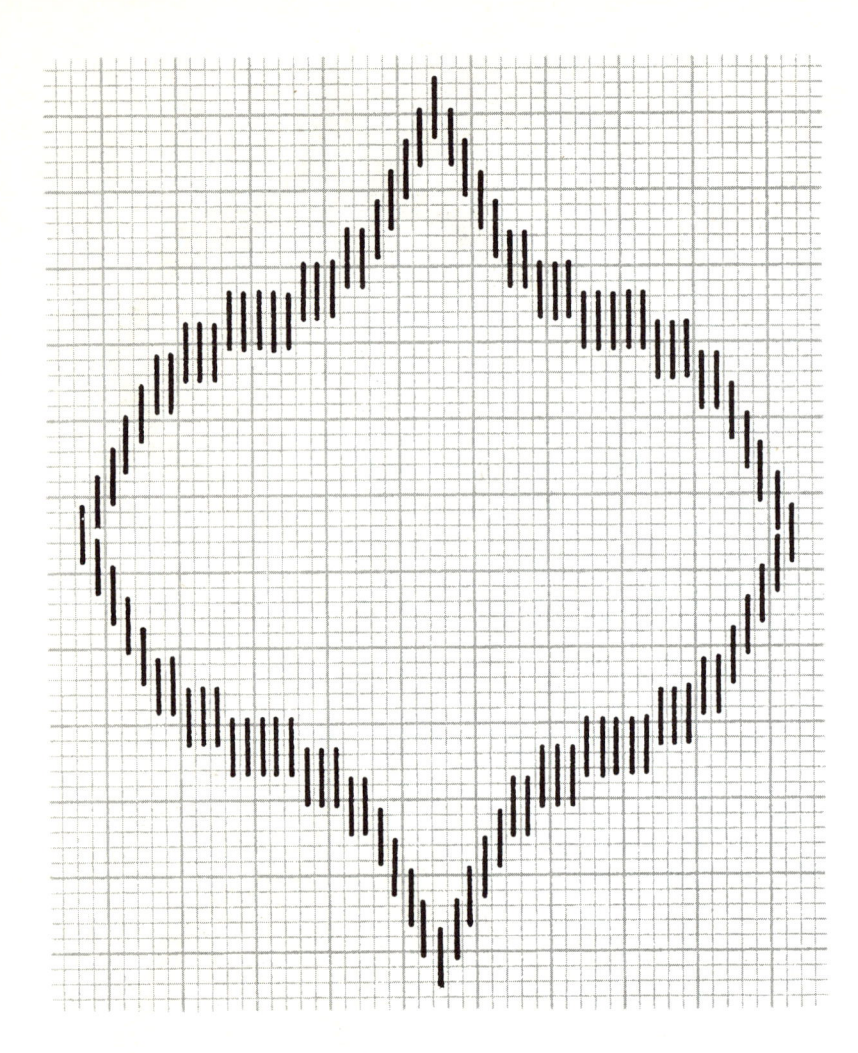

POMEGRANATE

This stitch pattern is basically the same as the popular Pomegranate - a self enclosed ogee type arch. Because these variations look so different, they have often been identified as separate patterns. Once you work with the Pomegranate and its many options, it will be one of the most versatile patterns you can use.

114

The 6 diagrams on the next page are not stitch diagrams but rather a guide to help you in planning your colors for the Pomegranate variations. The black areas are the pattern lines.

A. Work all the way around.

B. Work from the top down.

C. Work from the bottom up.

D. An auxiliary base row has been added at the top and the two areas were worked all the way around. The main portion takes on a heart shape.

E. The auxiliary base row has been added at the bottom. The main pattern is worked from the top down; it could also be worked around and around for an upside down heart effect. The lower portion was worked around.

F. Both auxiliary base rows were added creating two circles and two diamonds, or - an owl wearing a dunce cap!

The bell pull (N-18) used nine Pomegranates placed one stitch apart. From the top down, numbers 1,3,7, and 9 all used variation A. Numbers 2 and 8 followed variation B. Numbers 4 and 6 used variation C and number 5 used F. The textured background was created by following the same stitch rhythm in a solid color.

Whenever you have a self-enclosed area, formed by the addition of an auxiliary base row, it may be treated like any one of the Pomegranate variations.

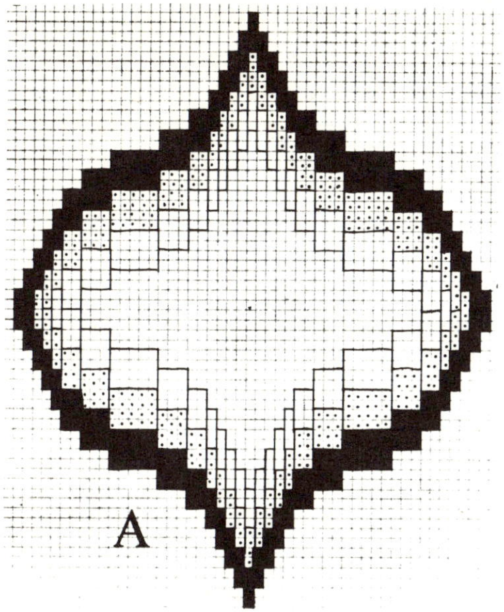
A
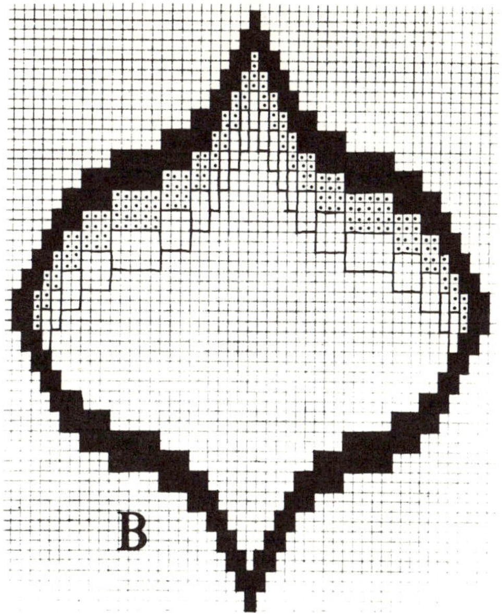
B
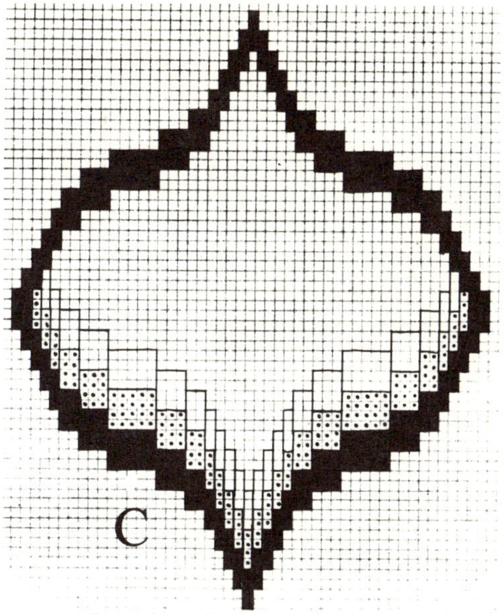
C
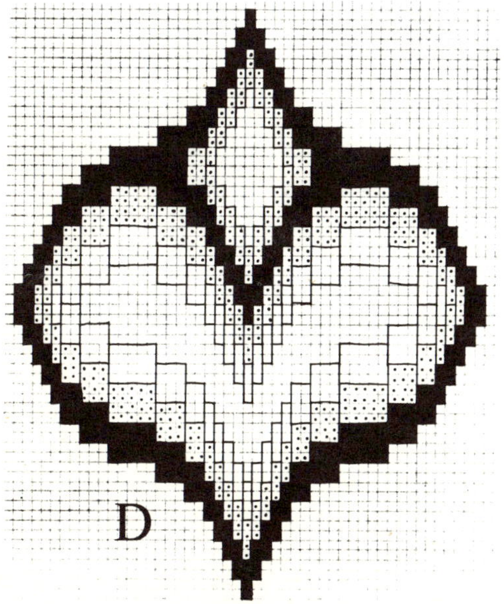
D
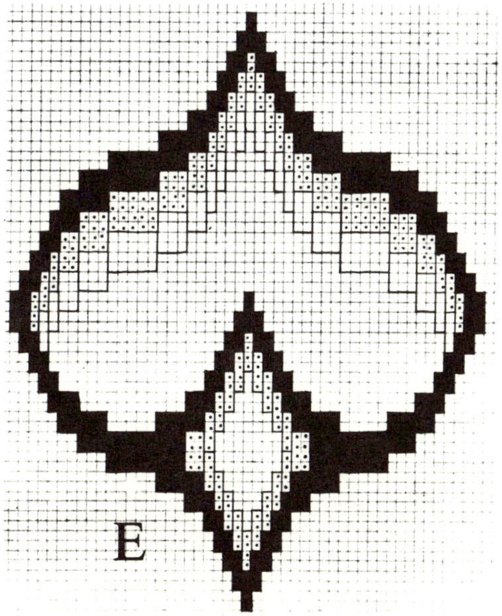
E
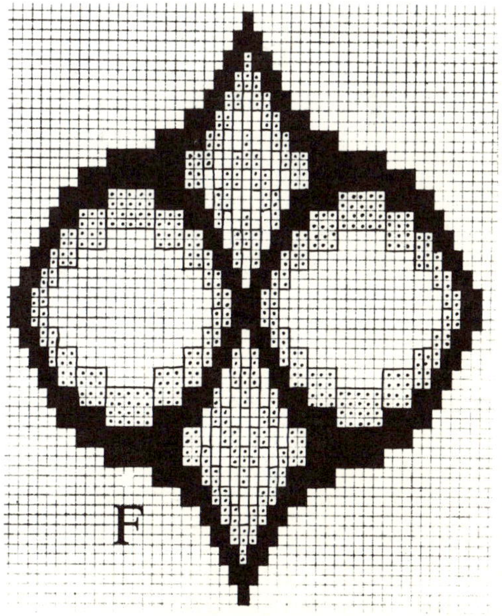
F

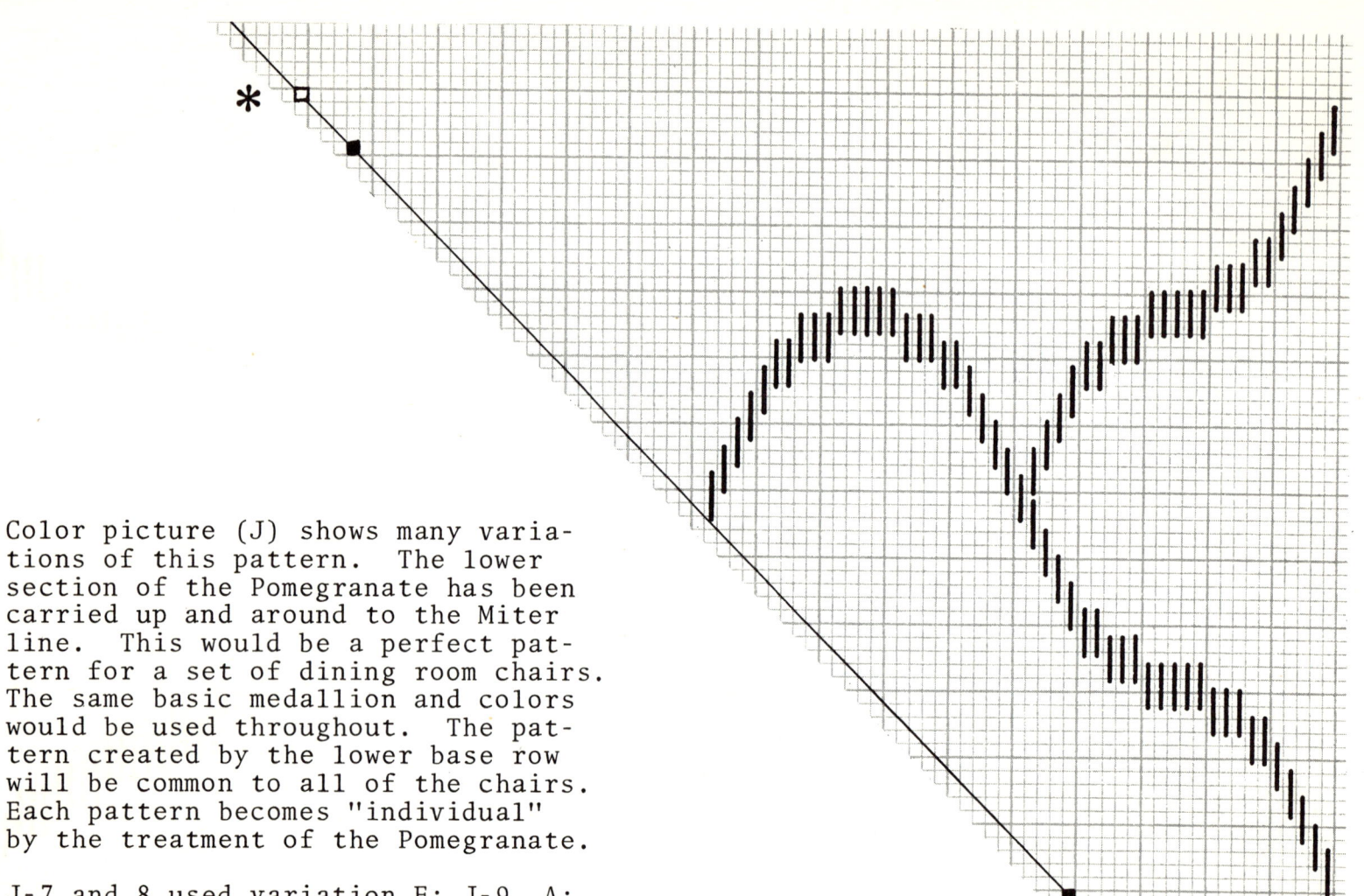

Color picture (J) shows many variations of this pattern. The lower section of the Pomegranate has been carried up and around to the Miter line. This would be a perfect pattern for a set of dining room chairs. The same basic medallion and colors would be used throughout. The pattern created by the lower base row will be common to all of the chairs. Each pattern becomes "individual" by the treatment of the Pomegranate.

J-7 and 8 used variation E; J-9, A; and J-12, B. J-10 used the lower auxiliary base row E and worked the main portion as an upside down heart. The introduction of the background color in the diamond shaped areas opens up the pattern.

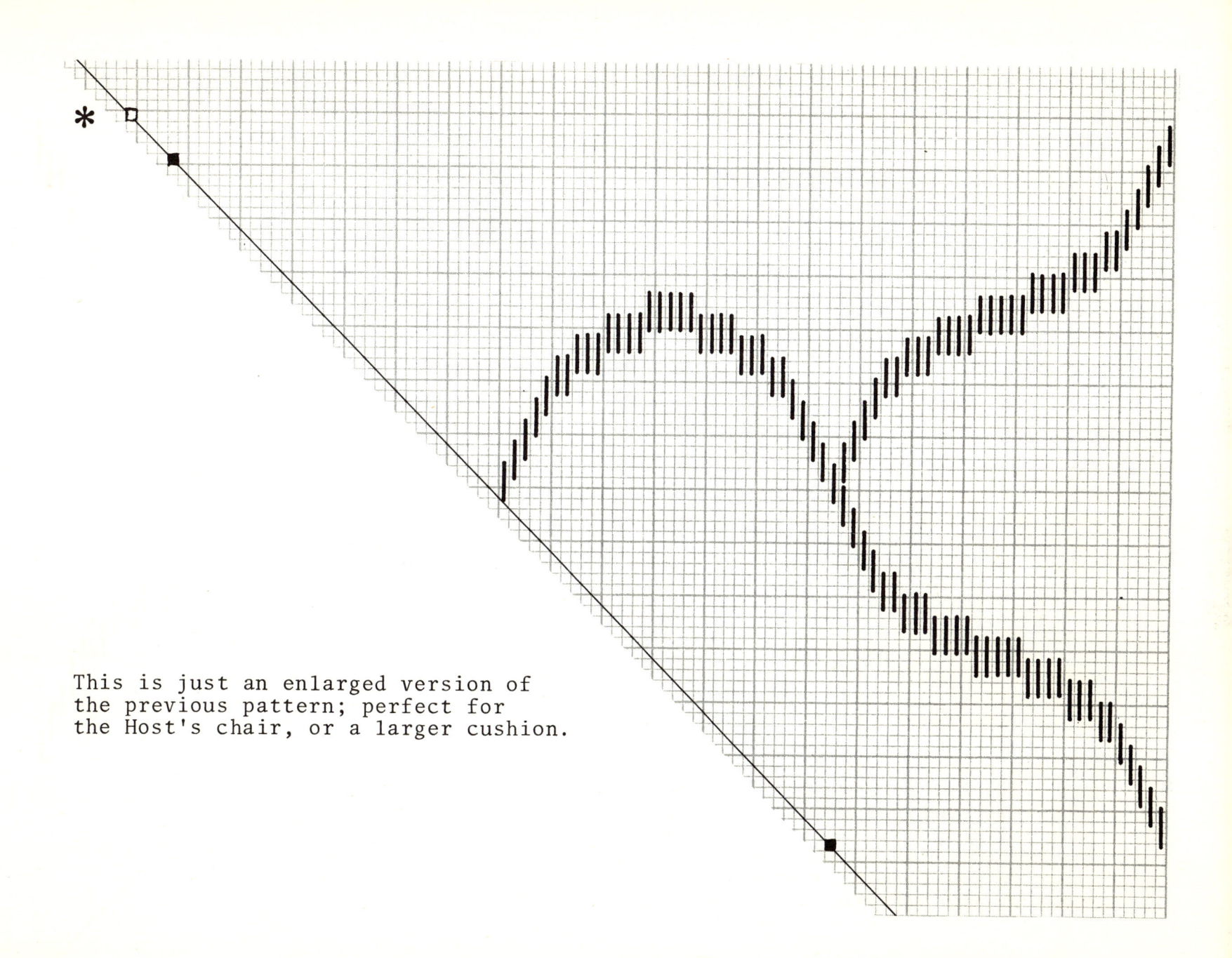

This is just an enlarged version of
the previous pattern; perfect for
the Host's chair, or a larger cushion.

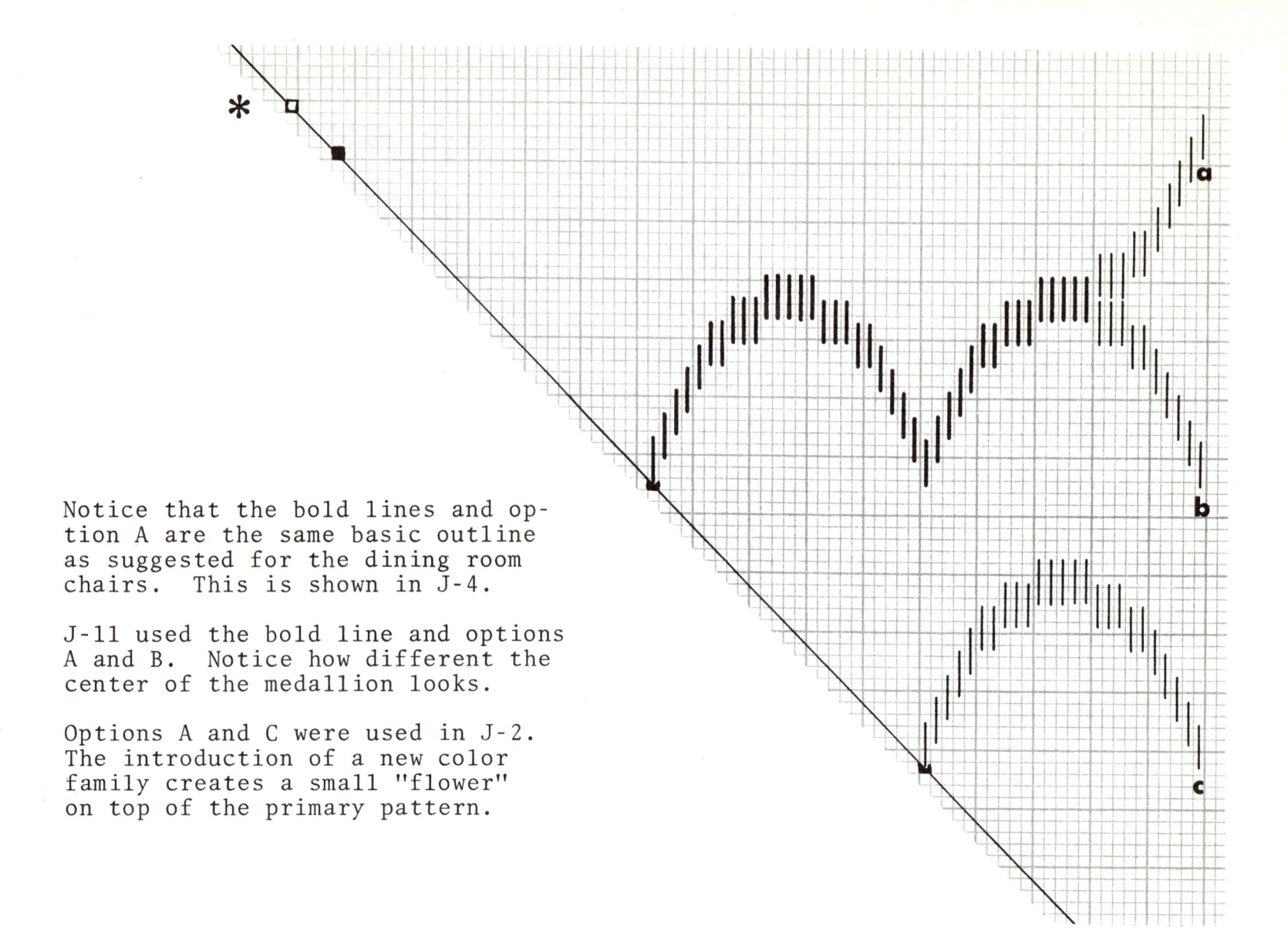

Notice that the bold lines and option A are the same basic outline as suggested for the dining room chairs. This is shown in J-4.

J-11 used the bold line and options A and B. Notice how different the center of the medallion looks.

Options A and C were used in J-2. The introduction of a new color family creates a small "flower" on top of the primary pattern.

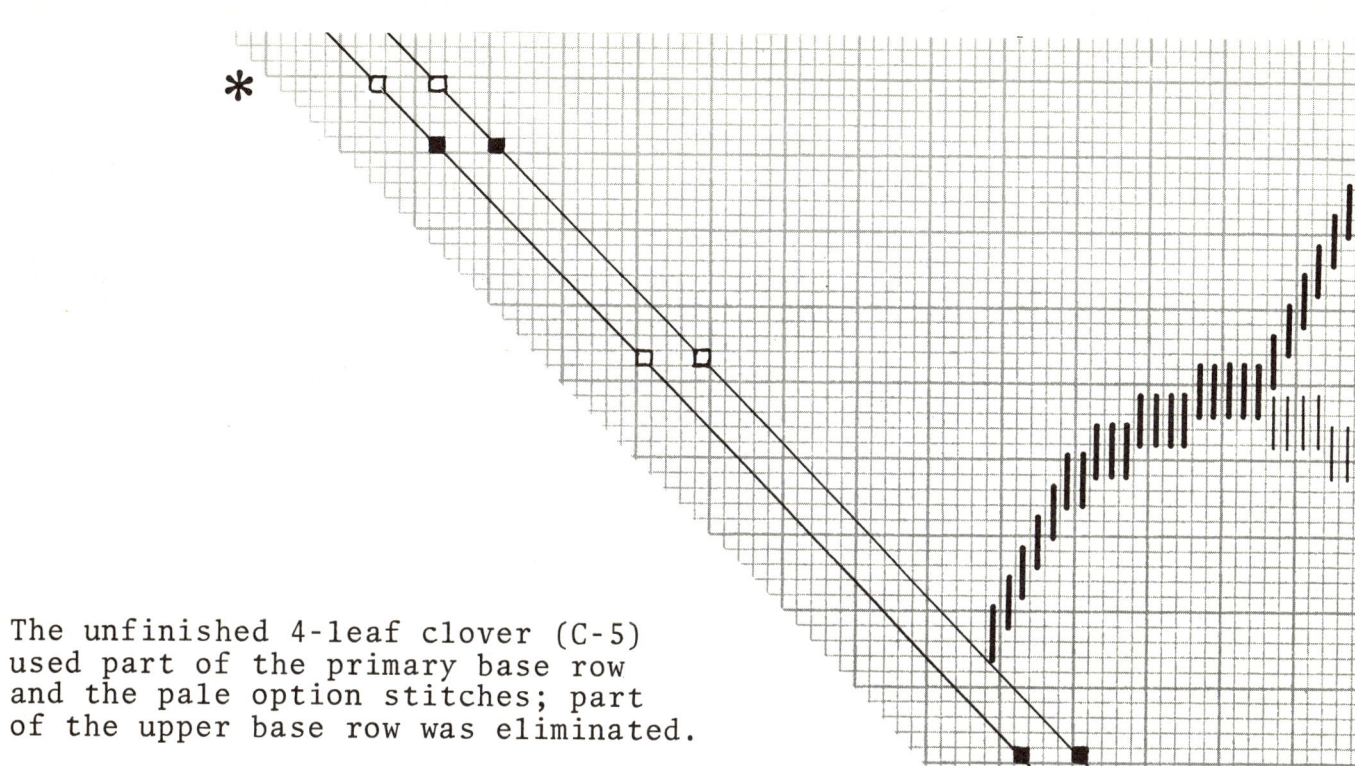

The unfinished 4-leaf clover (C-5)
used part of the primary base row
and the pale option stitches; part
of the upper base row was eliminated.

The pillow to its right (C-3) used
only the bold line. The Turkey
stitch in the center looks like a
fluffy button.

Both rows were used for (C-6). It
was first divided into 4 pie-shaped
sections by Gobelin. This created
a new Miter line which has been
diagrammed for you. You might like
to try this technique with some other
pattern.

119

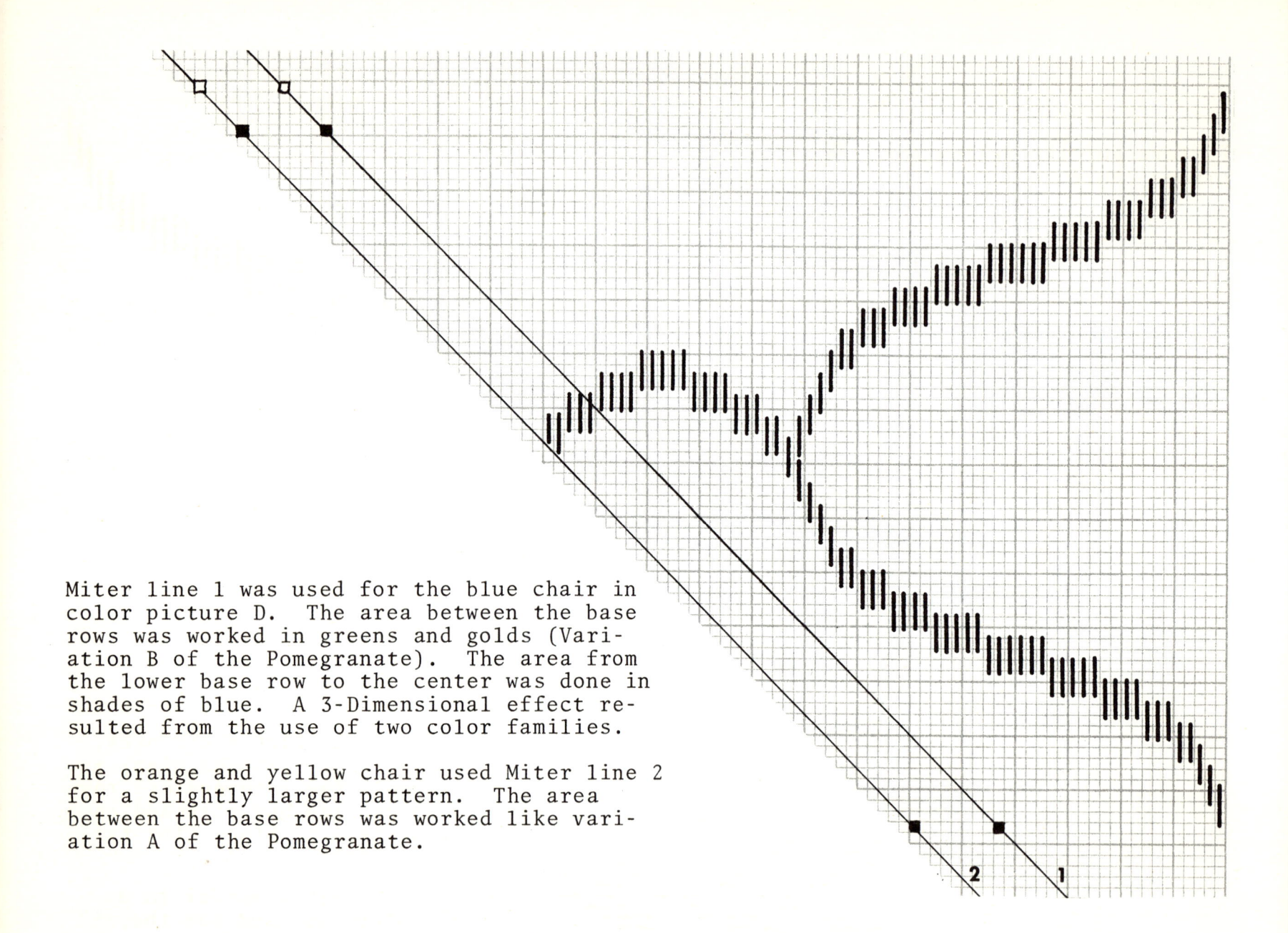

Miter line 1 was used for the blue chair in color picture D. The area between the base rows was worked in greens and golds (Variation B of the Pomegranate). The area from the lower base row to the center was done in shades of blue. A 3-Dimensional effect resulted from the use of two color families.

The orange and yellow chair used Miter line 2 for a slightly larger pattern. The area between the base rows was worked like variation A of the Pomegranate.

120

Pattern for the yellow and orange chair back.

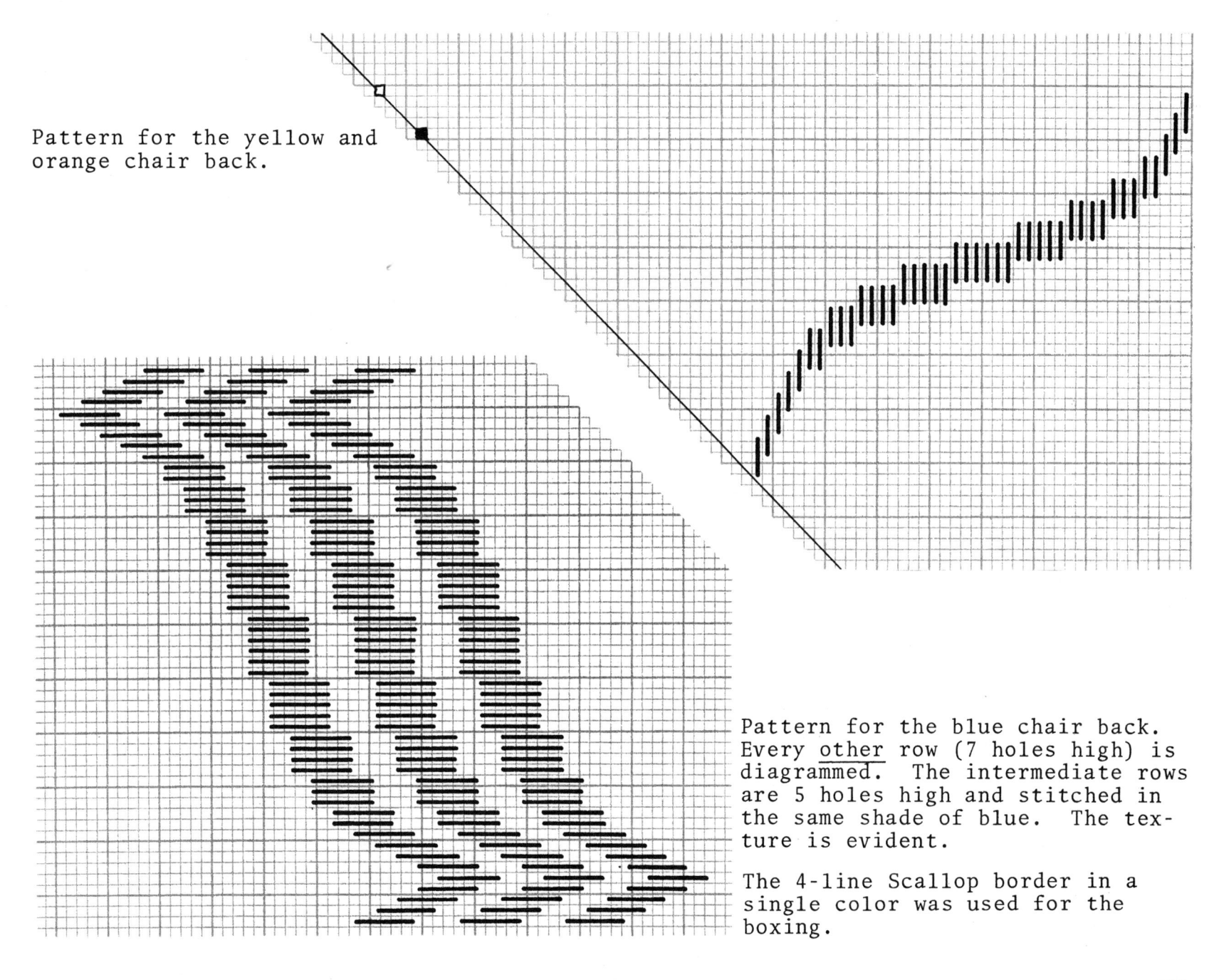

Pattern for the blue chair back. Every <u>other</u> row (7 holes high) is diagrammed. The intermediate rows are 5 holes high and stitched in the same shade of blue. The texture is evident.

The 4-line Scallop border in a single color was used for the boxing.

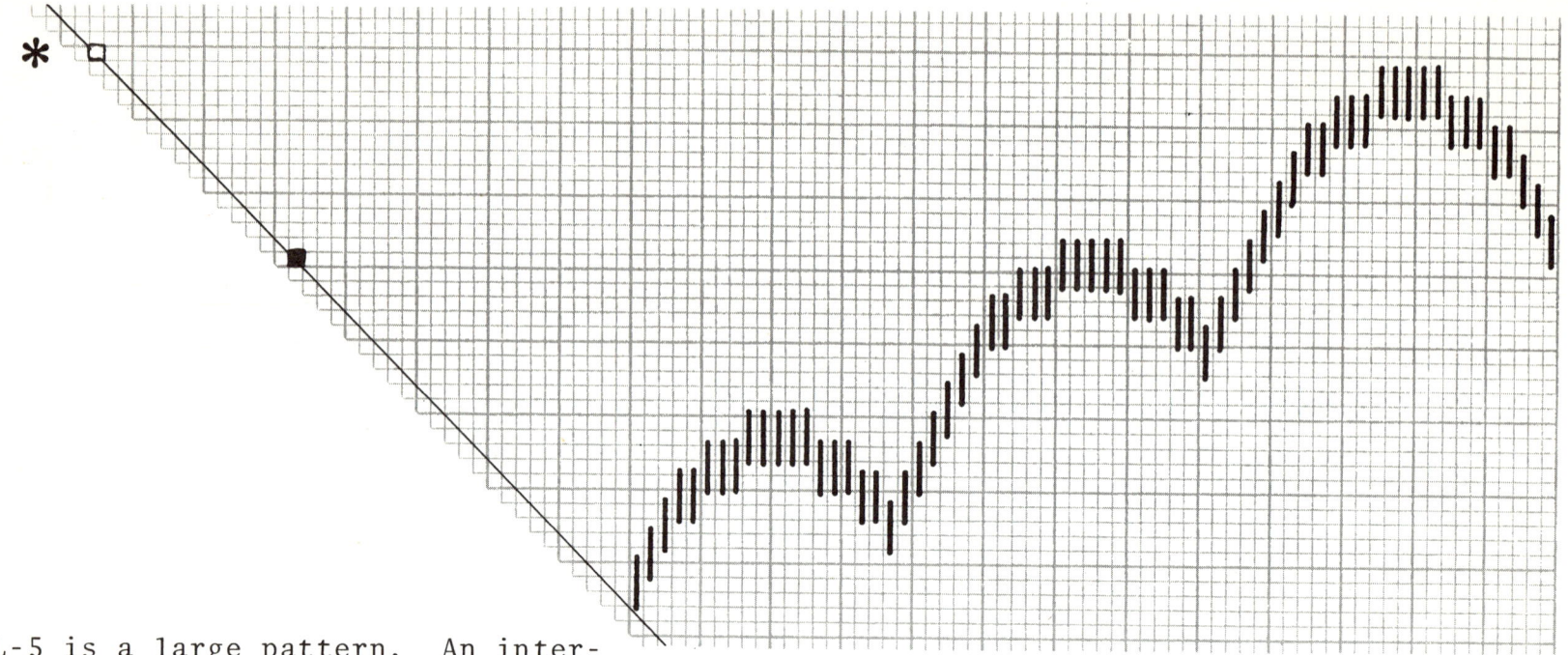

L-5 is a large pattern. An interesting effect has been created by the use of double rows and shading.

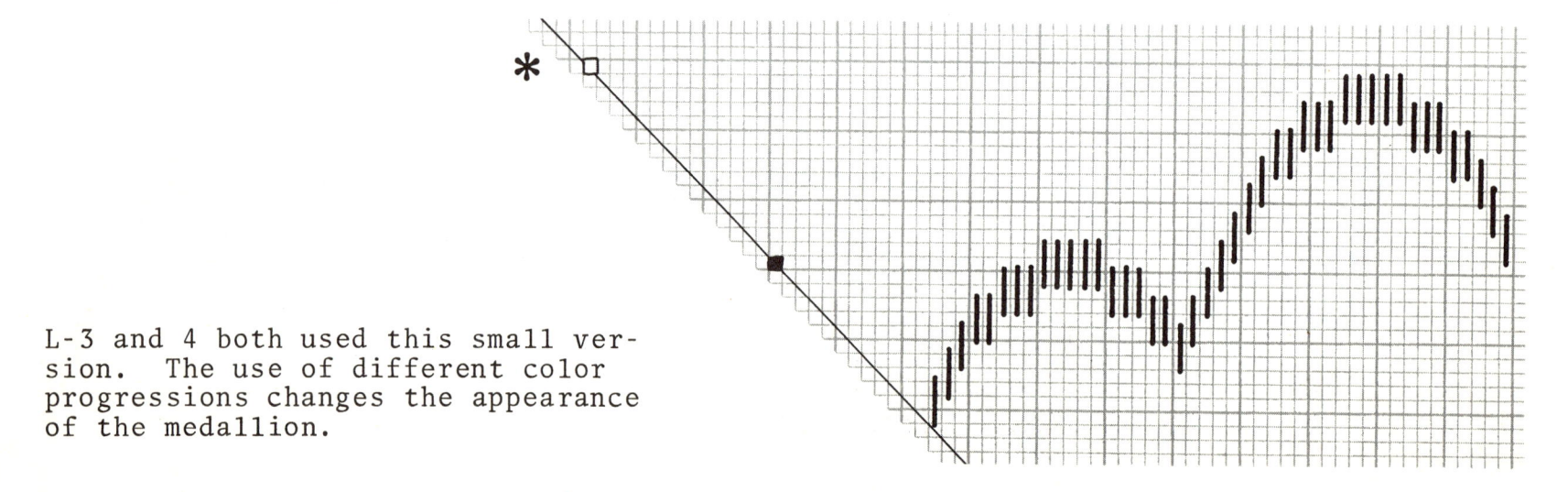

L-3 and 4 both used this small version. The use of different color progressions changes the appearance of the medallion.

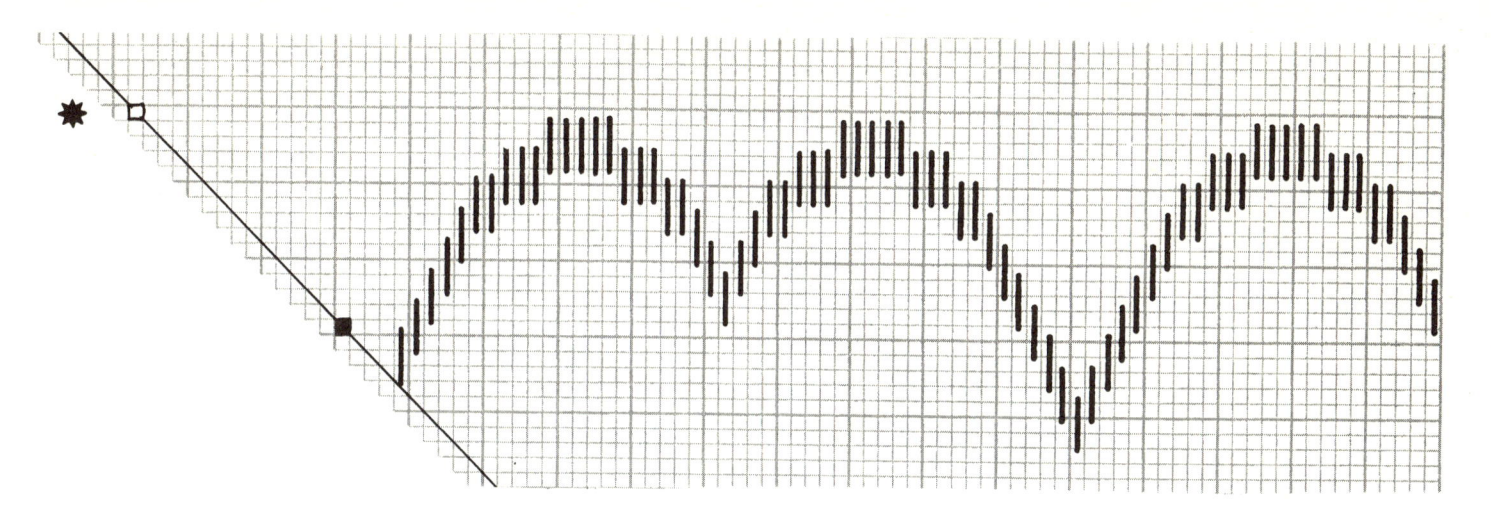

These two patterns are similar; but if you study the diagram and the photographs, the difference will become apparent.

I-4 used double and triple rows and a monochromatic color scheme.

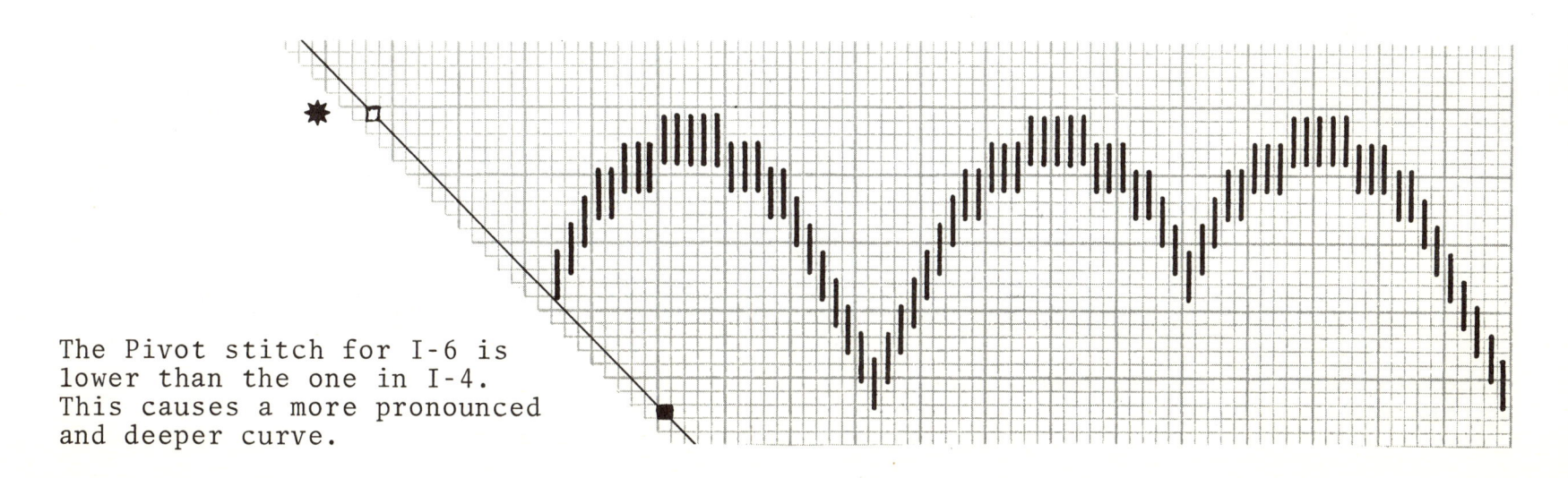

The Pivot stitch for I-6 is lower than the one in I-4. This causes a more pronounced and deeper curve.

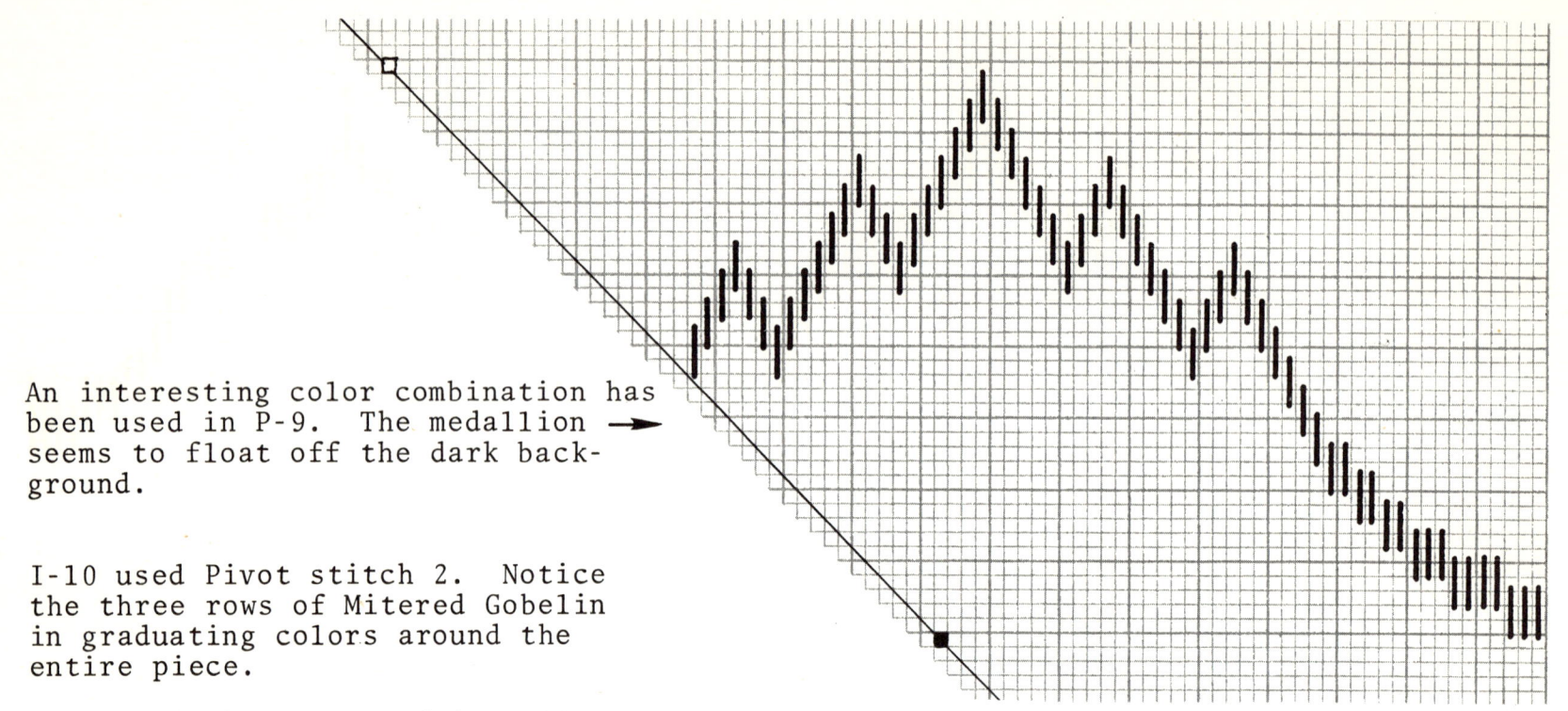

An interesting color combination has
been used in P-9. The medallion →
seems to float off the dark background.

I-10 used Pivot stitch 2. Notice
the three rows of Mitered Gobelin
in graduating colors around the
entire piece.

Pivot stitch 1 was used in I-12.
See how different the center looks
by changing the Pivot stitch.

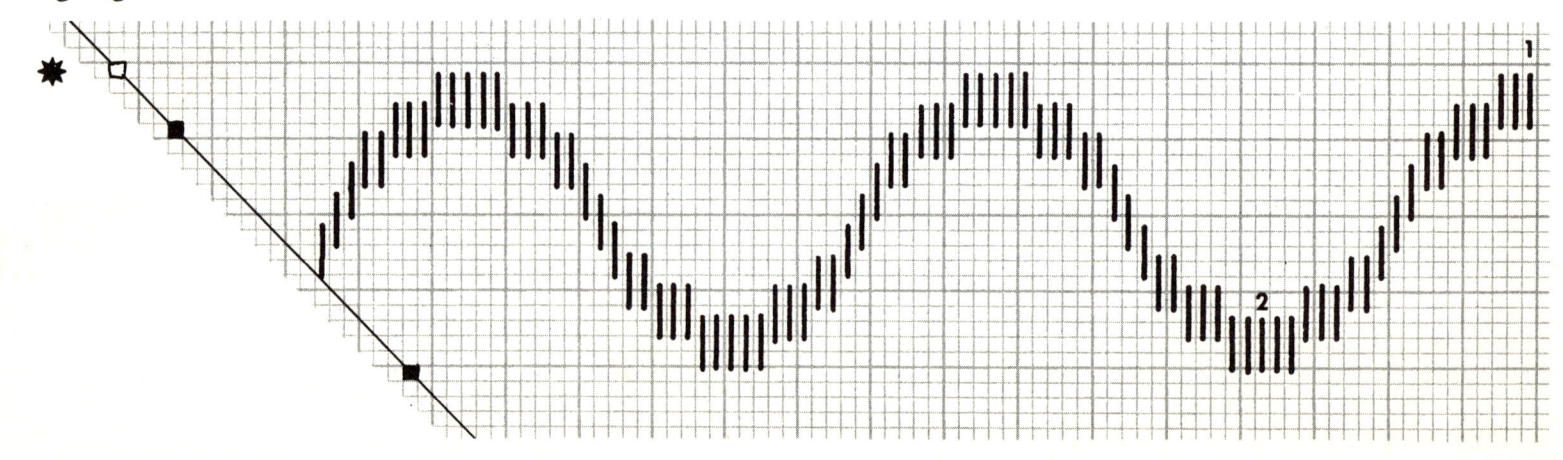

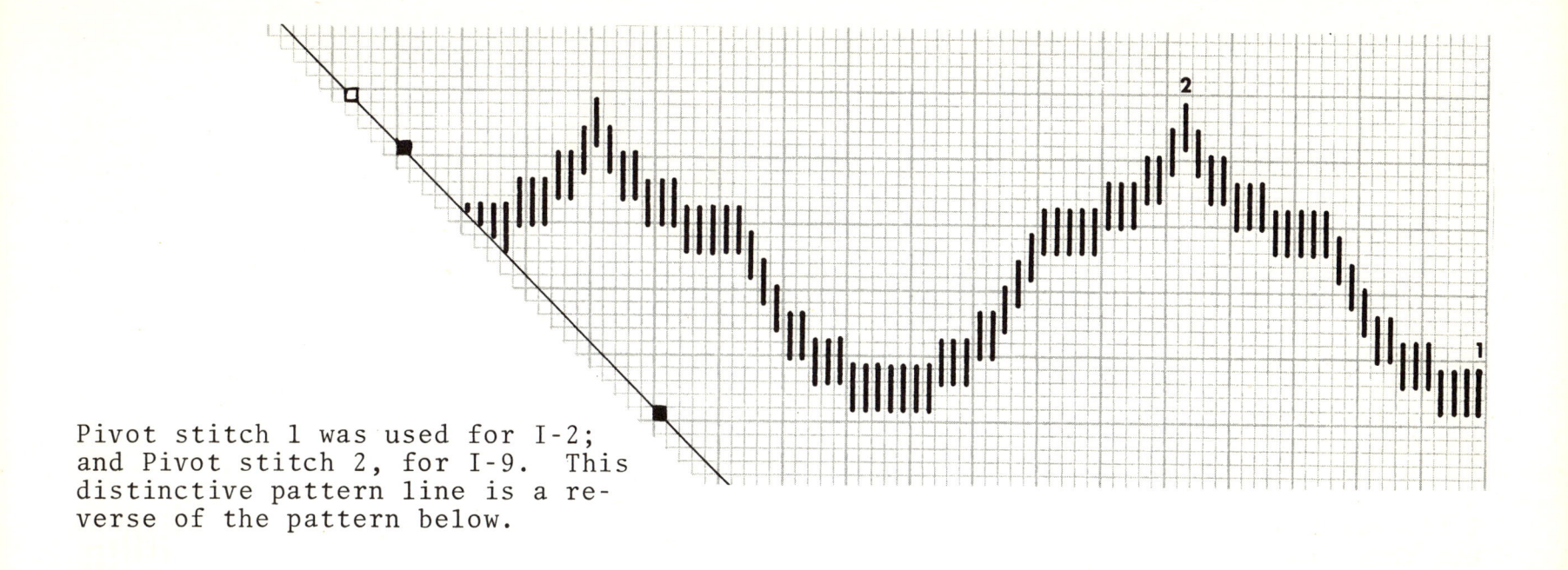

Pivot stitch 1 was used for I-2; and Pivot stitch 2, for I-9. This distinctive pattern line is a reverse of the pattern below.

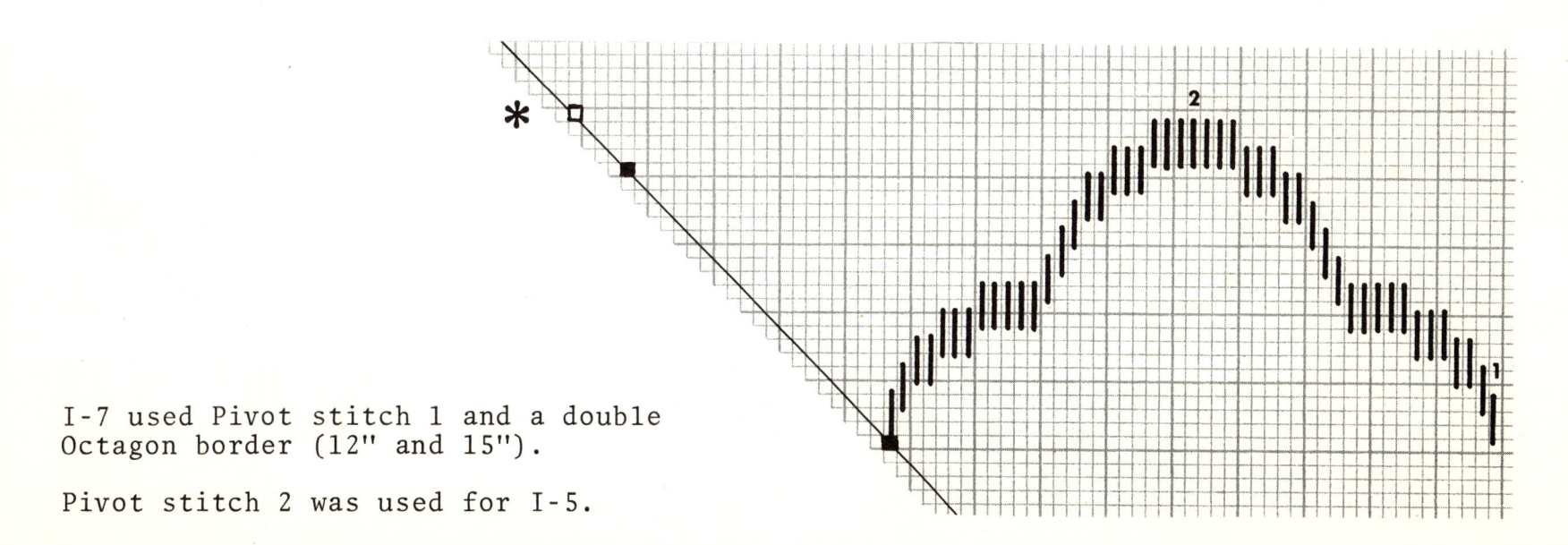

I-7 used Pivot stitch 1 and a double Octagon border (12" and 15").

Pivot stitch 2 was used for I-5.

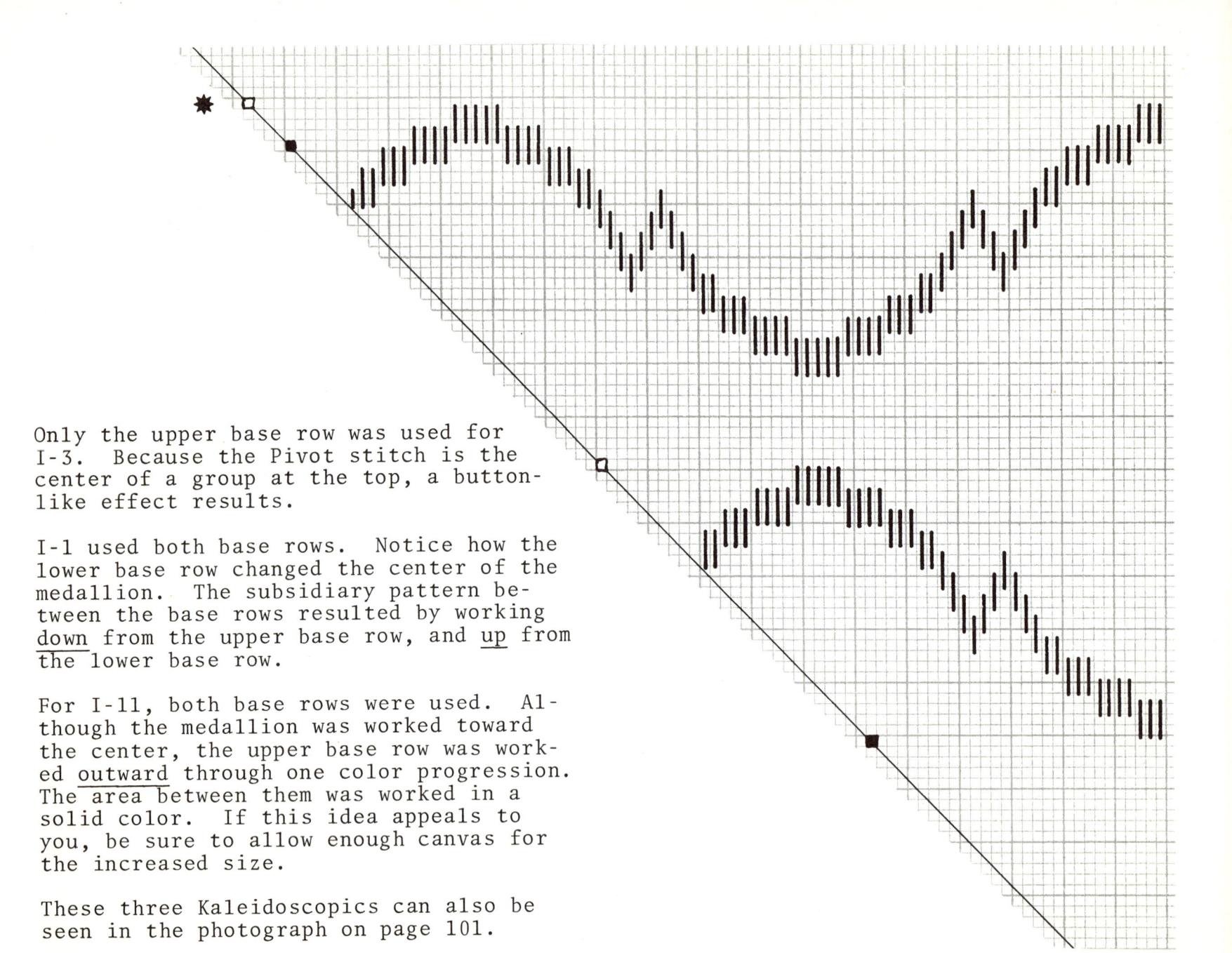

Only the upper base row was used for I-3. Because the Pivot stitch is the center of a group at the top, a button-like effect results.

I-1 used both base rows. Notice how the lower base row changed the center of the medallion. The subsidiary pattern between the base rows resulted by working down from the upper base row, and up from the lower base row.

For I-11, both base rows were used. Although the medallion was worked toward the center, the upper base row was worked outward through one color progression. The area between them was worked in a solid color. If this idea appeals to you, be sure to allow enough canvas for the increased size.

These three Kaleidoscopics can also be seen in the photograph on page 101.

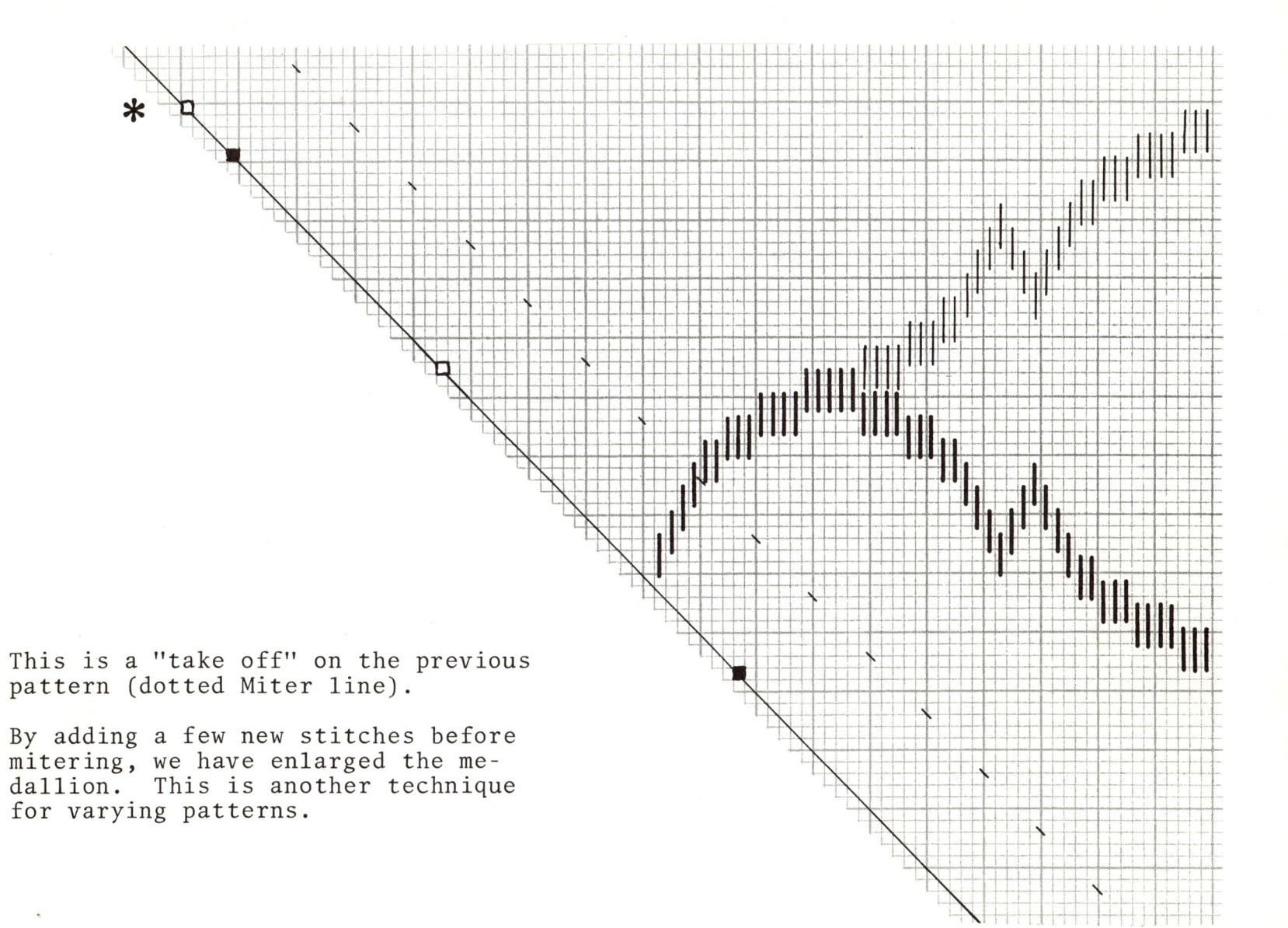

This is a "take off" on the previous pattern (dotted Miter line).

By adding a few new stitches before mitering, we have enlarged the medallion. This is another technique for varying patterns.

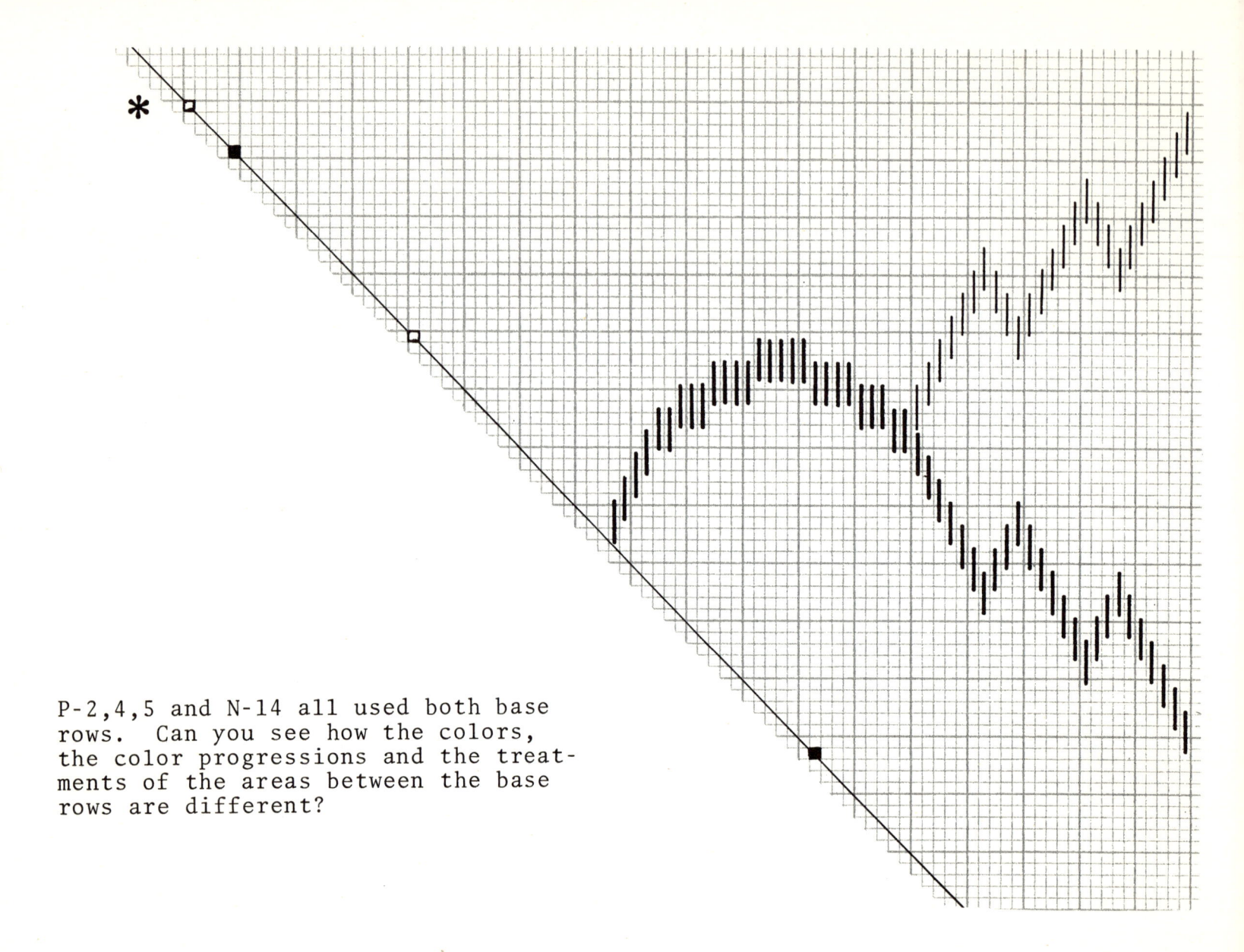

P-2,4,5 and N-14 all used both base rows. Can you see how the colors, the color progressions and the treatments of the areas between the base rows are different?

128

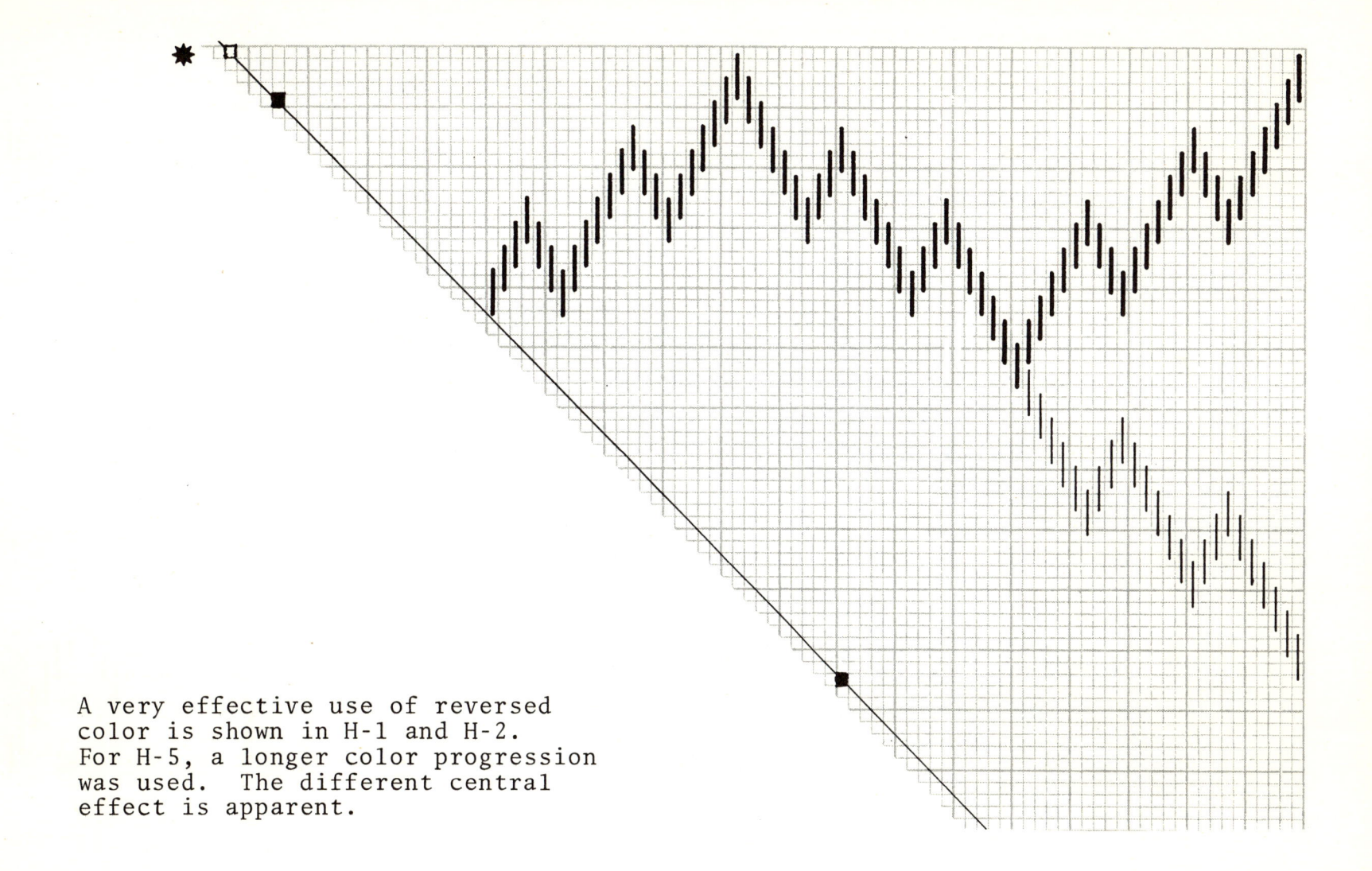

A very effective use of reversed
color is shown in H-1 and H-2.
For H-5, a longer color progression
was used. The different central
effect is apparent.

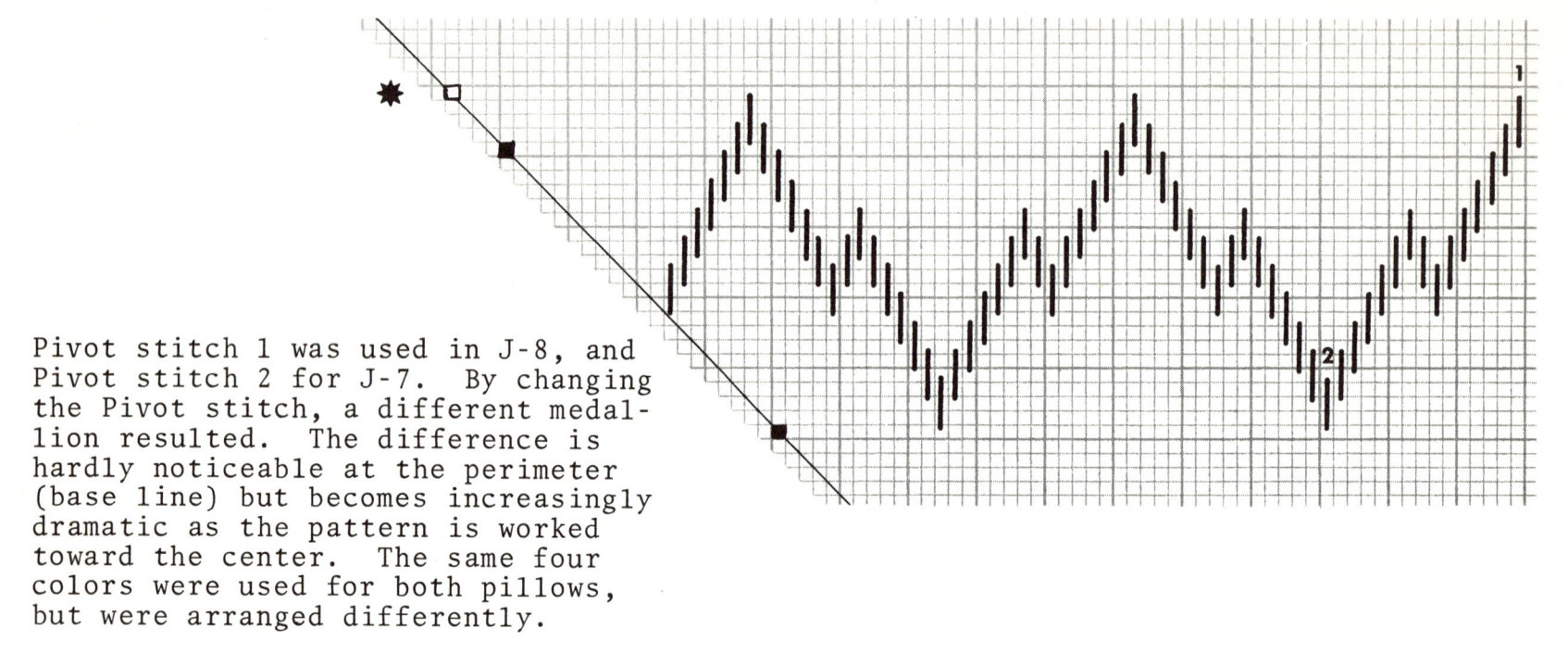

Pivot stitch 1 was used in J-8, and Pivot stitch 2 for J-7. By changing the Pivot stitch, a different medallion resulted. The difference is hardly noticeable at the perimeter (base line) but becomes increasingly dramatic as the pattern is worked toward the center. The same four colors were used for both pillows, but were arranged differently.

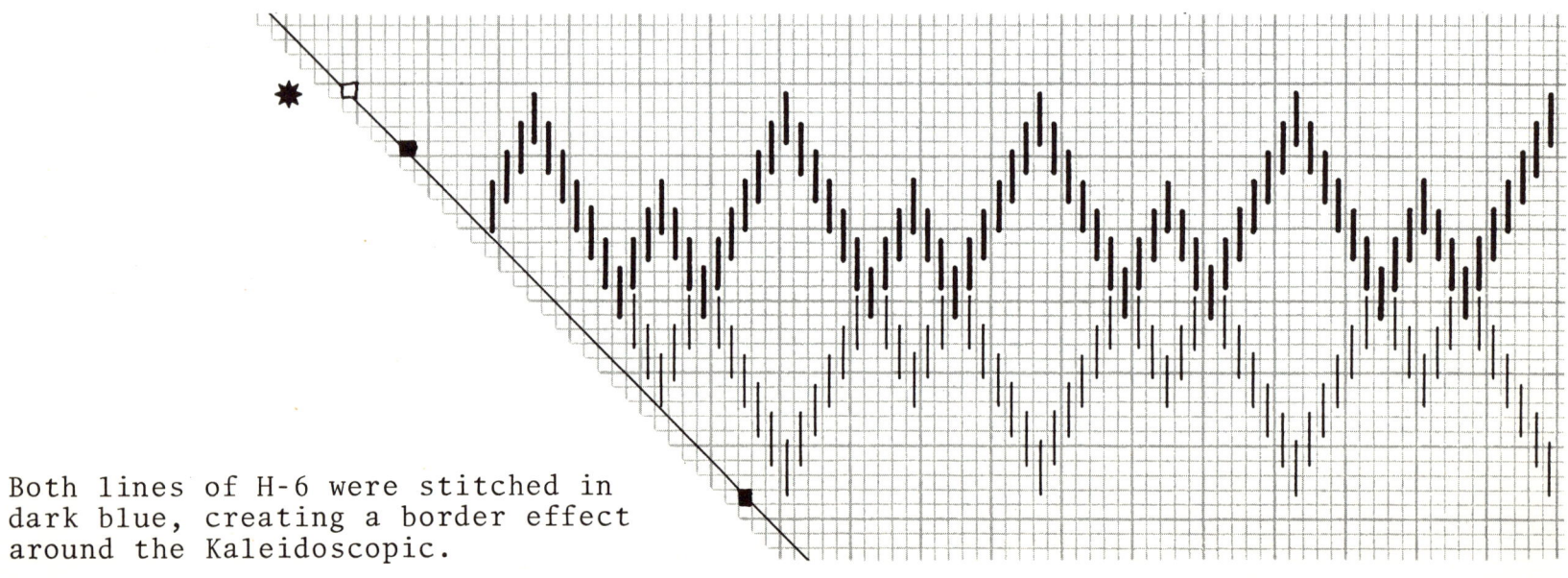

Both lines of H-6 were stitched in dark blue, creating a border effect around the Kaleidoscopic.

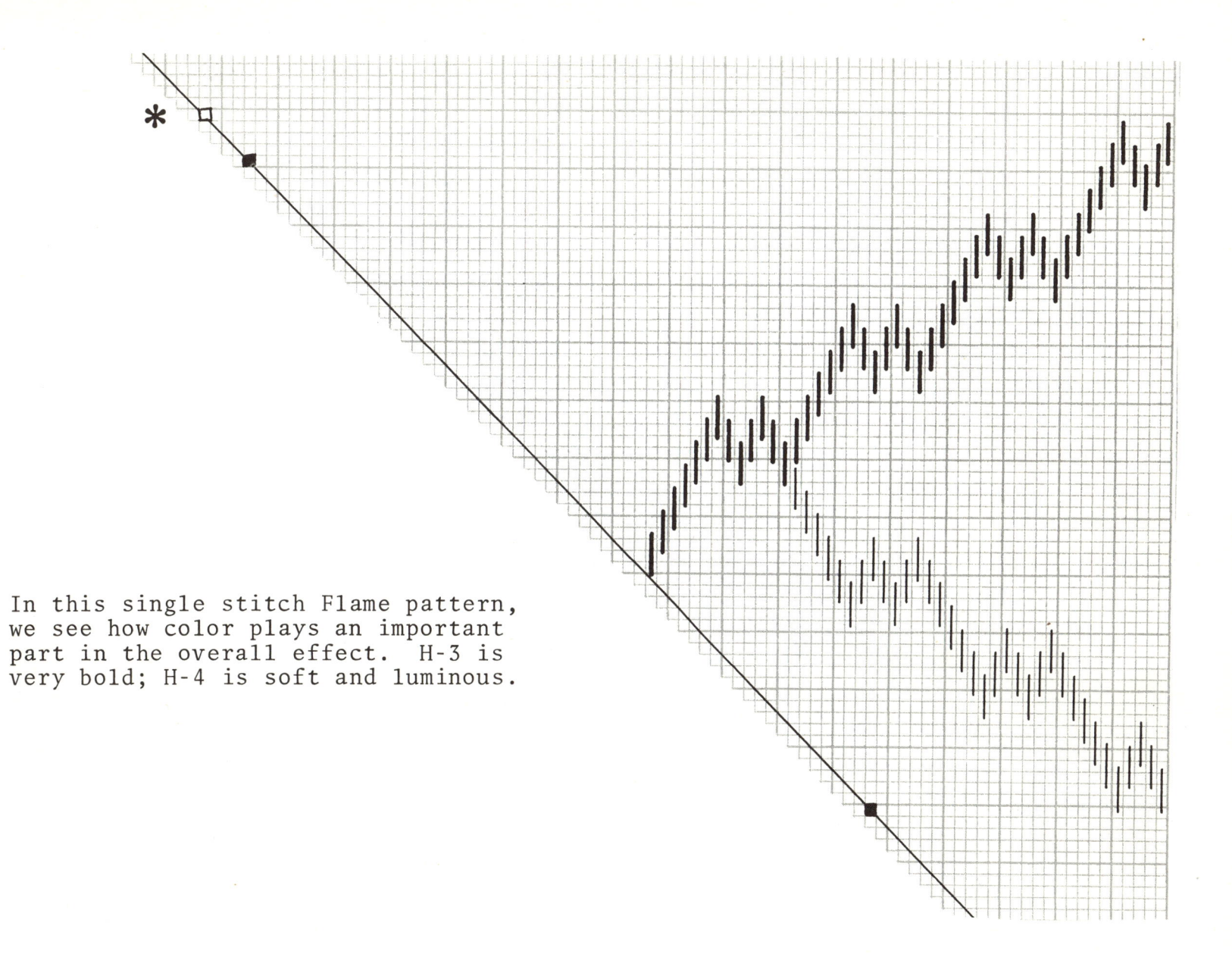

In this single stitch Flame pattern, we see how color plays an important part in the overall effect. H-3 is very bold; H-4 is soft and luminous.

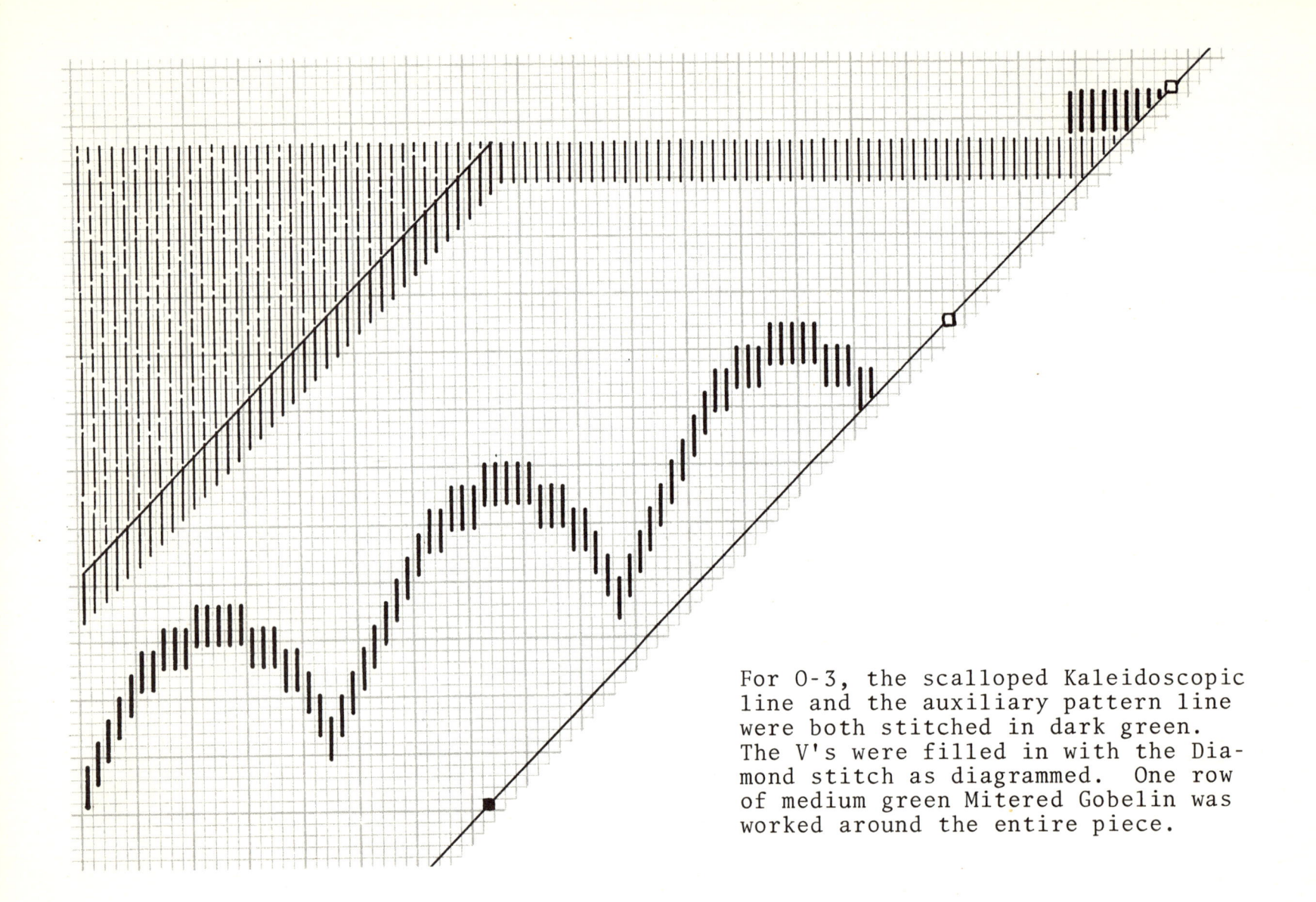

For O-3, the scalloped Kaleidoscopic line and the auxiliary pattern line were both stitched in dark green. The V's were filled in with the Diamond stitch as diagrammed. One row of medium green Mitered Gobelin was worked around the entire piece.

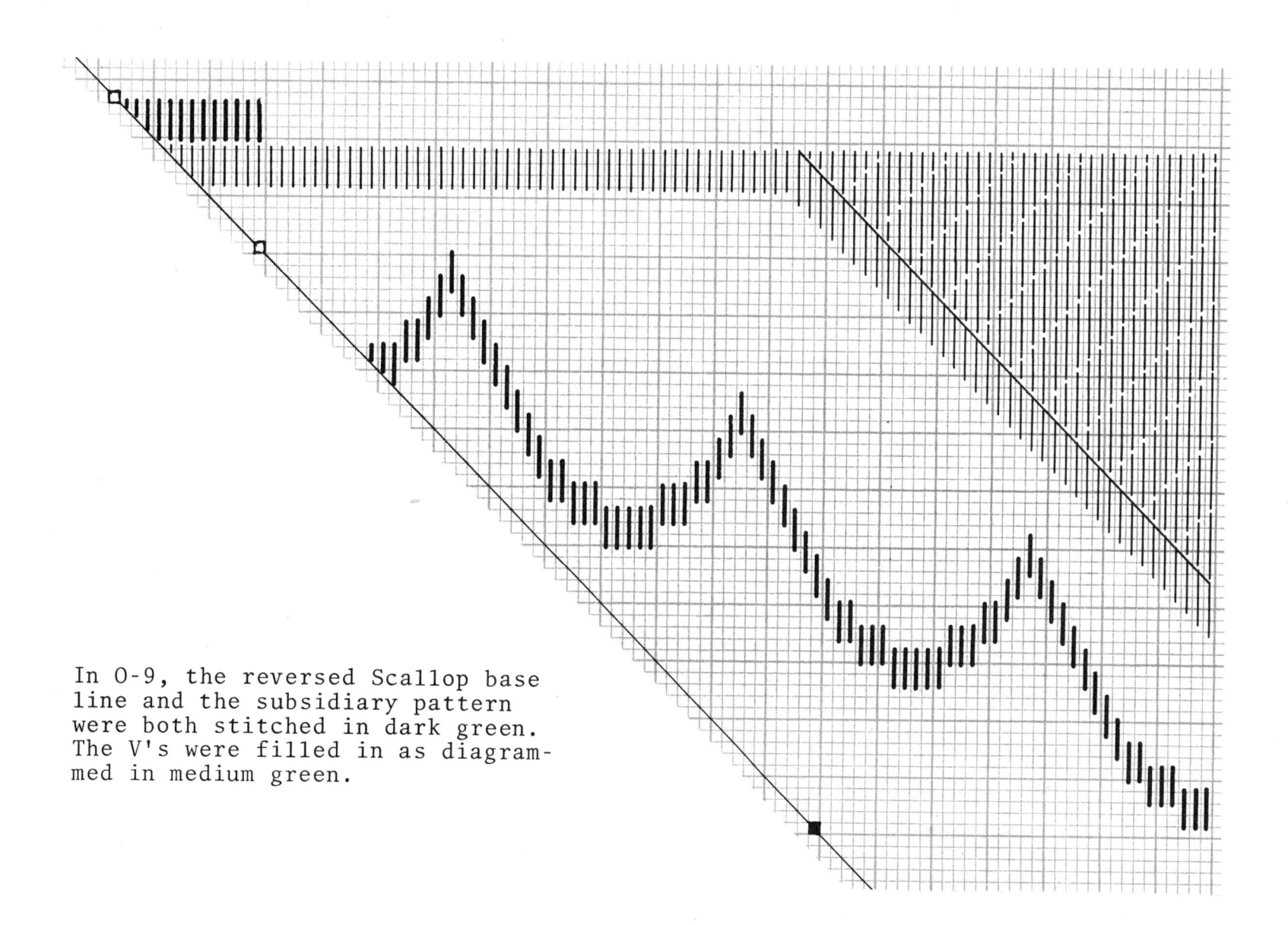

In O-9, the reversed Scallop base
line and the subsidiary pattern
were both stitched in dark green.
The V's were filled in as diagrammed in medium green.

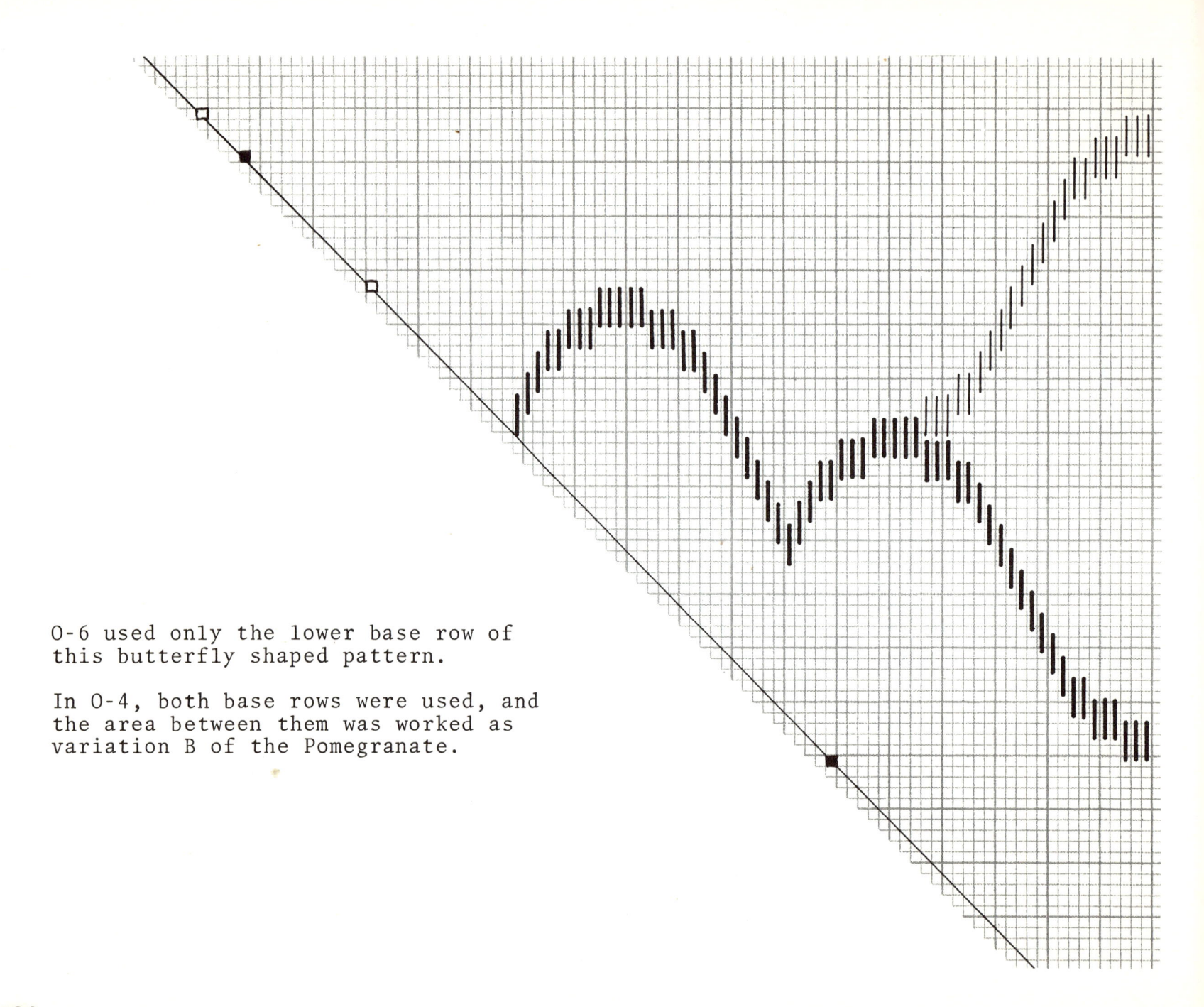

O-6 used only the lower base row of
this butterfly shaped pattern.

In O-4, both base rows were used, and
the area between them was worked as
variation B of the Pomegranate.

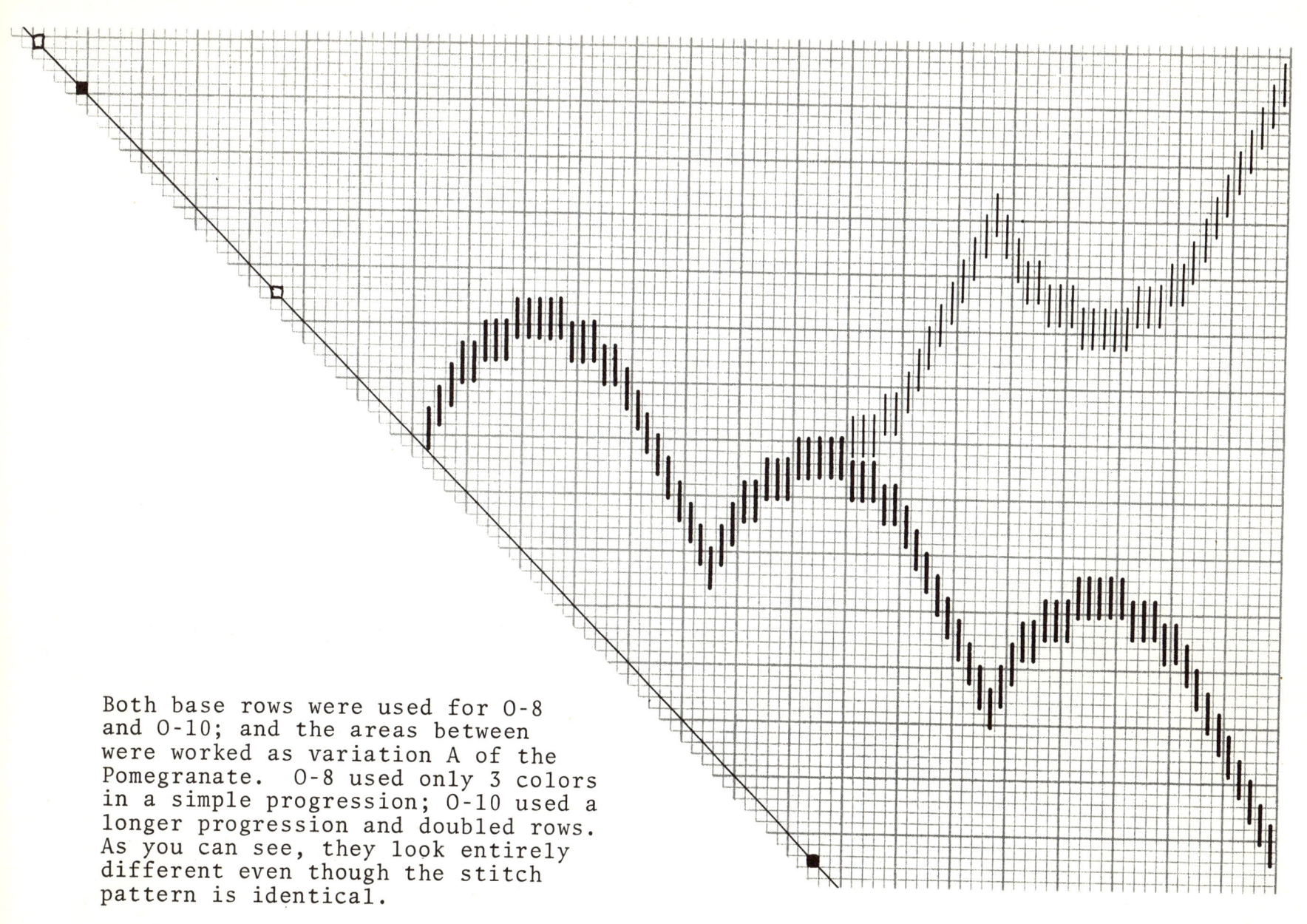

Both base rows were used for O-8 and O-10; and the areas between were worked as variation A of the Pomegranate. O-8 used only 3 colors in a simple progression; O-10 used a longer progression and doubled rows. As you can see, they look entirely different even though the stitch pattern is identical.

O-5 used only the lower base row.

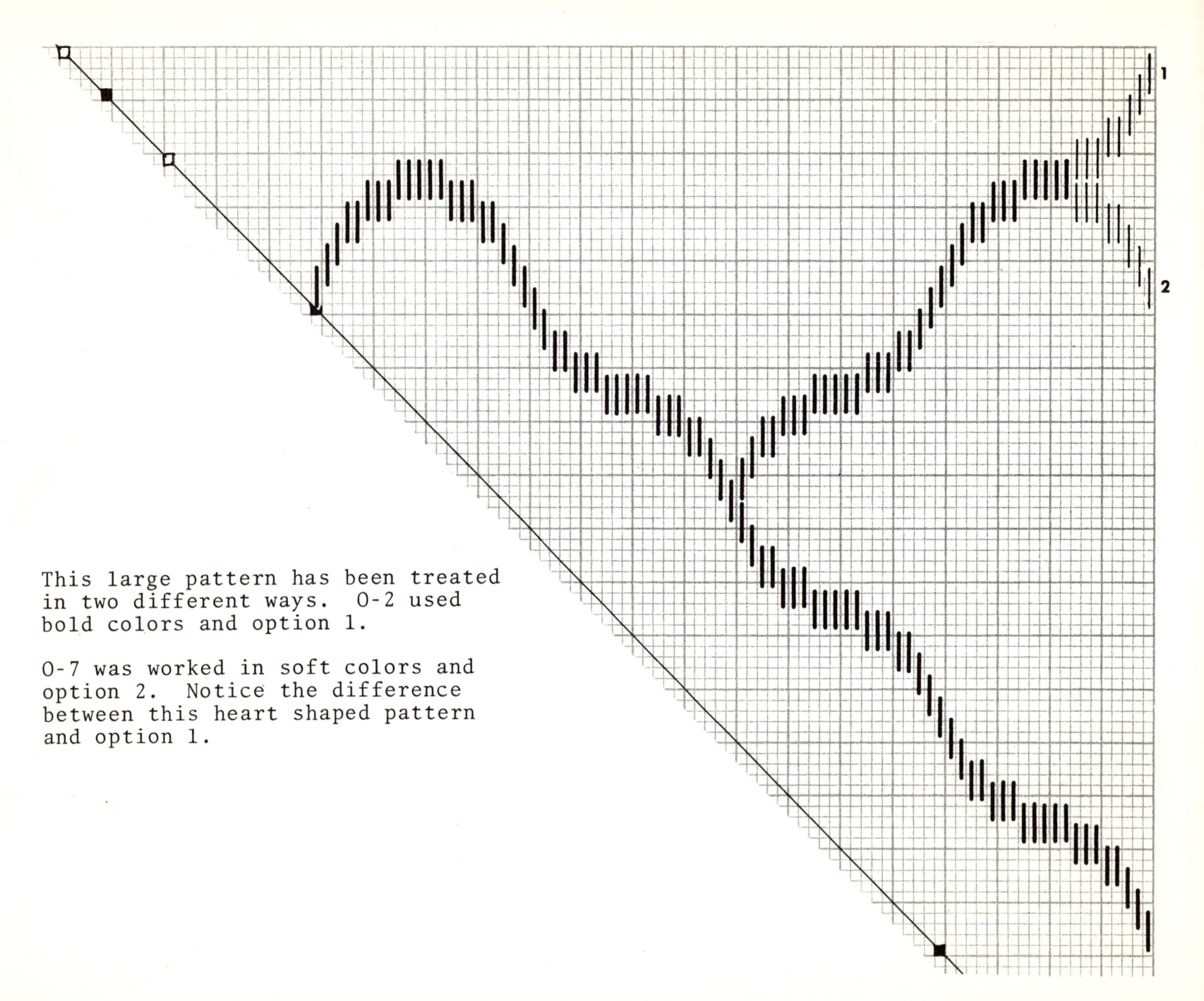

This large pattern has been treated in two different ways. O-2 used bold colors and option 1.

O-7 was worked in soft colors and option 2. Notice the difference between this heart shaped pattern and option 1.

In L-11, Pivot stitch 1 was used. The color progression was continued in the area between the base rows.

Pivot stitch 2 was used for I-8. The area between the base rows was worked in a solid color.

L-7 was done on a #18 canvas and used only two colors.

Pivot stitch 2 and only the lower base row were used for L-13. The triple Scallop border was stitched in a single color.

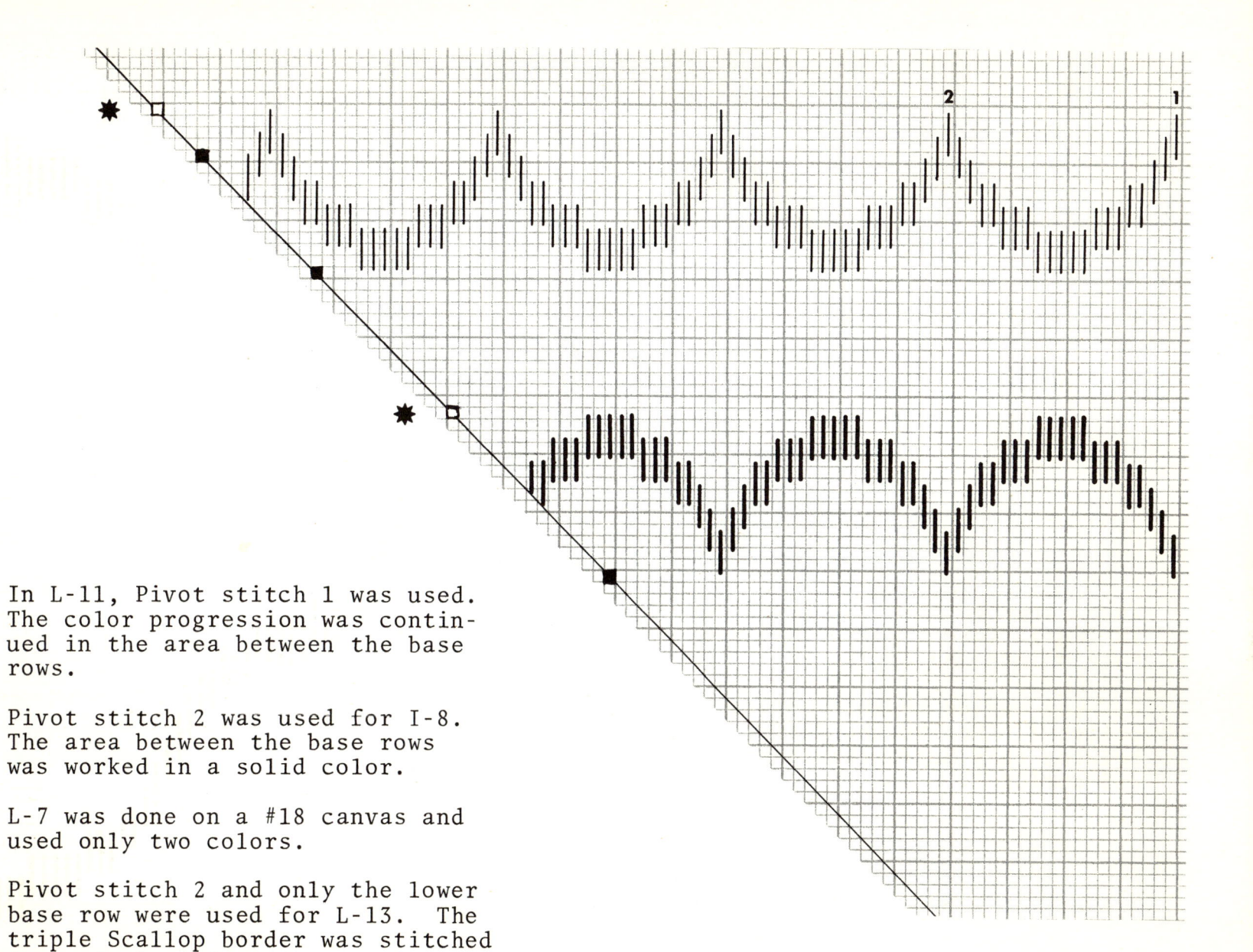

L-8 was worked on #18 canvas and uses only two colors.

L-9 looks like a "double-win" Tic-Tac-Toe game and is a good example of reversed shading.

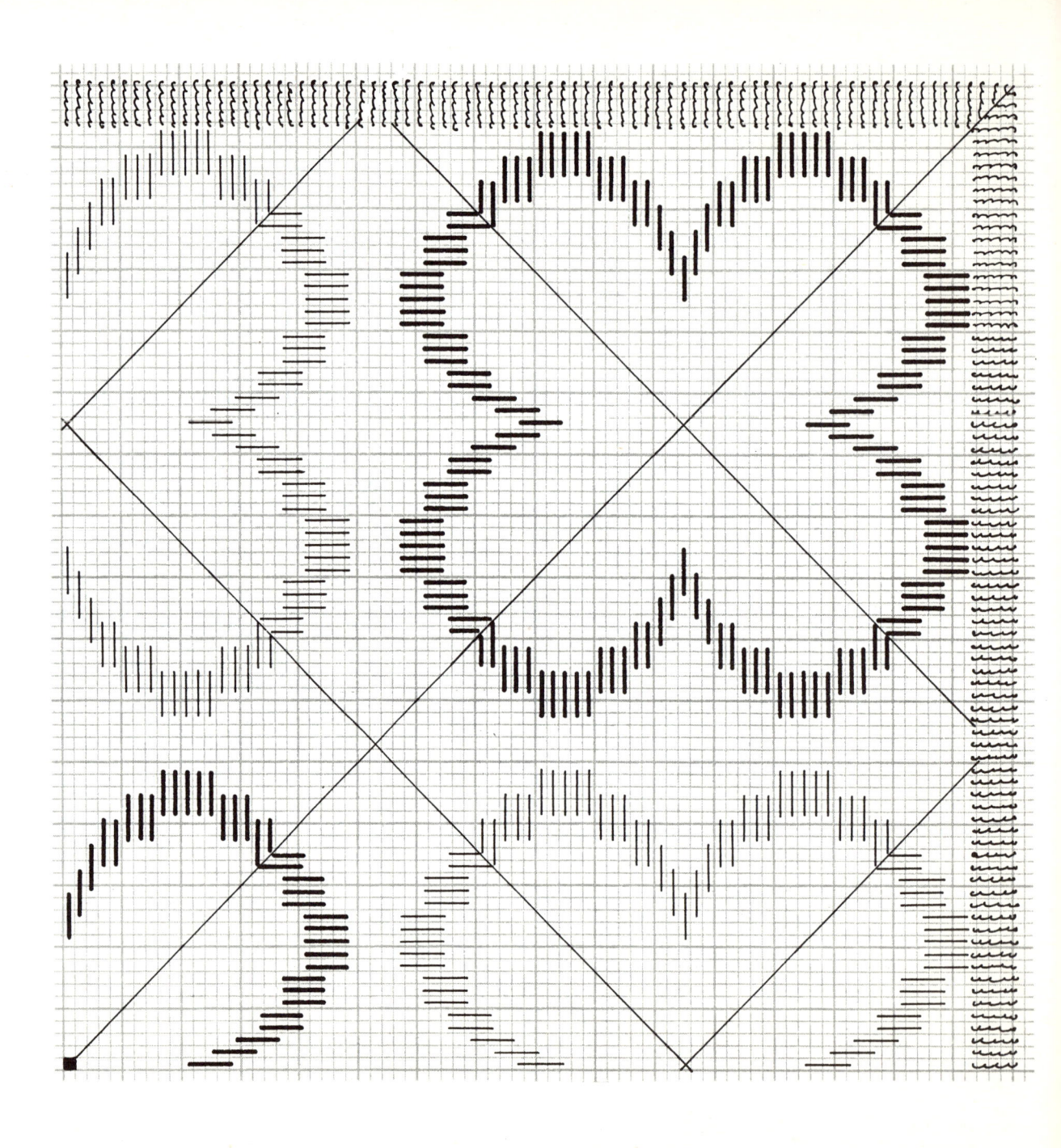

138

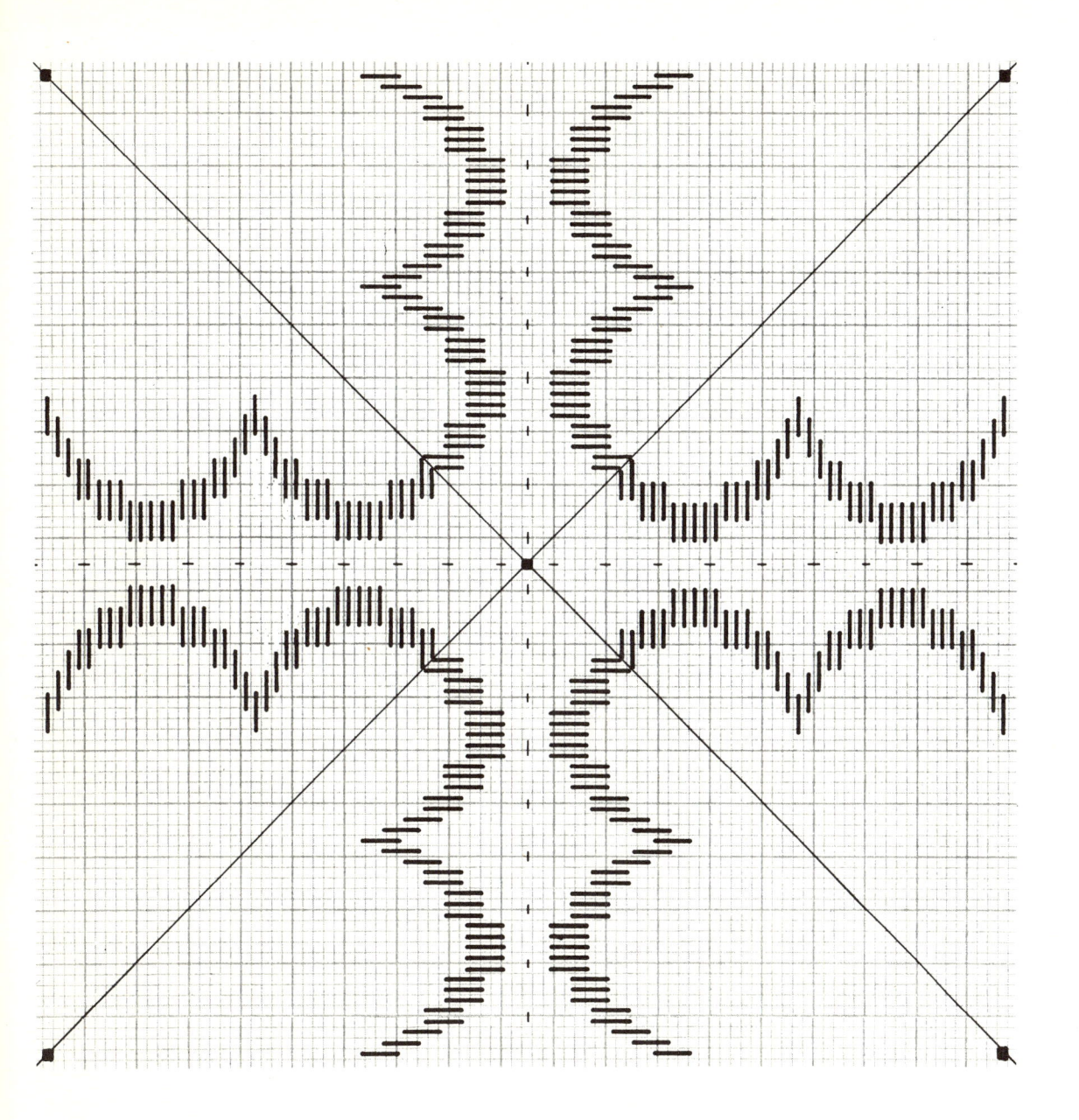

The Mitered Gobelin division lines in L-12 were stitched after the small medallions had been completed, but before the white background was started. These small flowers are the same as L-13 and L-7, but have been grouped on the canvas. This diagram shows the Center Hole and 1/4 of each pattern. The four black dots in the corners are the center holes for each flower.

139

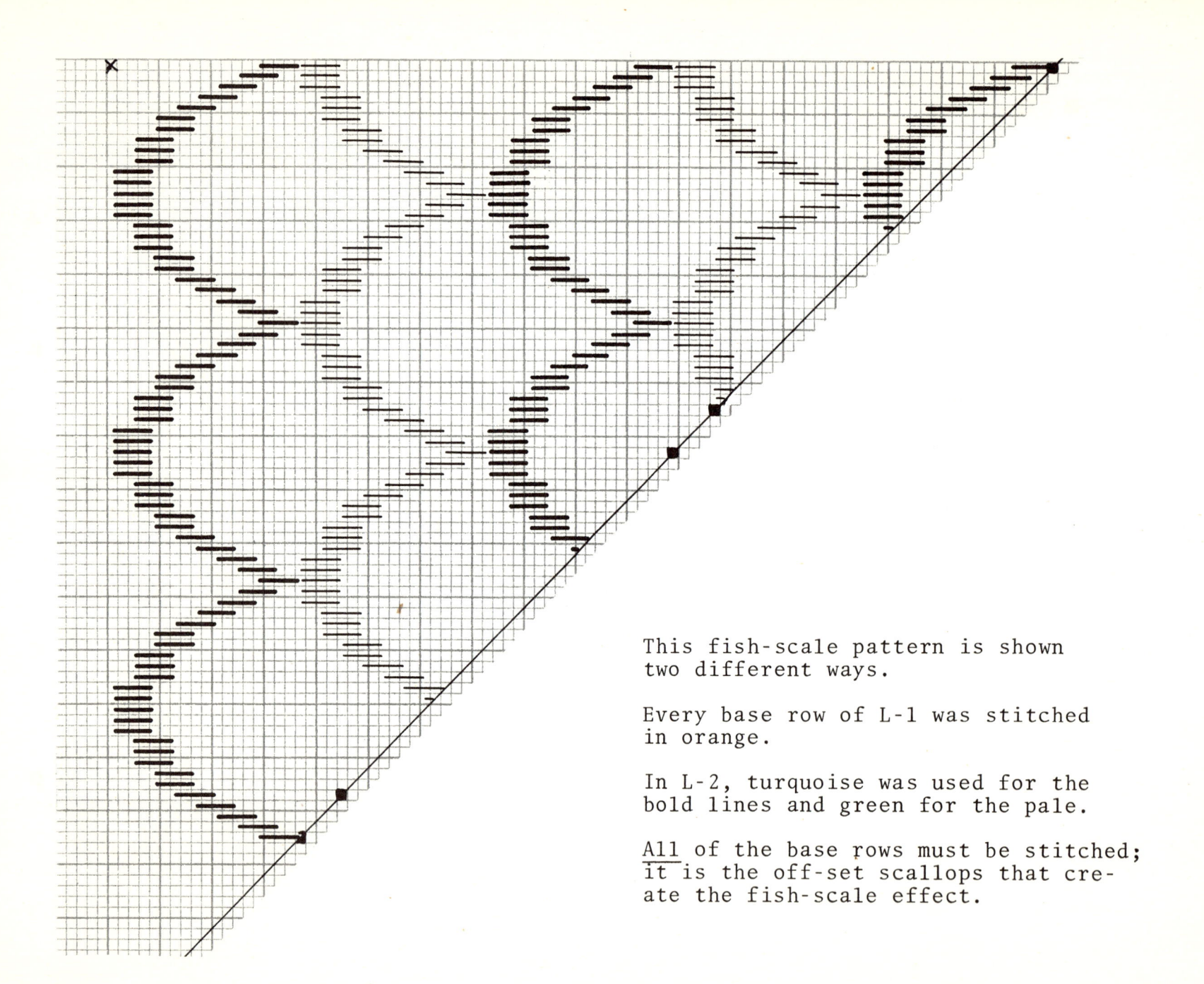

This fish-scale pattern is shown two different ways.

Every base row of L-1 was stitched in orange.

In L-2, turquoise was used for the bold lines and green for the pale.

All of the base rows must be stitched; it is the off-set scallops that create the fish-scale effect.

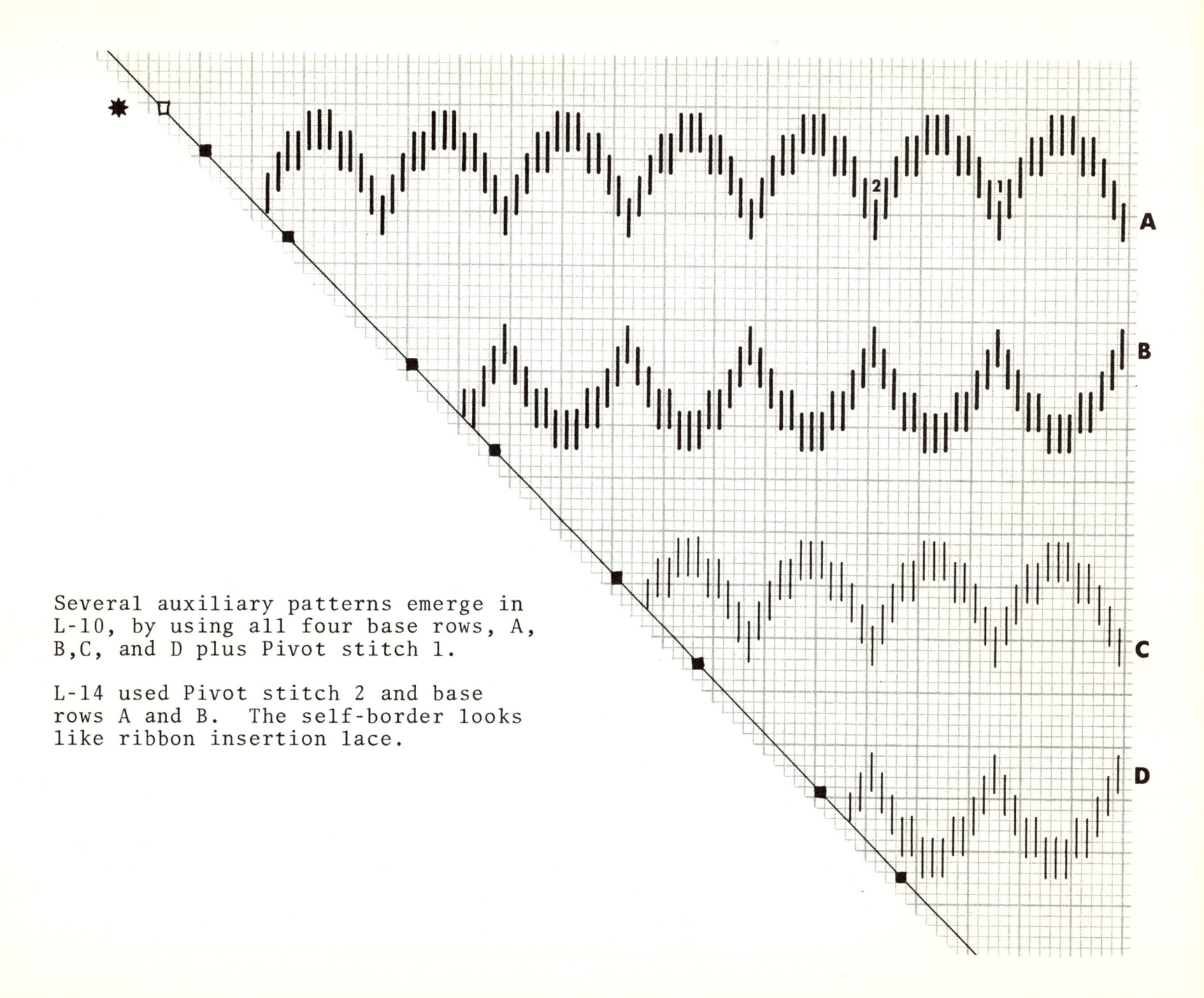

Several auxiliary patterns emerge in L-10, by using all four base rows, A, B, C, and D plus Pivot stitch 1.

L-14 used Pivot stitch 2 and base rows A and B. The self-border looks like ribbon insertion lace.

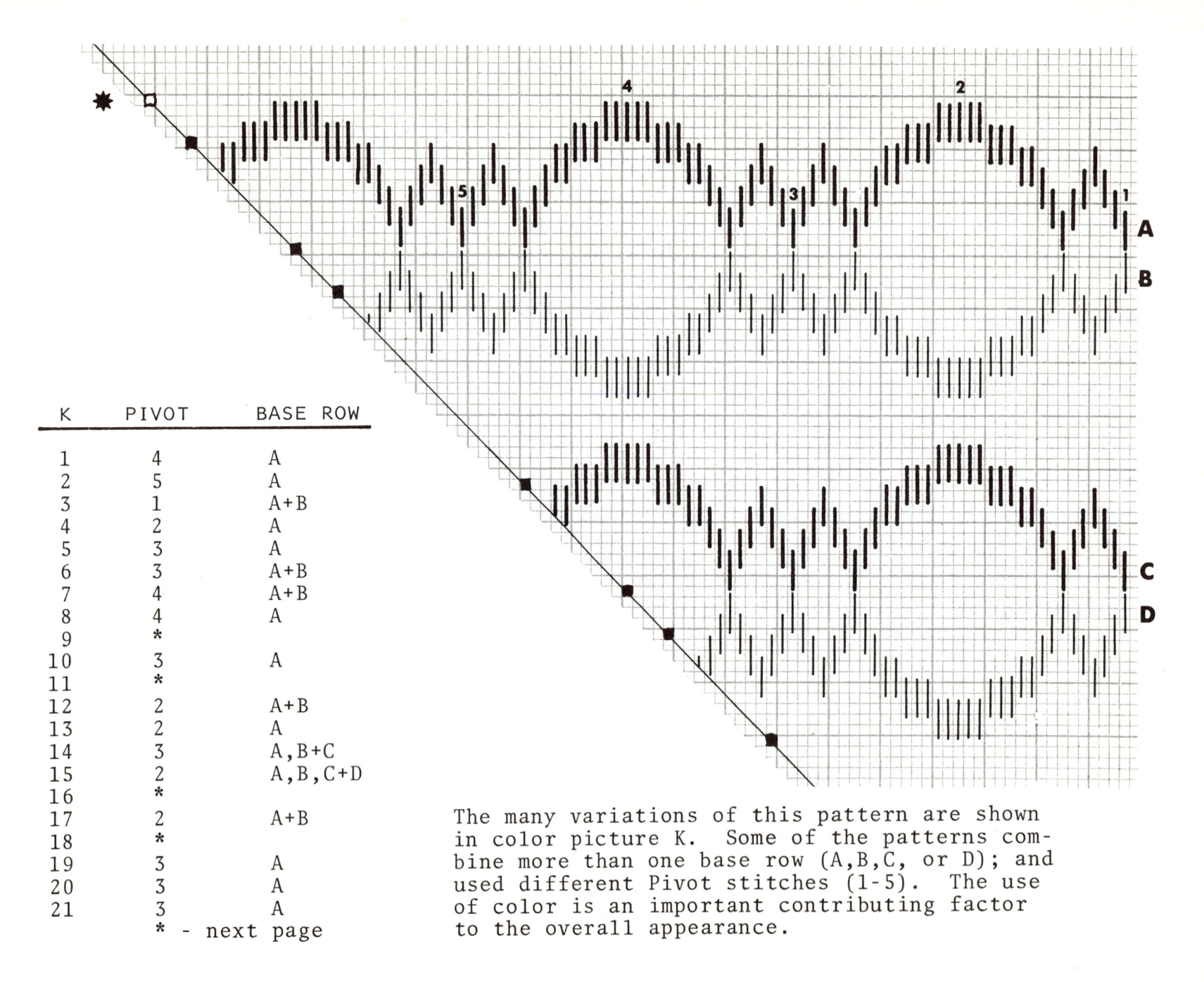

K	PIVOT	BASE ROW
1	4	A
2	5	A
3	1	A+B
4	2	A
5	3	A
6	3	A+B
7	4	A+B
8	4	A
9	*	
10	3	A
11	*	
12	2	A+B
13	2	A
14	3	A,B+C
15	2	A,B,C+D
16	*	
17	2	A+B
18	*	
19	3	A
20	3	A
21	3	A

* - next page

The many variations of this pattern are shown in color picture K. Some of the patterns combine more than one base row (A,B,C, or D); and used different Pivot stitches (1-5). The use of color is an important contributing factor to the overall appearance.

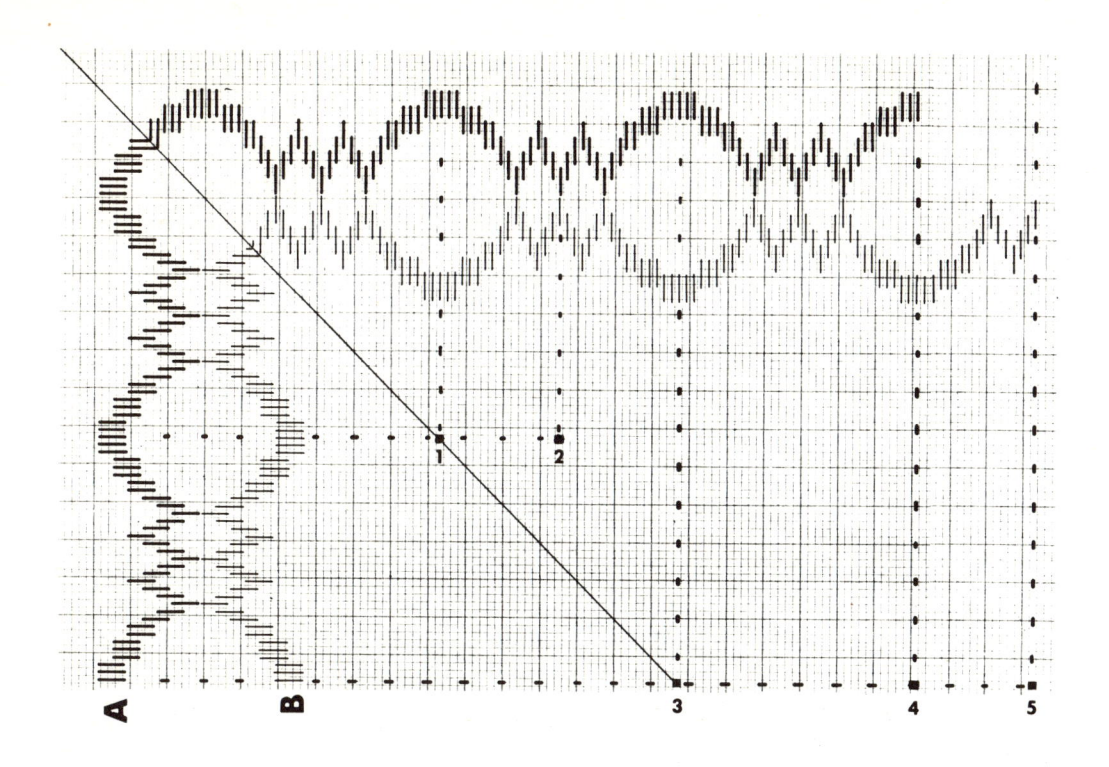

RECTANGULAR KALEIDOSCOPICS are fun to do, but take a bit more planning. Only square type patterns (✳) will lend themselves to this rectangular treatment. The pattern must be worked out on graph paper before you cut your canvas. You must chart 1/4 of the pattern - from Pivot stitch, around a miter, to the next Pivot stitch. The dotted lines on this diagram show the Pivot stitches for 1/4 of 5 different patterns.

The purse flap (K-1) used Center Hole 1, Base Row A and is a regular "square" Kaleidoscopic. The companion tote bag, (K-16) used Center Hole 2, Base Row A for a rectangular effect. Look at Center Holes 1 and 2; they are in the same horizontal row of holes. The Miter line passes through Center Hole 1, resulting in a square pattern. For a rectangular pattern, Center Hole 2 has been moved away from the Miter line. It is the very "Center Hole" on your canvas; but, no Miter lines radiate from it.

143

In preparing your canvas for a rectangular Kaleidoscopic, mark the vertical and horizontal center rows of holes. Center Hole 2 is at the junction of these two lines. Locate your Pivot and stitch your Base Row. Mark the two Miter lines at each end of the canvas; they will meet at Center Hole 1. Remember, you must "flip" the pattern to do the other half, so there will be a Center Hole 1 at each end.

Center Holes 3, 4, and 5 all share another horizontal row of holes. Center Hole 3 produces a square pattern because the Miter line passes through it. Pattern K-4, 12, 13, 15 and 17 all used Center Hole 3.

Base Rows A+B, Center Hole 4 is the pattern for the cushion on (K-9). The Base Rows were stitched in dark blue. Two rows of medium and two rows of light blue were stitched <u>outside</u> Row A and <u>inside</u> Row B. Petit-point rosebuds were inserted between the Base Rows for a delicate touch. The balance of this piece was stitched in white for a subtle texture.

Center Hole 5, Base Row B is the pattern for the tray, (L-11). Look at the center of the tray; an unexpected pattern resulted between the miters. These bonus patterns only occur in rectangular Kaleidoscopics. The size of the pattern repeat and the distance between the miters determines how many 'bonus patterns' you will have. The colors you work with and the progression you have planned determine how striking they appear.

The sleep mask, (K-18) uses the very center of the tote bag pattern (L-16). The solid black background makes it look like a cat's eyes shining in the dark.

By choosing different Pivot stitches and increasing the dimensions in either direction, you can create a rectangular Kaleidoscopic to fit any need. The only requirement is that you plan it on graph paper before you cut your canvas.

DESIGN YOUR OWN KALEIDOSCOPIC

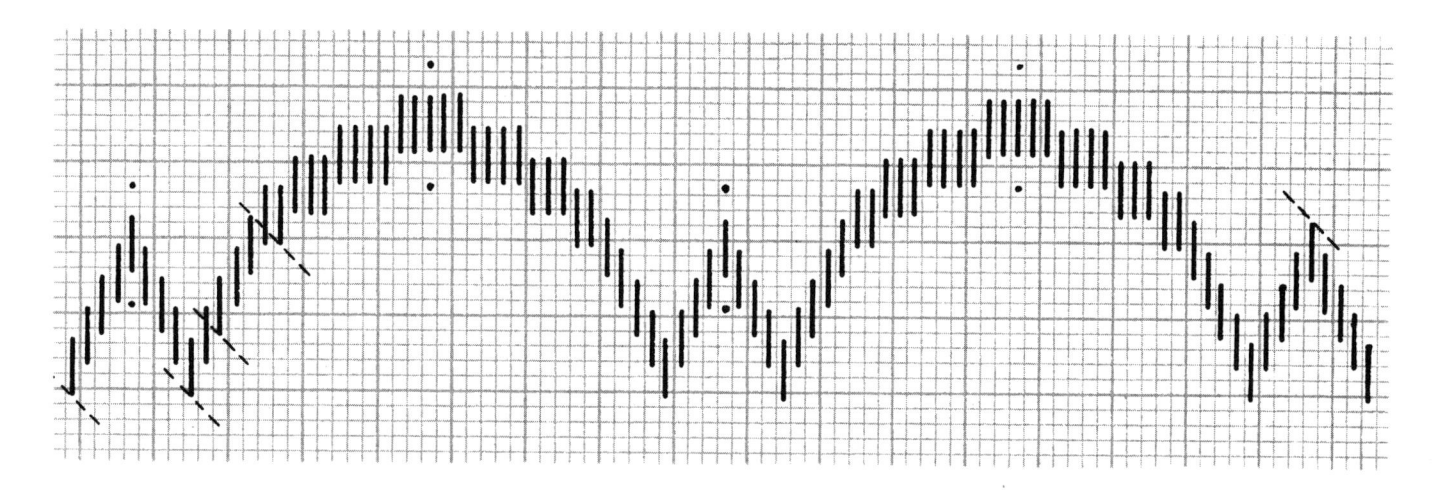

Diagram a straight Bargello line. Does the outside shape please you? Flip it; you might like it better upside down. Remember, the perimeter stitches control not only the shape of the medallion, but the central effects as well.

Where will you place your Miter line? You should always work down into the miter. The dotted lines on the left side of the diagram (upright or flipped) are the possible miter points. Eliminate any stitches on the diagram that would interfere with a smooth miter on your canvas.

Which stitch will you use as your Pivot? The dots indicate possible Pivot stitches.

Do you want to add an auxiliary base row? Remember, this is simply a reverse of a portion of the pattern. It may be above or below the primary line.

Follow standard Kaleidoscopic procedures: check the size, cut and prepare your canvas, plan your color progression, and stitch your "Original".

Finishing

There are two good reasons for finishing a project yourself. First, you have the satisfaction of seeing something through from conception to completion; and second, you can save yourself a lot of money.

Professional finishing is expensive; but there are some things that should be sent to a specialist. Your own upholsterer can do a beautiful job on chairs, benches, footstools, and will even box and cord a pillow. Needlepoint shops have accesss to people skilled in handling leather bound goods such as, slippers, wallets, purses, and telephone book covers. A frame shop can handle most framing needs; however, special items like mirrors and clocks might best be sent to a Gallery.

Pre-finished kits are the newest thing. They are available for many items such as tennis racquet covers, tote bags, golf club covers and purses. The items have already been assembled and bound; all you have to do is work the blank canvas.

What is left for you to finish? Pillows are simple; and any soft goods such as belts, pin cushions, eye glass cases, and check book covers can be finished with neat, professional results by following our methods. The Tender Loving Care you will provide is worth the additional time and effort it takes to do-it-yourself.

The finishing process is as simple as 1, 2, 3; and should be followed in that order. 1. Check it. 2. Block it. 3. Sew it or Bind it.

CHECK IT   Hold it up to the light. Have you made any mistakes or have you missed any stitches? Are all yarn ends securely anchored and closely clipped? Do you want to add anything - Crewel overlay or a row of Mitered Gobelin? Any corrections or additions should be made now.

Is the masking tape still firmly in place? If not, re-tape. The edges of your canvas will be subjected to considerable stress during the blocking process. Because the selvedge is tightly woven, it must be slashed at 1" intervals and allowed to spread for smooth blocking.

Do two rows of Tent stitch around the entire piece for a seam allowance. Hidden in the seam, these stitches strengthen the edges and give a smoother finish; one row is not enough and three rows are unnecessary. If you are determined to do an Octagonal shaped pillow, add ½" of Bias Tent along all 8 sides. As an alternative, you may square up the shape with a row or two of Mitered Gobelin and two rows of Tent. Do not add the Tent if you are using the Binding Stitch to finish the edges.

BLOCK IT   No matter how carefully you work, your piece will need some blocking, even Bargello. Vertical stitches do not ordinarily distort the canvas; but blocking smooths, freshens, and straightens your work. It is not a difficult process and it is worth while to do it properly.

The materials you will need are relatively inexpensive and are a one-time purchase.
1. Blocking board - You need a firm surface on which to pin your canvas. A frameless bulletin board or a piece of insulation board 2' square will handle most projects. Cover your board with ½" <u>woven</u> gingham (the lines on printed gingham may not be true). This not only looks attractive, but it is a perfect guide to aid you in blocking your canvas straight.
2. Push Pins - These aluminum, non-rusting pins have large heads and long points. They can be purchased at an Artist or Office Supply Store in packages of 20 or boxes of 100. It is more economical to buy the large quantity as you will need at least that many to block a 15" canvas.
3. Spray bottle - Fill a clean pump spray bottle with cool, not hot, water.

BLOCK FACE UP! Most blocking directions say, "Block face down"; DON'T! Blocking face up allows you to: see what you are doing, adjust tension for truer lines, and most importantly, allows the wool to "breathe".

With your dry canvas face up, line up the top left corner with the gingham. The squares serve as continuous reference points to aid in your blocking. Pin through the tape at A - never through the worked area. Work along line AB, smoothing and pulling the edge taut, and pinning at ½" intervals. Go back to A and align the left edge of your tape with the gingham checks. Pull down as you pin line AC. Is corner A square, and do the two taped edges look straight? If not, readjust some of the pins.

Things get just a bit tougher with line BD. If it has crept toward the center, just grab your spray bottle and "spritz" lightly. This will penetrate the wool, soften the canvas, and allow you to pull your edge straight. Is corner D in line with corners B and C? It should be; if not, adjust. It may take a bit of tugging to straighten CD; but when it is properly pinned, the tension will equalize along the four sides and the stitches will fall into their proper alignment.

Spray the entire piece until it looks wet. The moisture will penetrate the wool and soften the canvas sizing, allowing the needlepoint to dry to its true shape. Cover with a clean towel; lay it flat and out of the way. When your piece is dry (24-48 hours), the stitches will look bouncy and you may unpin your needlepoint.

SEW IT   Learning to put a pillow together can be a life saver. Many times a small needlepoint pillow would be the perfect remembrance or gift. But the cost involved, and the often lengthy wait for professional finishing, take it out of the category of a casual gift.

Contrary to popular opinion, it is not necessary to be an accomplished seamstress to assemble a simple pillow. If you have access to a sewing machine, it is a matter of just a few minutes work. We recommend doing things the easy way as long as the final result is acceptable.

A row of Mitered Gobelin does the same job as bias-covered cording; it is easier to do; and two extra layers of material are eliminated from the seam. Putting a knife edge pillow together without cording is no more difficult than sewing four straight lines. To make things even easier, we don't use zippers or inner pillows. Needlepoint should be spot cleaned or sponged - not dry cleaned or submerged. Because you

BLOCKING

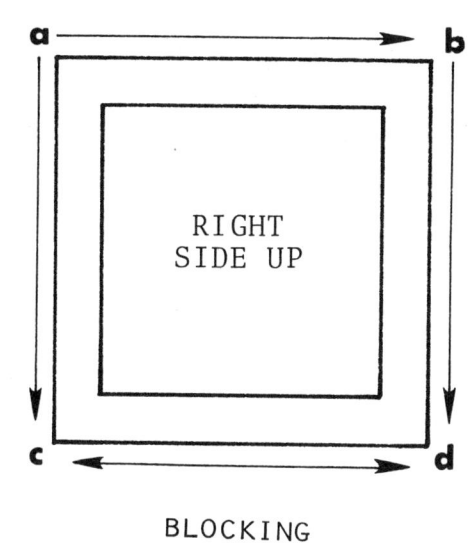

SEWING

do not have to take your pillow apart, why put in a zipper? By eliminating the two biggest head-aches, zippers and cording, even a novice can put a pillow together.

The material used for backing can be anything from chintz or gingham to velvet, corduroy, or cotton-backed vinyl; the choice is yours. The backing fabric does not have to match your background stitches. Many times it is more effective to "pick up" one of the secondary colors for the backing.

Set your sewing machine for a fine stitch and run two rows of straight stitching around the entire piece. These should be in the margin outside your seam allowance (Tent stitches). This will keep the canvas threads from unraveling when you trim the edges.

Pin the needlepoint to your backing material, right sides together. With the wrong side of the needlepoint facing up, start at A and machine stitch around the piece, ending at B. Be sure and leave an adequate opening between A and B so you can turn the pillow inside out. Your stitching guide will be the indentation between the Gobelin and the Tent stitches (the two rows of Tent will be in the seam allowance). This gives a smooth, even finish.

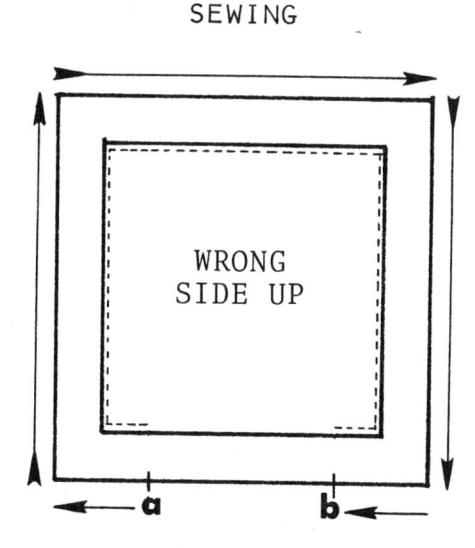

Trim the seam allowance to ½" and turn the pillow casing right side out. Stuff evenly and firmly with Dacron Polyester Pillow Stuffing; be sure the corners are well filled and the stuffing is evenly distributed. Do not use shredded foam or a rubber form (you don't want your pillow to look like it was filled with lumpy mashed potatoes or rubbery jello). Fold in the seam allowance of the backing at the bottom and pin. Slip stitch the seam and your pillow is finished.

If you want your pillow boxed (round and octagonal pillows should be), it is worth the cost to have it finished by an upholsterer. If you are an accomplished seamstress, you know how to handle boxing. One word of warning! Make an exact paper pattern of your needlepoint and add your seam allowances. Even though your piece is hole by hole symmetrical, the measurement will vary length to width by as much as 1". For no apparent reason, the canvas seems to "shrink" from top to bottom (with the selvedge on the side).

Even with a boxed pillow, cording is not necessary; the line of the border is an adequate finish. Unless very carefully applied, cording can detract from the appearance of your pillow.

KNITTED CORDING

If you like the round effect of cording, you can knit your own. It is fun to do and because you can work with your Persian yarn, you are guaranteed a perfect match. We learned this trick from the syndicated column "Pat's Pointers" by Pat Trexler; she calls it "Idiot's Delight". If you are not a knitter, maybe someone can help you get started; the directions are very simple.

The knitted cording requires a continuous strand of yarn (joinings or knots show) approximately 15 times the circumference of your pillow. A 15" pillow needs 60" of cording, or 25 yards of yarn. Be a bit generous in your measurement. You also need two double pointed knitting needles, size 2 or 3.

Cast-on 3 stitches. Slide them to the right end of the needle - do not turn it for the second row. Yes, the yarn is coming out of the left side of the stitches. Merely carry it around the back and pull tight as you knit the first of the three stitches. Again, slide them to the right, carry your yarn around, and pull tight as you knit. Continue until you have enough cording but do not cast-off yet; you might have to add or subtract from your estimate.

Begin attaching the "cast-on" end of the cord to the bottom seam of your pillow. Apply a light tension as you continue tacking it around the seam. When you near the starting point, add or subtract stitches as needed and cast-off.

If you need a matching "gimp" for an upholstered piece, cast-on 5 stitches (instead of 3) for a flat, matching braid. This requires a strand of yarn 25 times your estimated needs. The "gimp" may be glued in place with an extra tacky fabric glue.

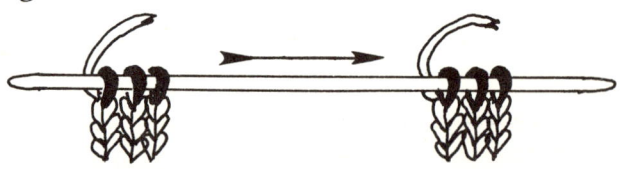

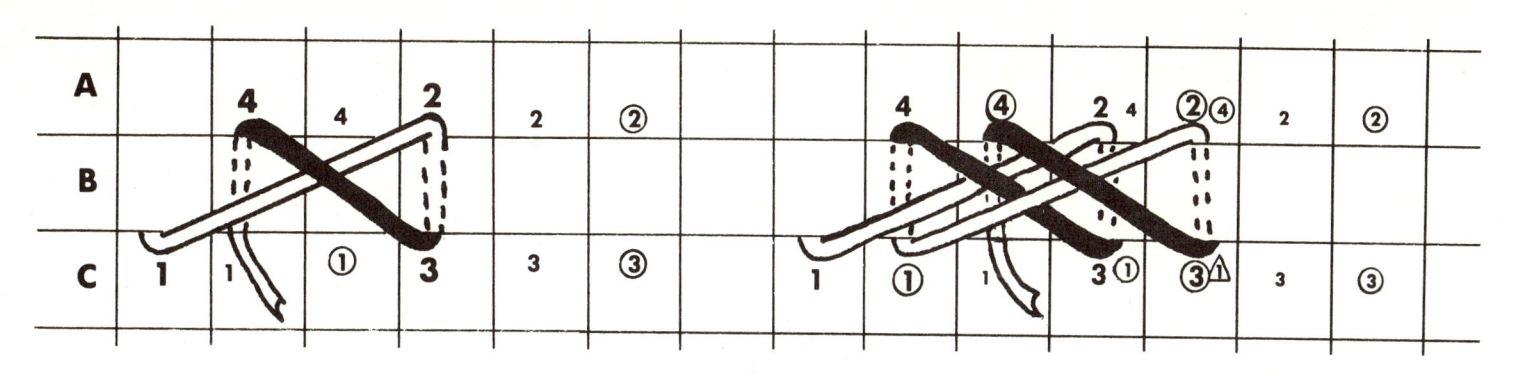

BIND IT

The Binding stitch is a flat woven braid that is worked over the folded edge of the canvas. It is worked in a straight line and can be carried around a square corner; it cannot be used successfully around curves or along an uneven edge. By mastering the Binding stitch, you can finish many things with "better than professional results".

Our approach to this stitch is unique. We begin by teaching it as a decorative stitch much like the Long-legged Cross. On a piece of scrap canvas, follow our directions until you understand the stitch progression.
1. You will only be working in row A+C. Row B never gets used.
2. Begin by bringing your needle up at 1.
3. Carry the yarn forward to 2. The needle goes straight from 2 to 3. Think of this as one stitch 2-3. Carry the yarn backward to 4 - from 4 straight through to the next "1". Think of this as 4-1. This backward progression from (2-3) to (4-1) skips a row of holes. You can easily see the "skip" on the diagram; but it will be more difficult to see it on your canvas.

You are now back at 1 and ready to start your next forward progression. As you carry your yarn forward, notice that 2 is the next empty hole along line A, and that 3 is the next empty hole along line C. Carry the yarn backward for stitch (4-1). This time the "skip" has yarn in it but it is still counted as a "skip". The progression to keep in mind is: Forward 1 - Back 2!

As before, the forward progression uses the next set of empty holes but at this point the backward progression (4-1) will use holes that already have yarn in them. Just remember - Forward 1 - Back 2!

151

Yarn

#18 - 1 ply
#14 - 2 ply
#10 - 3 ply

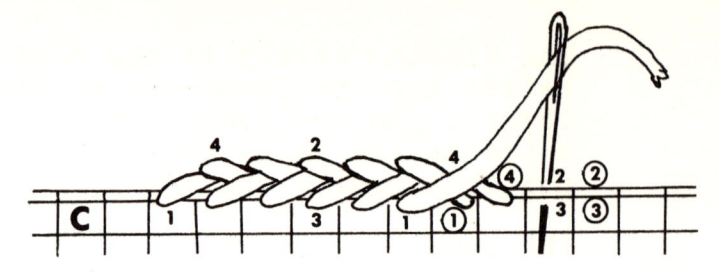

Practice until you feel confident. Now, fold your canvas so that row B and 2 canvas threads are on top of the fold. Continue the same stitch progression, only now pull your yarn quite tight. After working an inch or two, open up the flap. It looks quite different doesn't it? By pulling your yarn tight, you have created a flat, neat braid and your edge will stay down.

Before you begin "Binding", remove the tape and trim all edges to 1".

1. Turn the canvas so that the wrong side is facing you.
2. Row A is the last row of holes that has yarn in it from the central design.
3. Fold the canvas so that row B and 2 threads are on top of the fold.
4. Row C is now facing you.
5. Secure your yarn in the back of nearby stitches and come up at 1. Carry your yarn over the fold to 2-3. Backtrack to 4-1. Your needle is always coming straight toward you and the yarn is carried over the top of the fold. Do not let your tension get too loose. You don't want a floppy braid - pull a little tight!
6. When you run out of yarn, take the needle to the back at 2 and weave off through the back of nearby stitches. The new yarn is secured in the back and comes out at 3.
7. When approaching a corner, be sure that you have enough yarn in your needle (6-8") to take you around the corner. This is a crucial spot and no place to run out of yarn.
8. Fold the corner inward (A) so that one hole remains on the outside of the diagonal fold. Crease the adjacent side as in #3, (B) and re-fold the top edge. Holding all edges as well as you can, continue around the corner, adding a few extra stitches to cover the "point". Once around the corner, you can pick up your regular stitch progression. When you re-connect with the "beginning", take a few extra stitches so that all threads are covered.

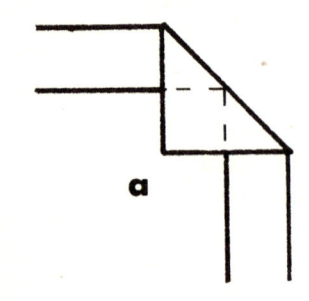

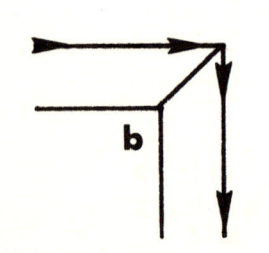

The Binding stitch is the perfect method for finishing many items with better than professional results. Belts, eye glass cases, check book covers, pin cushions, tote bags, purse flaps and wall hangings are just a few of the items that you can finish yourself. By using the Binding stitch to cover the edges, all you have to do is attach the lining.

The choice of lining fabric is the key to easy assembly. You must use a firm, non-raveling material. Felt comes in many colors and is perfect for any items that will not be subjected to wear or stress (purse flaps, wall hangings, pin cushions etc.). Tote bags, luggage rack straps and especially belts, require a stronger fabric. Synthetic suede cloth is ideal; however, some varieties do ravel. Be sure and test the cut edge before you buy. Ultra Suede by Skinner is superb; but, rather expensive - still a savings over professional finishing!

A needlepoint belt is a fast, easy project and a fun way to perk up your wardrobe. Purchase your buckle first because they vary in length and style. Measure it from bracket to bracket, and subtract this figure from "your" measurement (waistline or hip) to determine how much needlepoint to do. Remember if using belt loops, they determine how wide your belt can be. If the pattern you choose is too wide on a #14, try a #18 canvas. Don't forget to include the two threads on each side for the Binding stitch.

Cut your canvas and tape it - be sure to leave 1½" on all sides for blocking and finishing. When your pattern is complete, block it and let it dry. Apply the Binding stitch and trim the excess canvas to ½". You may also trim some of the bulk at the corners.

Cut a strip of material ½" wider on each side and 4" longer on each end than your belt. Center the needlepoint on the backing - wrong sides together, and pin. Machine stitch, using the groove between the Binding stitch and the pattern as your stitch guide. Double stitch the ends for added strength. Trim the excess suede cloth as close as you can on the sides (don't cut your Binding stitch).

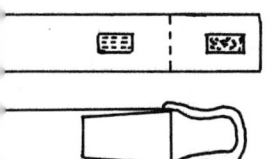

To attach the buckle to the belt, cut a 1½-2" strip of Velcro. Pull it apart and hand whip the smooth side to the lining of the belt, the burr side to the back of the flap. Pull the flap through the bracket and press the Velcro together. Many shops force the needlepoint through the bracket, fold it over and stitch it permanently. Not only is this bulky, but you can't remove the buckle, or slide the belt through loops. Our method is neater, and it allows you some flexibility. You can adjust the length of your belt by changing buckles or by changing the contact point of the Velcro. Another plus for doing it yourself!

This same method can be used for finishing many other items:

Luggage Rack Straps - Finish as for belts, wrap the flap over the frame and nail through the suede cloth. Camp stools are finished the same way. Or, trim all the edges of the lining, and attach the needlepoint to the frame with brass nail heads. Nail in the groove between the Binding stitch and the pattern.

Tie Backs - Line with felt, trim all the edges and sew on small rings.

Wall Hangings - Line with felt, trim all the edges and sew rings at the top, or attach self loops and hang from a decorative rod.

Needle Case - Use felt for the lining, trim all the edges, fold in half, and sew snaps at the corners to hold it shut.

Desk Pad - Cut a piece of canvas board (available at an Artist Supply Store) to size and paint it if desired. Line the blotter ends with suede cloth or felt and trim only the long sides closest to the center. The short ends and the "outside" edges should have a 1" flap. Position the needlepoint on the canvas board and pin it in place. Wrap the lining and glue. Because the lining does not ravel, you may trim some of the excess at the corners.

Pin Cushions - Use felt or suede cloth for the backing. Sew all the way around, leaving a small opening in the center of one side. Stuff, and hand stitch the opening.

Eye glass Case - Your case may be 3"-3½" x 6"-6½" depending on the size and style of your glasses. You must use a #18 canvas if you want to incorporate a small border and a monogram. With our fast, easy assembly technique, you only have to needlepoint the front of your case. After you stitch, block, and bind your needlepoint; cut two pieces of suede cloth or felt 1" wider and 1" longer than the front. For the lining, machine stitch one piece to the bound needlepoint, and trim all the edges. For the backing, machine stitch a ¼" hem on one short end of the remaining piece. Line up the top of the needlepoint with the top of the hem and pin the backing to the lined case. Machine stitch three sides and trim the edges.

Tote Bag - In I-1, the Kaleidoscopic tote bag was bound, lined and backed with suede cloth following the directions for finishing the eye glass case. A leather strap was attached for the handle.

Checkbook Cover - To make paying bills a bit more pleasant, needlepoint a checkbook cover. The finished, bound size should be 7½" high by 6½" wide. For this small project, a #18 canvas allows you more design detail. Line with suede cloth and trim all the edges. Cut two pieces of suede cloth 3" high by 7" wide for the pockets. Machine stitch a ¼" hem along one long side of both pieces. Place the needlepoint over one piece. The cut edges should extend ¼" on three sides. Pin in place, machine stitch and trim the three sides. Do the same for the other piece, forming the second pocket. If you are really ambitious, make a smaller version for a matching credit card case.

In case you wondered, N-7 and K-18 are sleep masks. Wouldn't the DO NOT DISTURB be a perfect gift for someone in the hospital? A gentle reminder to the nurse who invariably wakes the patient to take a sleeping pill. Trace the outline and transfer the pattern to your canvas, making sure the top edge is straight. Stitch your design and block it. Finish only the top edge with the Binding stitch. Pin the needlepoint face up over a piece of felt and stitch in the groove between the Binding stitch and the pattern. Now, machine stitch right on the curved edges, through the needlepoint and the felt. Run one more row of stitching just inside the first. Take courage, and cut away all of the excess canvas. Hand whip ¼" bias seam binding around the edges. Cut a piece of 3/4" elastic and attach the ends at the hash marks on the pattern.

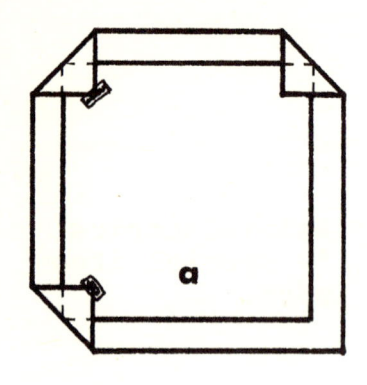

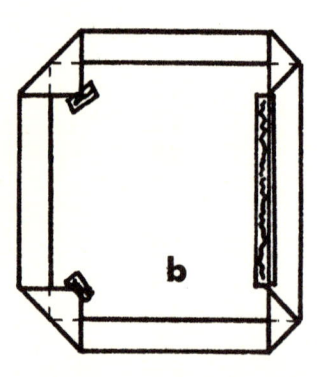

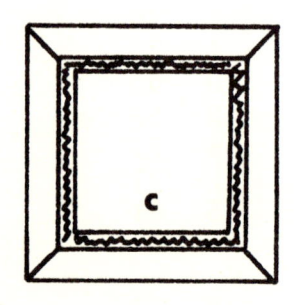

Needlepoint pictures present only one problem - the framing. It's difficult to achieve the exact dimensions for a ready-made frame. The yarn adds bulk to the canvas, changing the estimated size. What started out as 8" x 10" might end up 7½" x 9½" after it has been stitched and blocked. When you are working with the tight measurements of a frame, you can understand why this would be a problem.

It is much easier to have a frame custom made <u>after</u> your needlepoint has been blocked and mounted. There are many frame shops that offer fine work at reasonable prices. You may let the shop mount your needlepoint and frame it for you; or you can take it to them already mounted, ready for framing.

Cut a piece of canvas board 1/8" larger on <u>all</u> sides than your needlepoint. The lip of the frame overlaps the edge of the board by ¼" so a few of your stitches will be covered by the frame. Allow for this in your planning; you might want to add a few rows of Tent stitch to "hide" under the lip. Exact measurements and true right angles are essential. Apply a <u>light</u> coating of fabric glue to the rough side of the board. Center the needlepoint, pat it in place and let it dry.

Turn the board over, fold the four corner tips down and tape them in place (Fig A). Strapping tape is stronger than masking tape, and excellent for this purpose. Carefully miter the corners and fold the sides of the canvas to the back and tape them securely (Fig B). Figure C shows the back of the canvas board, with the needlepoint mitered and taped, ready for framing.

A glass covering is not necessary, but if you insist on glass, please use non-glare. Have the shop provide a spacer between the needlepoint and the glass so the stitches won't look crushed or flattened.

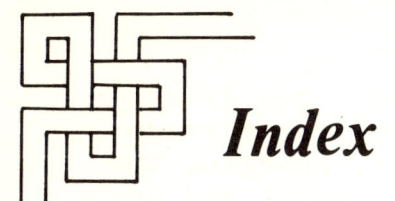

Index of Photographs

A key to this index: B= Borders, C= Corners, K= Kaleidoscopics, G= Geometrics, L= Lattice, *= special items handled at the end of the Index.

A
1. Nancy Hall — B 60
2. Jean Riley — B 60
3. Nancy Hall — B 60
4. Jean Riley — K 138
5. Nancy Hall — B 58

B
1. Joan Keller — B 60
2. Hi Smucker — B 41
3. Jean Riley — C 21
4. Nancy Hall — B 51
5. Jean Riley — C 26

C
1. Nancy Hall — B 69
2. Nancy Hall — B 58
3. Nancy Hall — K 119
    C 22
4. Nancy Hall — L 71
5. Nancy Hall — K 119
6. Nancy Hall — K 119

D
1. Jean Riley — K 120
2. Tifi Bander — K 120

E
1. Jean Riley — B 57
2. Nancy Hall — B 48
3. Nancy Hall — B 41
4. Jean Riley — P 98

F
1. Nancy Hall — B 19
2. Janet Grant — L 70
3. Nancy Hall — C 35
4. Nancy Hall — C 24
5. Nancy Hall — G 82
6. Nancy Hall — L 70
7. Nancy Hall — L 70
8. Nancy Hall — B 63
9. Nancy Hall — B 62
10. Nancy Hall — B 62
11. Nancy Hall — L 71
12. Nancy Hall — B 61

G
1. Bess Gorelick — B 53
2. Jean Riley — B 53
3. Ann Meyer — B 66

157

H
1. L. Dangovian — K 129
2. L. Dangovian — K 129
3. Marilyn Hayden — K 131
4. Lois Hausman — K 131
5. Jan Dailey — K 129
6. Barbara Samberg — K 130
7. Jean Riley — K 130
8. Jean Riley — K 130

I
1. Jean Riley — K 126
2. Jean Longon — K 125
3. Jean Riley — K 126
4. Dottie Chetter — K 123
5. Nancy Hall — K 125; C 31
6. Nina Schneyer — K 123
7. Nancy Hall — K 125
8. Jean Riley — K 137
9. Nancy Hall — K 125
10. Marsha Cohen — K 124
11. Ann Oancea — K 126
12. Gladys Barr — K 124

J
1. Carol McCarus — K 113
2. Marilyn Walters — K 118; C 23
3. Jean Riley — K 113; C 29
4. Ginny Richmond — K 118
5. Jean Riley — K 113; C 27
6. Jane Maxted — K 113; C 31
7. Anne Wilde — K 116
8. Gloria Armstrong — K 116
9. Loretta Rohan — K 116
10. Eunice Rarr — K 116
11. Irene White — K 118
12. Jackie Signore — K 116

K
1. Nancy Hall — K 143
2. Nancy Hall — K 142
3. Carol Kerber — K 142
4. By Parrott — K 142
5. Lorraine Fenster — K 142
6. Phyllis Hill — K 142
7. By Parrott — K 142
8. Margo Cohen — K 142
9. Linda Burton — K 143
10. Jean Brewer — K 142
11. Nancy Hall — K 143
12. By Parrott — K 142
13. By Parrott — K 142
14. Claudia Ireland — K 142
15. Nancy Hall — K 142
16. Nancy Hall — K 143
17. By Parrott — K 142
18. Nancy Hall — K 143
19. Ruth Hartman — K 142
20. Fran Berman — K 142
21. Jean Riley — K 142

L
1. Billie Harley — K 140
2. Sheila Bloom — K 140
3. Nancy Hall — K 122
4. Mary Ringstad — K 122
5. Beverley Garside — K 122
6. Joan Keller — B 60
7. Hi Smucker — K 137
8. Hi Smucker — K 138
9. Jean Riley — K 138
10. Joan Keller — K 141
11. Lis Andrews — K 137
12. Marsha Cohen — K 139
13. Sandy Holben — K 137; B 57
14. Vera Sklar — K 141

M
1. Nancy Hall   G 80
2. Marilyn Klein   G 83
3. Marilyn Klein   G 80
4. Nancy Hall   G 83
5. Jean Riley   G 82
6. Nancy Hall   B 68
7. Joan Keller   G 78

N
1. Jean Riley   B 59
2. Nancy Hall   B 59
3. Nancy Hall   B 59
4. Nancy Hall   B 59
5. Nancy Hall   K 113
6. Nancy Hall   G 78
7. Nancy Hall   * 155
8. Nancy Hall   B 58
9. Nancy Hall   G 82
10. Hi Smucker   G 87
11. Jean Riley   C 30
12. Nancy Hall   G 81
13. Nancy Hall   K 127
14. Jane Burgess   K 128
15. Hi Smucker   C 38
16. Nancy Hall   K 102
17. Nancy Hall   * 102
18. Gladys Barr   * 114
19. Jean Riley   C 38
20. Nancy Hall   C 38
21. Nancy Hall   B 56
22. Nancy Hall   C 31
23. Nancy Hall   C 31
24. Jean Riley   B 65
25. Jean Riley   C 29
26. Nancy Hall   C 36
27. Nancy Hall   B 68
28. Nancy Hall   B 57
29. Nancy Hall   B 67

O
1. Doreen Gordon   *
2. Ann Meyer   K 136
3. Beverley Garside   K 132
4. Jean Brenner   K 134
5. Doreen Gordon   K 135
6. Sandy Holben   K 134
7. Mildred Weiss   K 136
8. Marilyn Klein   K 135
9. Mildred Weiss   K 133
10. Genevieve Clark   K 135

P
1. Jean Riley   G 85
2. Jean Riley   K 128
3. Jean Riley   C 32
4. June Elkington   K 128
5. Carol McCarus   K 128
6. Yvonne Bowman   G 86
7. Ann Meyer   B 55
8. Ann Meyer   B 54
9. Judy Miller   K 124
10. Celeste Smart   B 68
11. Jean Riley   B 65
12. Ginger Marshall   C 22
13. Marilyn Hayden   B 51

*N-17 is the straight Bargello diagram on page 103.

*N-18 is the Pomegranate bell-pull explained on page 114.

*O-1 Mrs. Gordon's Cardiogram is a clever use of Bargello. In case any of you are concerned about her health, the pillow was photographed upside down.

To order a single copy of "BARGELLO BORDERS":

Send a check or money order for $9.95 + 50¢ postage and handling (Mich. residents add 4% sales tax) to:

NEEDLEMANIA, INC.
P. O. Box 123
Franklin, Michigan, 48025